T0301321

State and Local Fiscal Policy

STUDIES IN FISCAL FEDERALISM AND STATE–LOCAL FINANCE

Series Editor: Wallace E. Oates, *Professor of Economics, University of Maryland, College Park and University Fellow, Resources for the Future, USA*

This important series is designed to make a significant contribution to the development of the principles and practices of state–local finance. It includes both theoretical and empirical work. International in scope, it addresses issues of current and future concern in both East and West and in developed and developing countries.

The main purpose of the series is to create a forum for the publication of high-quality work and to show how economic analysis can make a contribution to understanding the role of local finance in fiscal federalism in the twenty-first century.

Titles in the series include:

Competition in the Provision of Local Public Goods
Single Function Jurisdictions and Individual Choice
Alexandra Petermann Reifschneider

Decentralization in Asia and Latin America
Towards a Comparative Interdisciplinary Perspective
Edited by Paul Smoke, Eduardo J. Gómez and George E. Peterson

The Politics and Economics of Regional Transfers
Decentralization, Interregional Redistribution and Income Convergence
Fabio Padovano

Fiscal Reform in Spain
Accomplishments and Challenges
Edited by Jorge Martinez-Vazquez and José Félix Sanz-Sanz

Fiscal Federalism and Political Decentralization
Lessons from Spain, Germany and Canada
Edited by Núria Bosch and José M. Durán

The Theory and Practice of Local Government Reform
Edited by Brian E. Dollery and Lorenzo Robotti

The Political Economy of Financing Scottish Government
Considering a New Constitutional Settlement for Scotland
C. Paul Hallwood and Ronald MacDonald

Does Decentralization Enhance Service Delivery and Poverty Reduction?
Edited by Ehtisham Ahmad and Giorgio Brosio

State and Local Fiscal Policy
Thinking Outside the Box?
Edited by Sally Wallace

State and Local Fiscal Policy

Thinking Outside the Box?

Edited by

Sally Wallace

Georgia State University, USA

STUDIES IN FISCAL FEDERALISM AND STATE–LOCAL
FINANCE

Edward Elgar

Cheltenham, UK • Northampton, MA, USA

Published by
Edward Elgar Publishing Limited
The Lypiatts
15 Lansdown Road
Cheltenham
Glos GL50 2JA
UK

Edward Elgar Publishing, Inc.
William Pratt House
9 Dewey Court
Northampton
Massachusetts 01060
USA

A catalogue record for this book
is available from the British Library

Library of Congress Control Number: 2009937773

Mixed Sources
Product group from well-managed
forests and other controlled sources
www.fsc.org Cert no. SA-COC-1565
© 1996 Forest Stewardship Council
FSC

ISBN 978 1 84844 424 9

Printed and bound by MPG Books Group, UK

Contents

PART IV   EVALUATING STATE AND LOCAL
           GOVERNMENT FINANCES AND BUDGETING

Contributors

Don Bruce is Associate Professor in the Center for Business and Economic Research and the Department of Economics at the University of Tennessee, Knoxville.

Ronald C. Fisher is Professor of Economics, Michigan State University.

Mary Mathewes Kassis is Associate Professor of Economics, University of West Georgia.

Daniel R. Mullins is Associate Professor and Co-Director of the Center for Public Finance Research in the School of Public Affairs at American University. His PhD is from the Maxwell School of Citizenship and Public Affairs at Syracuse University.

Igor Popov was, at the time he contributed to this chapter, a senior economics major at Stanford University, interning with the New England Public Policy Center at the Federal Reserve Bank of Boston.

Jonathan Rork is Assistant Professor of Economics and Faculty Research Associate of the Fiscal Research Center, Andrew Young School of Policy Studies, Georgia State University.

Jason S. Seligman is Assistant Professor, John Glenn School of Public Affairs, Ohio State University.

David L. Sjoquist is Professor of Economics and Director, Fiscal Research Center, Andrew Young School of Policy Studies, Georgia State University.

William J. Smith is Assistant Professor of Economics, University of West Georgia.

Robert Tannenwald is the Vice President and Economist Director, New England Public Policy Center at the Federal Reserve Bank of Boston.

Kurt Thurmaier is Director and Professor of Public Administration in the Division of Public Administration at Northern Illinois University.

Bert Waisanen is a Program Principal for Fiscal Affairs at the National Conference of State Legislatures in Denver.

Sally Wallace is Professor of Economics and Associate Director, Fiscal

Research Center, Andrew Young School of Policy Studies, Georgia State University.

Robert W. Wassmer is Professor and Chairperson of the Department of Public Policy and Administration at California State University, Sacramento. At Sacramento State he also directs the Master's Program in Urban Land Development and is associate director of the Doctorate Program in Education Leadership and Policy.

Jennifer Weiner is policy analyst with the New England Public Policy Center, at the Federal Reserve Bank of Boston.

Laura Wheeler is Senior Research Associate, Fiscal Research Center, Andrew Young School of Policy Studies, Georgia State University.

Katherine Willoughby is Professor of Public Management and Policy, Andrew Young School of Policy Studies, Georgia State University.

PART I

The perfect storm?

1. Introduction and overview

Sally Wallace

The period since 1990 has presented a new set of challenges and opportunities for public finances in the USA. Demographic trends have put substantial pressure on non-discretionary public expenditures such as health care, legal challenges have put pressure on education financing, and aging infrastructure continues to call for more federal, state and local investment. Policy changes at the federal level such as changes in income tax policy affect states tied to the federal income tax, and revised and new mandates for issues such as water and air quality reduce state and local governments' fiscal 'space'. Control over many of these challenges is beyond the bailiwick of state and local governments, but dealing with their repercussions on public finances is a central job of state and local governments. Dealing with these forces has arguably become increasingly difficult due to domestic and international competition for economic development and the politics associated with holding down local taxes such as the property tax.

The economic downturn of the early 2000s and the 2008 recession underscore the volatility of the economic landscape facing state and local governments. Because of the overarching landscape of pressures outside their control and difficult economic times, state and local governments are more hard-pressed than ever to find creative solutions to long-term financing issues. How can state and local governments cope? Is there room for more tax revenue at the subnational level? Do states need to reduce expenditures? Are there means of creative financing out there? These questions and more were the focus of a conference sponsored by the Fiscal Research Center of the Andrew Young School of Policy Studies, Georgia State University, in May 2008. The conference brought together state and local public finance scholars and practitioners to share their research and experiences regarding state and local governments' use (or potential use) of 'out of the box', or novel, new public finance mechanisms to deal with the demographic, economic and political pressures facing them. The conference participants presented original work that asked whether state and local governments have 'gone outside the box' to deal with the strains on current public finances – or whether they have gotten along by adhering to the status quo. Some of the papers looked toward the future by analyzing the applicability of out of the box policies for the future.

Brought together in this volume, the chapters and comments by discussants provide an extensive landscape of state and local fiscal policy today and for the future. The chapters thereby provide students and policy-makers with evaluations of actual practices and analysis of potential policy changes for the future – made by well-known scholars in the area of state and local public finance.

Part I of the book provides insight into the major state and local policy challenges and why and how states have become creative in their response. In Chapter 2, Ronald Fisher posits six 'headliner' challenges to state and local fiscal policy: health care costs and provision; assessment, productivity and accountability in education; privatization of higher education and related issues of access; corrections and public safety; resurgence of the property tax revolt; and the expectation that economic development is a primary objective or responsibility of state–local government. Fisher provides data and analysis to demonstrate the magnitude of the growth in public health care costs and points out that the complications of health care as a social issue merit a federal–state–local policy discussion regarding the reform of financing. Fisher points out three other expenditure-related issues likely to be problematic for state and local governments: the need for real advances in achievement in education; the increased private cost of higher education; and the need for re-evaluation of 'policy and approach' to criminal justice. In addition, he notes that the continued attack on property taxes will further constrain local government choices as they deal with demographic and economic pressures. Finally, Fisher highlights the potential damage done to state and local choices by the focus of state and local economic development policy. In conclusion, he calls for more practical research in areas that focus on these larger issues in state and local budgets to help governments overcome these challenges.

Chapter 3 by Robert Tannenwald, Jennifer Weiner and Igor Popov presents two alternative explanations of state policy-makers' increasing creativity: 'alienation' and 'tax obsolescence'. The alienation hypothesis holds that as the economic status of the average American has stagnated and state and local spending has increased, there has been a voter backlash against 'big government' and additional tax hikes. The obsolescence hypothesis is one that has been uttered by many public finance economists – state and local tax polices simply do not fit today's economy. As a result, the growth in tax revenues has not mirrored the economic growth of the nation. Tannenwald et al. support these main hypotheses by presenting data demonstrating the reluctance of governments to increase tax rates for corporate and individual income and sales taxes over the last 20 years. They also show us data on the increasing disparities in income distribution and lack of public confidence in government. However, they also point out that spending did not decrease over the same period of time – thereby increasing the pressure for new levels of creativity in state budgets in this millennium.

The obsolescence hypothesis is supported in the chapter by exploring the following trends: the intensification of interjurisdictional competition; the shift in the nation's mix of production and consumption from goods to services; the proliferation of electronic commerce; and the tendency of state courts to invalidate the local property tax as the principal means of financing public primary and secondary education. The chapter summarizes by pointing out that future pressures – less buoyancy to the property tax and a tough federal budget deficit – may reduce state–local tax policy creativity and call for good old-fashioned tax increases to deal with the pressures from 2009 forward.

David Sjoquist presents an interesting tax counterfactual in Part II, Chapter 4. What do states without an income tax do? How do they raise revenue – or do they simply make do with less? To provide insights into these questions, Sjoquist selects a sample of income tax states and compares a number of fiscal characteristics between the no-income tax states with that sample. He carefully decomposes the various possible differences including expenditures per capita, grants, composition of revenue and relative state versus local revenue. Excluding Alaska, the no-income tax states carry a higher sales tax burden than the income tax states – other tax burdens are similar between the two groups.

Chapter 4 ends with an interesting hypothetical: if an income tax state eliminated their income tax, what changes would have to occur to other components of the revenue structure to keep the state finances whole? This exercise uses the state of Washington as the no-income tax example, and calculates changes in the revenue necessary for the average income tax state to obtain Washington's revenue structure. The changes are substantial (measured as dollars per capita) – state property taxes would have to increase by over 1000 percent on average (the largest percentage change) and state general sales and gross receipts taxes would have to increase by over $600 per person to attain Washington's revenue distribution. It is questionable as to whether income tax states would be willing to make such changes – or whether there is much public sentiment for eliminating the state income tax regime.

Robert Wassmer (Chapter 5) takes a look at the impact of California's Proposition 13 on the state and local revenue structure in California. Since Proposition 13 was instituted, property taxes as a share of state and local tax revenue in California have fallen from 26 percent to 13 percent.

The state is now in the lower quartile in terms of property tax reliance. Wassmer asks how California has coped with the reduction in property tax reliance and what state and local governments might do in the future to cope with property tax limitations.

Between 1977–78 and 2005–06, total state and local revenue in California increased relative to the US average as a share of personal income and on a per capita basis. According to Wassmer, a large share of the increase in state and local revenue in California came from an increase in personal income tax revenues. Because of the concentration of personal income tax revenues from high-income taxpayers, Wassmer points out a potential instability in the share of income tax revenues from the capital income attributed to individuals at higher income levels. He points out that until recently, the general growth of the economy masked some of the fiscal stress accompanying the change in the composition of revenue.

Accompanying the revenue shifts post-Proposition 13, the state's education spending per student fell from the top five in the nation to 33rd. Wassmer argues that further financing and school expenditure initiatives have severely restricted state and local government budget discretion in the state. The budget crisis of 2007–09 in an environment of decreased budgetary flexibility has led to a number of proposed solutions, including revising the budget process and revenue reform to move to a more stable revenue structure (such as a less progressive income tax and a significant state-level property tax). Wassmer suggests there are other alternatives and offers us an 'out of the box' solution involving the use of a cap-and-trade agreement to enable companies to reach the state's greenhouse gas emissions goals. In this case, the state could benefit by retaining a portion of the revenue earned from auction sale of initial allocations.

The two chapters in Part III of the book look at alternative forms of state income taxation. Rork and Wheeler (Chapter 6) focus on alternative corporate income tax forms and Wallace (Chapter 7) focuses on the potential of an integrated income tax. In Chapter 6, the authors analyze the implications of moving from factor apportionment corporate income taxes to a gross receipts tax (GRT) at the state level. Gross receipts taxes have gained in popularity, evidenced by the adoption of the GRT in four states since 2002 (joining Washington). Using micro-level corporate data for Georgia, the authors analyze the impacts of moving from a standard state corporate income tax to a GRT.

Rork and Wheeler do a good job of providing us with the basics regarding how a GRT works in most states. As a broad-based tax on receipts, it is a potentially powerful revenue engine and relatively simple from a tax administration standpoint. However, as they point out, it may be criticized on the basis of its turnover nature – whereby the tax gets embedded and passed forward in multiple-stage production processes. They provide us with an interesting empirical analysis of the change in the concentration of tax payments among firms from moving a state's corporate income tax to a gross receipts tax (adjusting the GRT tax rates so that there is no net revenue change and using a one-factor apportionment formula as an intermediate step). Using a panel micro data file of more than 90,000 state corporate income tax returns, they simulate the impacts of a GRT in Georgia. They find that there is little change in the concentration of tax payments moving from a state corporate income tax to a GRT.

In Chapter 7, Wallace develops an empirical analysis of the revenue impact of moving a state income tax system (corporate and individual) to a consumption tax. With a proliferation of federal consumption tax proposals in the US and their increased use around the world, it is natural to ask whether a 'true' consumption tax is feasible for a US state. The objective of this chapter's analysis is to demonstrate how a conventional income tax system could be converted to a flat rate consumption tax in a US state under a revenue-neutral scenario. Wallace uses data for Georgia to decompose the revenue impacts of the main changes need to move a standard income tax system to a consumption-based tax system. As she points out, there are some major revenue swings; the loss of itemized deductions and personal exemptions will be burdensome to all taxpayers and may be particularly so to low-income taxpayers. Taxing fringe benefits and eliminating tax benefits for retirement contribution increase revenue, but at a high political cost. However, she demonstrates that there are reasonable ways to estimate the impacts of such a change and, in the case of Georgia, some of the distributional implications of the change can be offset with an overall rate reduction.

The final section of the book, Part IV, contains two chapters that highlight the budgetary aspects of state and local governments' fiscal choices. In Chapter 8, Katherine Willoughby examines state government leaders in 'structural balance' as determined by the Government Performance Project (GPP). Structural balance is the ability of government to support ongoing expenditures with ongoing revenues, and consideration is given to tax structures, countercyclical devices, financial management strategies and various fiscal ratios. The research uses information generated by the most recent iteration of the GPP 50-state survey, conducted in 2007. Willoughby first provides an overview of the current fiscal condition of state governments and relays the concerns of current governors regarding reaching and maintaining structural balance. She includes a helpful accounting of the GPP methodology and criteria used to measure state budget and financial management. Using the GPP results, she assesses the characteristics of strong states (those with structural balance) as well as states that are not in as positive a budget balance position.

Willoughby identifies nine state governments as leaders in reaching and maintaining structural balance and finds that there are some characteristics that define these states that could provide useful examples to other states. On the revenue side, these states are characterized as follows: they did not transfer earmarked funds into the general fund, increase short-term borrowing, draw down budget stabilization or contingency funds or accelerate tax payments. Additionally, on the expenditure side, these states did not use hiring or program increase freezes but they were more likely to require employees to contribute additionally toward health benefits and to implement privatization initiatives.

In Chapter 9, Daniel Mullins brings the tax and expenditure limitation (TEL) information and debate up to date. Mullins argues that while TELs have been around for more than 100 years, the TELs since the 1970s have brought in more rigorous constraints to state and local fiscal policy. He also demonstrates that the impact of TELs increases over time, so that it becomes difficult to analyze the impact of any one TEL policy given that often many have come before.

Mullins provides a great deal of detail on the types of TELs that have been passed since 1990. He also summarizes the literature on why we have this continued passage of TELs. Various explanations abound, including 'runaway' property taxes, mistrust of government and a demand for increased efficiency in government. The impacts of the TELs also vary. Mullins summarizes a wide-ranging literature, and suggests that TELs have little effect on the overall size of the state and local public sector and have decreased the use of local broad-based taxes (specifically property taxes), have expanded the fiscal role for state governments, and have altered the composition of the local public sector, increasing the use of special districts (special purpose districts designed to meet specific needs of the local population including security, sanitation, and recreational services). The chapter provides a large amount of specific and timely data on TELs.

Finally, in Chapter 10, Bert Waisanen brings together the lessons learned from the individual chapters to draw conclusions regarding the future of state and local tax and expenditure policy.

2. Major state–local policy challenges: outside-the-box solutions needed

Ronald C. Fisher[1]

INTRODUCTION

What are the key or most fundamental fiscal policy challenges currently facing state and local governments in the United States? That simple question is the somewhat daunting topic for this chapter. Of course, this requires that the characteristics that make a challenge 'key' or 'fundamental' be identified. The objective here is to identify long-run issues that are fiscally important for states and localities, have been relatively intractable in a policy sense, and have a broad impact on society beyond the solely fiscal implications for subnational governments.[2]

I anticipate (and indeed hope) that the views expressed in this chapter will be somewhat controversial, challenging and contrary. They should be controversial because the reader may believe that the wrong issues have been selected and identified. Perhaps one believes that some of these do not meet the four characteristics noted above, or readers may believe that other issues are more fundamental or important than the six selected (see below). The discussion should be challenging because part of the objective is to stimulate creative thinking and new ideas that may help to resolve these difficulties, both for the state and local governments and for the broader society. And the issues may be a bit contrary from the perspective of economists who work on subnational government fiscal policy. Only two of the six issues discussed are tax policy issues; the others reflect spending or programmatic activities of state and local governments. This is not the first time it has been noted that research by public finance specialists tends to focus more on taxes and revenue than on expenditure and service issues.[3]

The six key long-term substantial, intractable and socially broad issues[4] identified and discussed in the chapter are:

1. Health care costs and provision.
2. Assessment, productivity and accountability in education.

3. Privatization of higher education and related issues of access.
4. Corrections and public safety.
5. Resurgence of the property tax revolt.
6. The expectation that economic development is a primary objective or responsibility of state–local government.

THE 'DIRTY' HALF-DOZEN

Health Care Costs and Provision

The magnitude and growth rate of health care costs is an important economic issue throughout the economy, so it is not surprising that the issue of health care costs is also a crucial one for state and local governments. Although the policy focus is sometimes on those without health insurance coverage, it seems clear that the more comprehensive issue is the cost of health care, whoever pays (see Samuelson, 2008). Obviously, the issues surrounding Medicaid are well documented and have received substantial attention, but state and local government budgets are also substantially affected by health care issues from other sources – including employee benefit costs, health care costs for the institutionalized population, and public health programs.

Here are the facts:

- Nearly one in five persons now receives health care services financed by Medicaid (58 million in 2005, 19.5 percent of the population; US Social Security Administration, 2006).
- State Medicaid direct expenditure for services in 2007 was estimated at about $310 billion, about 21 percent of total state government spending according to the National Association of State Budget Officers (NASBO) (including administrative and insurance premiums costs, Medicaid expenditure was estimated at about $340 billion or 23 percent of state spending; National Association of State Budget Officers, 2007).
- The relative fiscal importance of Medicaid has increased substantially, from 12 percent of state spending in 1990 to the 21 or 23 percent in 2007; aggregating state and local governments together as one entity, Medicaid spending amounts to about 13 to 14 percent of total state–local expenditure.
- The state government share of aggregate Medicaid expenditures (23 to 50 percent of the total) requires about 15 to 16 percent of state own-source revenue.

- The Congressional Budget Office estimates that Medicaid expenditure will grow at an annual average rate of about 8 percent through 2017.
- Best estimates suggest that total health care spending amounts to between 25 and 30 percent of state–local budgets, second only to education as a component of spending.

In addition to Medicaid, the other components of health care spending or costs for state and local governments are substantial. In a report on the issue by NASBO (2004), it was estimated that total health care spending by states represented about 31.5 percent of state government expenditure in 2003 (with Medicaid at 22.5 percent, various public and community health services at 4.9 percent, and health care benefits of state employees at 2.6 percent). Using Census data for state–local governments for 2005, the sum of expenditures for Medicaid, public hospitals, public health programs and employee health costs is about $600 billion. This represents about 25 percent of total state–local expenditure and nearly 30 percent of state–local general expenditure.

It is sometimes overlooked that state and local governments are major employers, as well as service providers. For 2006, state–local FTE employment was about 16.1 million, with annual payroll (wages and salaries) of about $728 billion. If the overhead rate for health care benefits is 15 to 16 percent of payroll (the amount implied by the NASBO health care expenditure report and compensation analysis by industry by the Bureau of Labor Statistics), then state and local governments have annual health care costs for employees of about $110 to $115 billion. And this does not include health care costs for retired employees that state and local governments may still cover.

Although health care costs are, therefore, one of the largest categories of state–local spending (about equivalent to education spending) and the one where costs continue to increase at the greatest rate, it seems inappropriate to think of this issue as a state–local government issue, per se. Rather, this is a social issue, affecting every industry and person. Nor does it seem to be an issue that state and local governments will be able to resolve independently. Certainly a number of states have experimented with different health care financing mechanisms, consistent with the traditional notion that states can be effective 'experimental laboratories' for social policy solutions. But some of the state initiatives are more cost transfer programs than overall cost reduction, and others rely on rationing mechanisms. Until these issues are resolved nationally, health care costs will seemingly continue to be a major factor for state–local government fiscal health, as they are for many other sectors of the economy.

Assessment, Productivity and Accountability in Education

The focus on educational resource differences – equity – that dominated in
the 1970s and 1980s has, in large part, given way to a focus on measuring
and improving educational results – productivity. Just as with the earlier
expansion in state financing of education, these changes have reduced the
autonomy of local education governments. But the fundamental issue –
how to improve the educational level of students – remains.

Here are the facts:

- In 2004–05, only 74.7 percent of public high school students graduated within four years after beginning their freshman year; only
  about half of students in the major urban schools graduate on time.
- The percentage of the 16- to 24-year-old age group who has not
  completed a high school program ('dropouts') remains substantial, at 9.3 percent in 2006, (although it declined from 12.2 percent
  in 1986). Although the dropout rate declined for both Blacks
  and Hispanics also during this period, their dropout rates (10.7
  and 22.1 percent, respectively) remained higher than the rate
  for Whites (5.8 percent) in 2006 (US Department of Education,
  2008).
- Nearly two-thirds of high school graduates still do not have sufficient academic preparation for college. Only 36 percent of students
  graduating in 2005 completed the 1983 National Commission on
  Excellence recommendations for college-bound students (4 units
  of English, 3 units of social studies, 3 units of science, 3 units of
  mathematics, 2 units of foreign language and 0.5 units of computer
  science).
- Eighth-grade reading scores in the National Assessment of
  Educational Progress increased very modestly since 1992, but
  there was no change in differences between White and minority students; eighth-grade NAEP mathematics scores increased
  substantially for all groups, but racial and ethnic differences were
  unchanged.
- Based on NAEP mathematics tests of 17-year-olds, fewer than 7
  percent score at the highest level implying capability of multistep
  problem-solving and algebra.
- All but three states (Iowa, Montana and Rhode Island) now have
  substantial state-set academic requirements for high school graduation (many of which were established or strengthened since 1985);
  23 states now require students to pass a competency test in order to
  graduate from high school; and all the US states have report cards

on schools and rate schools or identify low-performing schools (US Department of Education, 2007).

State governments initiated the emphasis on accountability during the 1990s, resulting partly from the legal decisions that forced states to take more fiscal responsibility for the distribution of educational resources and for ensuring adequacy of educational production. A second driving force was the long-run trend of continuous increases in real per student spending by public schools and decreases in average class sizes, whereas student performance either declined or did not improve nearly as fast as spending grew. With the adoption of the No Child Left Behind Act in 2002, the federal government became an additional force encouraging educational assessment and accountability.

Although there has been some improvement in the NAEP test scores, particularly since 1997, the results remain quite uneven. Improvements have occurred for some subject areas more than others, and there remain wide differences in measured outcomes among different states and different segments of the population. Recent attention has also focused on a set of student assessments used internationally, which show that achievement by students in the US remains below that of students in many other nations that have lower educational spending. There also is concern about 'dropouts' – students who do not complete high school. Although the dropout rate (the percentage of 16–24-year-olds who are not high school graduates in any way) declined from 12.2 percent to 9.3 percent from 1986 to 2006, it also remains quite uneven and is substantially higher in some locations and for some types of students. Only about three-quarters of high school freshmen graduate four years later. Recent attention has focused on high schools in major urban areas, where one analysis (Swanson, 2008) found that: 'only about one-half (52 percent) of students in the principal school systems of the 50 largest cities complete high school with a diploma'.

The clear challenge is to explore mechanisms to improve educational outcomes, not just to assess better. For some students, improvement or success requires achieving a higher level of educational attainment – graduating at a minimum level or moving on to higher education levels. For others, improvement or success requires advancing the level of competence in specific subjects or disciplines. To a state–local public official, the issue is how to make the educational system work better.

The Privatization of Higher Education and Implications for Access[5]

A substantial increase in demand for higher education and the resulting strong growth in the number of higher education students have contributed to increased costs of providing post-secondary education. These cost increases are due partly to the required expansion in capital facilities, partly to increasing costs of scientific research facilities, partly to increased competition for faculty with private sector, non-academic jobs, and partly because of rising health care costs for all employees. State and local government support for public higher education has not increased in real, per-student terms, and thus has not kept pace with the increase in costs of providing higher education. Consequently, students are bearing a larger share of the costs for higher education than in the past, leading some to the view that a process of 'privatization' of higher education is under way in the US.

Here are the facts:

- Public higher education (full-time equivalent, FTE) enrollment was about 10.2 million in 2007, and has increased about 36 percent since 1982. Expansion has been especially substantial recently, with 15 percent growth since 2002. Public colleges account for 75 percent of higher education enrollment in the US.
- Public higher education expenditures per student (Department of Education, constant 2006–07 dollars) were $24,024 in 2000, up from $17,780 in 1985.
- Average tuition at public, four-year institutions was $10,913 in 2006–07, an increase of 72 percent from the $6351 level in 1997–98.
- In 2003–04, the average undergraduate student at public, four-year institutions borrowed $12,707 to pay college costs.
- State–local expenditures accounted for 63 percent of revenue for all public higher education institutions in 2007, down from 78 percent 1982 (SHEEO, 2008).
- Net tuition (net of financial aid) increased from 22 percent of public higher education revenue in 1982 to 36.6 percent in 2007 (SHEEO, 2008).

Over the 25-year period since the early 1980s, state and local government support for public higher education increased in nominal terms, but not enough to offset increases in the number of students and costs. State expenditures for higher education have remained at about 10 percent of total state expenditure since 1992. Real state–local support per student for higher education was the same in 2007 as in 1982. But higher education revenue per student in real terms increased. Consequently, real net tuition paid by students increased. In essence, the increased relative costs of higher education and the increase in the number of students has been

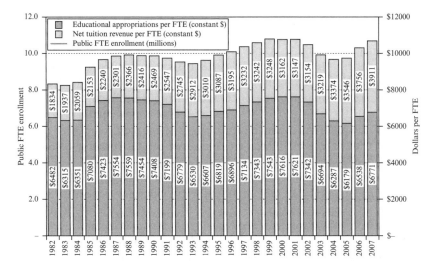

Note: Constant 2007 dollars adjusted by SHEEO Higher Education Cost Adjustment (HECA).

Source: SHEEO 2008.

Figure 2.1   *Public FTE enrollment, educational appropriations and total educational revenue per FTE, US, Fiscal 1982–2007*

financed by students paying higher tuition and bearing a larger fraction of costs. Simply put: more students, higher costs, all covered by higher tuition.

This result is illustrated especially clearly in Figure 2.1. The bottom of the bar that represents government support for public higher education, while varying over the period, is relatively constant. The top of the bar, representing real net tuition, has clearly increased in size.

The substantial increase in higher education enrollment has been concentrated in public higher education institutions. This growth has led to higher education spending per student, reflecting higher costs. Public support, although increasing, is now a smaller fraction of that expenditure than in the past. Consequently, tuition costs are substantially higher than in the past, increasing by 72 percent from 1997 to 2007. Even after allowing for increases in financial aid for students, tuition net of financial aid has increased from 22 percent of public higher education revenue in 1982 to 36.5 percent in 2007. In contrast, state–local expenditures accounted for 78 percent of revenue for public higher education institutions in 1982, but only 63 percent in 2007. Therefore, the average bachelor's degree recipient now leaves a public university with nearly $13,000 of debt.

The increase in costs (expenditure) and the increase in the relative importance of tuition have created pressures for both students and universities. As tuition increases in real terms, there is concern about access to higher education opportunities for students from less affluent families, and implications for both economic growth and economic equality. For universities, the relative decline in public support has required higher education institutions to seek alternative sources of private funding, furthering the notion of 'privatization'.

The growth in higher education enrollment has been fueled by an increase in demand in the labor market for individuals with post-secondary degrees, and the resulting growing wage difference between students with a high school education and a college education. In 2006, median annual earnings in the US for individuals with a high school education only were $27,383, whereas median annual earnings for individuals with a bachelor's degree were $46,435, a nearly 70 percent difference. That difference has been growing substantially, providing an incentive for more individuals to enroll for post-secondary education. The irony, and related public policy issue, arises from the fact that just at a time when post-secondary education seems essential for continued economic growth and vitality, the nation is requiring that higher education be financed privately to a much greater degree than in the past.[6]

Corrections and Public Safety

Despite the fact that corrections represents less than 3 percent of state–local spending, and criminal justice services in aggregate less than 7 percent, and that both the incarceration rate and share of state–local spending going to criminal justice activity has stabilized (or even declined), corrections and criminal justice activities in general remain on this list of six key state–local issues. The issue remains fundamental, in my opinion, because of the differential application and impact of our criminal justice policy in society.

Here are the facts:

- State–local governments spent about $60 billion on corrections in 2005, representing about 3.5 percent of state direct spending (3.4 percent in 2007 – NASBO, 2007; 3.6 percent in 2005 – US Census Bureau, various years b).
- Corrections spending increased substantially as a share of state budgets in the 1980s and 1990s, but has stabilized (or even declined a bit) since (see Figure 2.2 for spending increases).

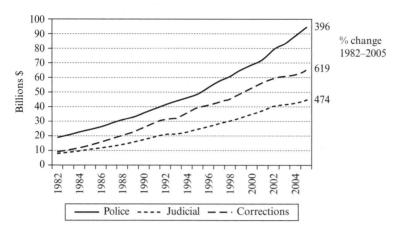

Source: Reprinted from Office of Justice Programs, US Department of Justice, Bureau of Justice Statistics.

Figure 2.2   Direct expenditure by criminal justice function, 1982–2005

- State–local governments spent about $169 billion on criminal justice, in aggregate, in 2005 (police protection, corrections, and the judicial and legal system), representing about 6.1 percent of state spending and 8 percent of local spending in 2005.
- Criminal justice expenditures increased as a share of state and local budgets in the 1980s and 1990s, but have declined modestly since.
- The US has the highest incarceration rate (number per 100,000 population) in the world (501 in 2006). The US incarceration rate doubled in the 1980s, and increased by 60 percent in the 1990s, but has grown only 5 percent since 2000 (see Figure 2.3).
- More than 7.2 million people were in jail or prison, on probation, or on parole in the US in 2006 – 3.2 percent of the adult population, with about 1.6 million persons incarcerated in federal and state prisons.
- 93 percent of prisoners are male, about 58 percent are African-American, Hispanic or Latino, and half of inmates in federal or state prisons are parents of minor children.
- Only 52 percent of state prisoners were sentenced for violent crime, whereas 20 percent are in state prison for drug offenses. About 23 percent of federal prisoners were sentenced for violent crimes or weapons charges, and 53 percent were sentenced for drug offenses.
- The violent crime rate in the US has declined since 1992, and property crime rates have generally declined since the mid-1970s.

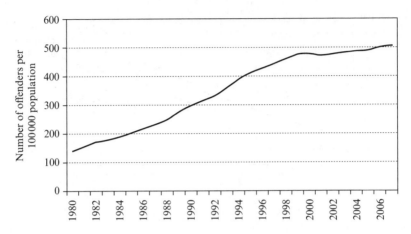

Source: Reprinted from Office of Justice Programs, US Department of Justice, Bureau of Justice Statistics.

Figure 2.3 Incarceration rate, 1980–2006

It is well known that the United States has the highest rate of imprisonment of any nation (suggesting, I suppose, that public safety is a normal good). With about 5 percent of the world's population, the US has about 25 percent of incarcerated persons. Among the states, incarceration rates vary from 151 per 100,000 population (Maine) to 846 (Louisiana). Similarly, corrections spending varies from 1 percent of state expenditure (West Virginia) to more than 5 percent (Michigan). The incarceration rate for African-American males is 3042 (per 100,000 in the population), much greater than for Hispanic and Latino males (1261) or White males (487). According to research reported by Loury (2007), an African-American male has a 32 percent chance of serving in a state or federal prison during his lifetime. There also is substantial variation in the type of criminal activity that leads to prison. The most recent report from the US Bureau of Justice Statistics (Sabol et al., 2007) finds that 'three offense categories – drug, weapons, and immigration offenses – accounted for 87 percent of the growth in Federal prisoners' since 2000.

Criminal justice activity, and corrections specifically, seems to be an area of state–local service where both the fiscal cost and the social cost suggest that a re-evaluation of policy and approach may be appropriate. States and localities are spending a substantial and increasing amount even when most measurements suggest serious crime has declined. The focus on drug and immigration incidents seems to have contributed to the concentration of criminal justice activity on minorities, and especially minority males, which creates social and economic consequences in those communities. There seem to be a number of obvious questions. What types of criminal activity should be the primary focus for state–local law enforcement? Is incarceration the appropriate response for drug and immigration offenses, especially with so many minor children involved in those families? What are the alternatives? How might states and localities reduce direct and social costs?

The Resurgence of the Property Tax Revolt

Property taxes are one of the fundamental fiscal foundations for local government in the US, but they remain exceptionally controversial. The tax is criticized for its incidence and distributional implications, for its effect on specific groups of taxpayers, for the incentives it creates, and because of disparities in the tax base among localities. Because of these concerns, the property tax seems continually to be under assault, and the target for reform, reduction or even elimination (Fisher, 2008).

Here are the facts:

- In fiscal year 2005, property taxes generated $346.3 billion of revenue and accounted for about 28 percent of all local government general revenue and more than 72 percent of local government taxes (see Figure 2.4).
- Property taxes provide about one-third of general revenue for public schools nationally, 55 percent of revenue for townships, a quarter of revenue to county governments and about one-fifth of revenue for cities, on average.
- In aggregate nationally, property taxes ($346.3 billion) are of roughly the same order of magnitude as corporate income taxes ($355 billion) and sales taxes ($271.2 billion from general taxes and $197.8 billion from selective taxes).
- In 2005, aggregate property taxes were 3.15 percent of personal income, the same ratio that existed in the 1950s. The tax-to-income ratio was higher in the 1970s and 1980s, but has remained near 3 percent since 1982.
- According to the American Housing Survey for 2005, the median market value for year-round, owner-occupied housing was $165 344, and the median monthly real estate tax was $127. This suggests annual property taxes of $1524 and an effective property tax rate on owner-occupied homes of less than 1 percent. Other recent analyses suggest median effective property tax rates on all real property of about 1.6 percent, in both cases relatively low rates.

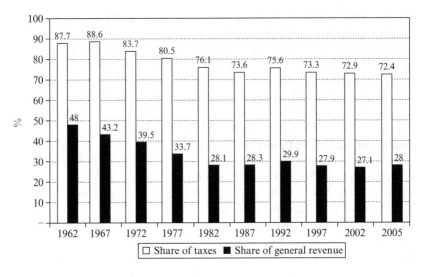

Source: US Census Bureau (various years b).

Figure 2.4   Local government property taxes as a percentage of all taxes and general revenue, 1962–2005

The initial 'property tax revolt' was tied to Proposition 13, adopted by California voters in 1978. Subsequently, property tax reform and reduction was often related to financing of K–12 (Kindergarten to grade 12) education because of the resource disparities between school districts implied by property tax reliance for funding schools (Kenyon, 2007). In the last several years, the 'property tax revolt' seems to have gained new life as a number of states have acted to reduce the property tax by expanding alternative revenues and some states have considered serious proposals to eliminate the tax. Florida considered such a plan, which would have involved substituting sales tax, in 2007. Georgia considered various property tax elimination options in 2007 and 2008. Similar discussions have taken place in Indiana and Texas, among other states.

The latest version of property tax opposition may have been fueled partly by the substantial increase in housing values that occurred since 1990, especially in certain parts of the country. In some states, average ratios of home value to income exceeded five, implying that monthly mortgage payments were high relative to income by historical standards. If households had made housing purchase decisions based on an expectation of a fixed monthly payment, and if those payments were high relative to income, then an increase in monthly payments – from interest rate or property tax changes – could be problematic.

A state representative in Georgia made the argument as follows:

> The biggest part of the problem is that property taxes are increasing faster than personal income . . . Even though people are not earning more income, the government is requiring that they pay more taxes. Because of this phenomenon, a family can live in a home for 30 years and suddenly find they cannot afford it anymore because their property taxes have increased so much. (Lunsford, 2007)

One might think that the bursting of the housing market bubble and subsequent decline in housing prices would mitigate the pressure for property tax reduction. I think just the opposite. Concerns about housing affordability seem greater now than ever, with a variety of schemes suggested to maintain home ownership. And in some states with limitations on the growth of property taxes or taxable values, property taxes may be able to continue to increase even while property values decline.[7] Neither of these two observations, it seems to me, is likely to lessen the call for property tax reduction.

Proposals to eliminate the property tax might be of four types:

1. Eliminate the property tax with no revenue replacement.
2. Eliminate the property tax and substitute (in full or in part) revenue from other local government taxes or fees.
3. Eliminate the property tax and substitute (in full or in part) a state property tax, possibly coupled with a state aid mechanism to distribute the state revenue.
4. Eliminate the property tax and substitute (in full or in part) revenue from other state government taxes, again possibly with a state aid program.

These are very different options with substantially different implications. It is clear that in addition to an issue of relative tax mix (sales–income–property), there also are issues about the provision of public services and the relative role of state compared to local governments. Many proposals for property tax relief would not only change tax reliance, but also greatly reduce the autonomy of local government. Citizen concern and opposition to property taxation is long-standing, but until these issues are resolved, the fiscal health of state–local governments will continue to be at risk. Moreover, the structure of fiscal federalism in the US itself may be at risk, if eliminating property taxation comes to mean eliminating autonomous revenue sources for local government.

The Expectation that Responsibility for Economic Development is a Primary Role of State and Local Governments

'Get jobs': I am not sure precisely when it began, but at some time the responsibility to 'get jobs' – to stimulate local economic development – became a standard expectation or role for state and local government and its officials. It is also not clear how or whether this fits with Musgrave's traditional characterization of the allocation, distribution and stabilization functions of government. Encouraging economic growth might be thought of as part of the stabilization function, but Musgrave (and others) viewed this as a national government responsibility. Today, this is an expectation for every mayor, governor or influential state legislator. It is often a (sometimes *the*) key issue in political campaigns. Every state and major city has an economic development agency, tax incentives for investment or job creation are ubiquitous, and 'trade' missions to other nations are common. Is this a good direction for state and local government to take?

Here are the facts:

- Differences in income among states and regions in the US have been reduced continually and dramatically over the twentieth century.
- One estimate in the 1990s (Bartik, 1994) suggested that states and localities spent up to $70 per person annually on direct and indirect economic development incentives.
- Although (or perhaps because) fiscal incentives for investment are offered by every state and most large counties and cities, Wasylenko (1997, p. 47) concludes: 'Taxes do not seem to have a substantial effect on economic activity among states'.

The direct cost of state–local economic development activity is unclear, at best. These expenditures are difficult to measure, partly because responsibility is often diffused among many departments and many governments, partly because many incentives are offered as tax reductions rather than direct spending (requiring measurement of revenue lost through tax expenditures), partly because incentives may take the form of reduced-interest or guaranteed loans, and partly because incentives are sometimes operated through quasi-governmental agencies. In addition, net cost depends on the effectiveness of the incentives. If an incentive generates a sufficient amount of economic activity that otherwise would not have occurred (and resulting tax revenue), then the net cost could be reduced or even become negative.

One recent analysis for Michigan (Bartik et al., 2003) calculated that about $700 million of public resources was devoted annually to economic development activity in the state. If accurate, this level of expenditure represents about 1 percent of total state–local government spending in the state. Even if inaccurate by a factor of two, this is still a relatively low level of state–local expenditure (certainly compared to education or health care). From that perspective, it may not seem to matter much that the overwhelming implication of a number of studies is that many (if not most) state economic development incentives are ineffective, or at least not worth the cost.

The most serious cost of the state–local governmental focus on stimulating economic development may, therefore, be an opportunity cost. One aspect of that is the time and effort that public officials and staff spend on development activity, rather than the more traditional subnational government responsibility of producing public services. Similarly, citizens' expectations of public officials and state–local governments may be based more on 'creating jobs' than what seems often to be perceived as the more mundane task of running effective schools, maintaining a well-functioning transportation system, and so on. The issue, then, is whether state and local governments would be better served focusing relatively more on the traditional allocation function – how to provide more or better public services at lower cost – rather than on an elusive and often unsuccessful competition for private sector jobs.

RESOLUTIONS

How important are these six topics or issues for state–local fiscal policy? Although all of the magnitudes may not be identifiable, it seems inescapable that these account for the great bulk of state–local budgets. A conservative estimate suggests that these six issues represent at least two-thirds of state–local budgets. Property taxes account for about 20 percent of state–local own-source revenue. Health-related expenditures represent 20 to 25 percent of state–local spending. Support for public higher education amounts to 8 percent of state–local spending, and criminal justice services account for about an additional 7 percent. Therefore, these four areas represent roughly 55 to 60 percent of budgets of state–local governments. K–12 education, in aggregate, represents nearly 30 percent of state–local spending, but only a portion of that is related marginally to assessing, reporting and improving educational performance and attainment. One analysis suggests that the annual cost of implementing only the NCLB law is between $2 billion and $8 billion. And there is no single measure of direct costs for economic development activity by state–local governments. For that issue, the opportunity cost – the deflection or misdirection of interest and effort away from providing traditional public services – may be greater than direct expenditure, in any case.

Are these issues new? In a similar review of key financing issues facing state and local government in the 1980s, Roy Bahl (1984) focused on: the importance of slower economic growth on state–local budgets; regional shifts in economic activity and population, and the implications for high- and low-spending states; the difficulty of maintaining the public capital infrastructure; the tax and expenditure limitation movement; the need for development of an urban policy and revitalization of central cities; and changes in the relationship between the federal government and the state–local sector. It is interesting that although the key fiscal policy issues seem to be quite different 30 years after Bahl's analysis, many of the exogenous factors influencing fiscal policy – variable national economic conditions, uneven regional growth, aging of the population, and changes in the racial and ethnic composition of the population – are similar.

What are the solutions? The ultimate goals from addressing these major policy challenges are easy to list: improve educational outcomes and strengthen post-high school preparedness; improve access to post-secondary or college education; re-evaluate criminal justice and imprisonment strategy and adopt alternatives; contain health care costs; maintain the fiscal viability of local government and improve perception of the property tax; and refocus state–local government effort on the provision of basic services. But achieving such objectives remains elusive.

What to do? For many of these issues, there has been no shortage of research, journal articles, books, reports and conferences. But real understanding, policy change or different outcomes have been more difficult to achieve. Economists and other academic specialists who study state–local government seem more comfortable and successful as analysts rather than engineers – explaining why or how something happens rather than identifying how to do it better. But engineering may be precisely what is needed. In some cases new ideas or options may be necessary; in others, existing ideas may need to be implemented. This may be a particular role for the public policy schools, as some have already embraced.

Changes in academic research direction may also be appropriate. For instance, public finance analysts have devoted substantial research and effort to the issues of state–local business taxation. Should a tax be on gross receipts, value added or profits, or should there be a business tax at all? And if there is one, how should it be apportioned? Does a lack of uniformity raise the efficiency cost, and by how much? And for taxpayers, how should economic activity be organized to minimize that tax burden? Yet, state–local direct business taxes account for less than 3 percent of own-source revenue for state–local governments. Surely some redirection of that research effort toward the issues discussed in this chapter might be welfare-enhancing.

This volume is focused on 'thinking outside the box' in the world of state–local fiscal policy. I suggest that there is no greater area of need for such thinking than the six issues identified and discussed in this chapter. Surely these issues have been intractable, which is one reason why they were selected for discussion. Though difficult, they also seem to be ones where even modest improvements can have a substantial impact on not only the fiscal position of state–local governments, but also the functioning of our economy and society.

NOTES

1. I benefited from comments and suggestions by many participants at the conference in May 2008 organized and hosted by the Andrew Young School of Policy Studies, with comments by Roy Bahl and Kurt Thurmaier especially helpful.
2. The definition excludes, therefore, the current fiscal difficulties faced by states and localities arising from the national macroeconomic slowdown (or recession) and the credit market crisis, reflected most obviously in the decline of housing prices, the reduction in liquidity, and increase in foreclosures. This situation certainly seems likely to affect subnational government substantially over the next several years and is a short-run challenge. But the focus in this chapter is on more continuing, long-run concerns.
3. For discussion of how these issues overlap and interact, see Fisher (2007).
4. It may be important to distinguish these fiscal issues under the control of state and local governments from external or exogenous factors that currently are important and affect state and local finances and policy. The aging of the population, changes in ethnic composition of the population, regional population shifts, growing income inequality, the rising relative cost of energy and increasing environmental concerns are all among the key external factors that are influencing state–local finances and policy choices.
5. Several participants at the conference held by the Andrew Young School suggested that perhaps higher education finance and provision should not be included among the six major issues facing state–local government. Alternatives suggested included transportation and population change. A strong case might be made, I think, for transportation to supplant higher education on this list. Many roads and bridges are old and require substantial maintenance or replacement; road congestion in major metropolitan areas is substantial and increasing; rising energy costs are increasing attention on mass transit options; gasoline excise taxes may no longer be the preferred mechanism for financing roads; and so on. I decided to keep higher education on the list instead of transportation primarily because the higher education issue seems newer. Many of the current transportation issues could have been (and were) raised in the 1970s. So, this issue seems to be a perennial one for states and localities. But the change in higher education funding and resulting shift of costs to students has been a fact since 2000 at a time when demand for higher education (and the return to it) is increasing.
6. The challenges and contrasts are apparent in my own state of Michigan. The Governor's administration has set as a state goal to: 'double the number of residents with a college degree'. The finance system for K–12 education was changed substantially in the 1990s. State high school graduation requirements were established for the first time in 2006. The Governor has proposed raising the high school dropout age to 18. But the high school

completion rate for the Detroit public school district is about 25 percent, the lowest in the nation. And state government financial support for higher education has declined as a share of the state budget and has even declined in nominal amounts in some years.
7. In Michigan, for instance, annual increases in taxable property values are limited to the lesser of 5 percent or the rate of inflation. Assessed values are set at 50 percent of market value, but because of the taxable value limitation, taxable values are substantially less than assessed values for many properties. Thus, taxable value might increase by the rate of inflation. Even with falling market values, taxable value could still be less than 50 percent of market value.

REFERENCES

Bahl, R. (1984). *Financing State and Local Government in the 1980s.* New York: Oxford University Press.

Bartik, T.J. (1994). Jobs, productivity, and local economic development: what implications does economic research have for the role of government? *National Tax Journal* 47: 847–61.

Bartik, T.J., Eisinger, P. and Erickcek, G. (2003). Economic development policy in Michigan. In C. Ballard, P. Courant, D. Drake, R. Fisher and E. Gerber (eds), *Michigan at the Millennium.* East Lansing, MI: Michigan State University Press.

Fisher, R.C. (2007). *State and Local Public Finance.* Mason, OH: Thomson South-Western.

Fisher, R.C. (2008). Property taxes for local finance: research results and policy perspectives. Report prepared for the Lincoln Institute of Land Policy, Cambridge, MA.

Kenyon, D.A. (2007). *The Property Tax – School Funding Dilemma.* Cambridge, MA: Lincoln Institute of Land Policy.

Loury, G. (2007). Racial stigma, mass incarceration and American values. Tanner Lectures in Human Values, Stanford University.

Lunsford, J. (2007). A GREAT plan for Georgia: the elimination of all property taxes. www.johnlunsford.com.

National Association of State Budget Officers (NASBO) (2004). *State Health Care Expenditure Report, 2002–2003.* Washington, DC: NASBO.

National Association of State Budget Officers (NASBO) (2007). *State Expenditure Report.* Washington, DC: NASBO.

Sabol, W.J., Couture, H., Paige, M. and Harrison P.M. (2007). *Prisoners in 2006.* Washington, DC: US Department of Justice, Bureau of Statistics Bulletin.

Samuelson, R.J. (2008). Getting real about health care. *Newsweek*, 15 September.

State Higher Education Executive Officers (SHEEO) (2008). *State Higher Education Finance, Early Release 2007.* Boulder, CO: SHEEO.

Swanson, C.B. (2008). *Cities in Crisis: A Special Analytic Report on High School Graduation.* Bethesda, MD: Editorial Projects in Education.

US Census Bureau (various years a). *Census of Governments, Compendium of Government Finances.* Washington, DC.

US Census Bureau (various years b). *State and Local Government Finances.* Washington, DC.

US Department of Education, National Center for Education Statistics (2007).

State Education Reforms. Washington, DC: US Department of Education, National Center for Education Statistics.

US Department of Education, National Center for Education Statistics (2008). *Digest of Education Statistics: 2007.* Washington, DC: US Department of Education, National Center for Education Statistics.

US Department of Justice, Office of Justice Programs, Bureau of Justice Statistics. Washington, DC. http://www.ojp.usdoj.gov/bjs.

US Social Security Administration (2006). *Annual Statistical Supplement to the Social Security Bulletin, 2006.* Washington, DC: Social Security Administration. http://www.socialsecurity.gov/policy/docs/statcomps/supplement/2006.

Wasylenko, M. (1997). Taxation and economic development: the state of the economic literature. *New England Economic Review, Proceedings of a Symposium on the Effects of State and Local Policies on Economic Development*, March/April.

3. Genesis of state–local creativity

Robert Tannenwald, Jennifer Weiner and Igor Popov[1]

INTRODUCTION

The premise of this chapter is that state and local governments in the USA have been forced to become more creative in raising revenue in recent years. Actually, states have exhibited creativity in raising revenues when confronting past challenges. In each recession, and with each wave of increased responsibility, states have come up with all sorts of clever ways to boost receipts. The Great Depression spawned state sales taxes. The property tax revolt of the late 1970s and early 1980s induced greater reliance on user fees and charges. The severe contraction in state revenues in the early 1990s inspired creative 'Medicaid arrangements' – a euphemism for clever exploitation of loopholes in federal regulations to divert money intended for health care into state general funds.

Nevertheless, some 'bread and butter' options, such as surcharges and increases in statutory tax rates, have been enacted less frequently during the 1990s and 2000s than they were in the 1970s and 1980s. Indeed, the 1990s were marked by a proclivity for tax cuts, a few years of discipline on the spending side, and increased federal aid (relative to very depressed levels in the 1980s), leading to a build-up of reserves. States have been drawing down these reserves since the mid-2000s to help make ends meet.

Furthermore, interest has intensified in forms of taxation not as widely or seriously considered in the past. Gross receipts taxes and value added taxes are perhaps the most prominent cases in point. 'Loophole closing', including combined reporting, although not as novel, has become more prevalent. Slow but steady growth in support for the Streamlined Sales Tax Agreement (SSTA) is another manifestation of states' 'thinking outside the box' to augment revenues over the long run. More and more states are also expanding casino gambling as a means of augmenting revenues (see Prah, 2004, 2007, 2008; Peterson, 2006; Butterfield, 2005).

In trying to explain why state tax policy-makers have become increasingly creative in their revenue-raising strategies, we posited two explanations: 'alienation' and 'tax obsolescence'.

The Alienation Hypothesis

The prototypical American has become disillusioned and alienated, in large part because their material well-being has, at best, improved little since the early 1980s, while the income and wealth of the nation's richest households have skyrocketed. Inequality has widened sharply, especially during the 1980s. To the extent that incomes grew at all in the lowest two income quintiles, they did so primarily because of an increase in labor force participation of the lower-earning spouse. In effect, as asserted in the title of an article published in the *New York Times* during the spring of 2008, which reprints a chapter of a new book by Steven Greenhouse, the prototypical American has been 'Worked over and overworked' (Greenhouse, 2008a, 2008b).

Meanwhile, Ronald Reagan began his presidency (during a recession) by blaming the nation's economic woes on 'big government'. In his first inaugural address, he asserted: 'It is no coincidence that our present troubles parallel and are proportionate to the intervention and intrusion in our lives that result from unnecessary and excessive growth of government'.[2]

When, following several years of rapid growth in state and local spending, large state fiscal deficits surfaced in the late 1980s and early 1990s, states enacted tax increases that, in the aggregate, were unprecedented in magnitude. Angered voters, their dissatisfaction stoked by the ideology of many of their national leaders, took out some of their frustration on elected state officials. Even if they did not necessarily throw out incumbents, they let their elected representatives know that they were fed up with what they perceived as large, inefficient government that did not seem to be helping 'average Americans'. They would not tolerate additional, visible, direct tax hikes. Governors and legislators got the hint. Their tax policies still reflect their fear of voter backlash.

The 'Obsolescence' Hypothesis

State and local tax systems, designed decades ago, are poorly designed to 'meter' and 'tax' the stocks and flows that have assumed an increasingly important role in the twenty-first century's economy. As a result, state and local governments have been compelled to tweak their tax systems in novel and creative ways, or to introduce taxes radically different from traditional levies, in order to raise needed revenues. Factors contributing to this growing obsolescence include: (1) the eviscerating impact of intensifying

interjurisdictional competition in a global economy; (2) the rising importance of hard-to-tax services in the mix of consumption and intermediate
purchases; (3) the spread of difficult-to-tax electronic commerce; and (4)
constraints imposed by state court cases on local governments' authority
to finance public education through the property tax.

The Role of Changing Public Attitudes

Since the alienation hypothesis has been less widely discussed and is more
controversial than the obsolescence hypothesis, this chapter focuses primarily on evidence supporting the former. Though such evidence is weak,
we still believe that a change in public attitude towards government spending has constrained the choices of state tax policy-makers. We are less
certain about our hypothesized explanation for this shift in attitude, that
is, public disgruntlement over a lack of economic progress for the prototypical American and growing inequality.

THE STATES' GROWING RELUCTANCE TO RAISE TAXES

Since 1993, the states have become less likely to raise, and more likely to
lower, statutory tax rates on personal income, corporate income and retail
sales, the 'big three' taxes imposed by most states. From 1974 through 1994,
we recorded 53 instances in which states raised statutory personal income
tax rates, including temporary surcharges, compared to 26 instances of
reductions in such rates. In every year for which data were available during
this period, instances of tax rate increases were greater than tax rate reductions, with the exception of 1974 and 1984. Since 1994, only two states
have reported a statutory personal income tax increase. By contrast, there
have been 23 reported reductions in tax rates during this period (Figure
3.1). (However, there have been recent instances in which scheduled statutory rate reductions have been postponed, such as in Massachusetts, in
2001). Propensities to raise or lower corporate tax rates and sales tax rates
have exhibited a similar intertemporal trend (Figures 3.2 and 3.3).

When looking at the net revenue consequences of all state tax changes,
not just changes in the statutory rates of the 'big three' state taxes, one also
sees a decreasing propensity to raise taxes and increasing willingness to
lower them. According to the *Fiscal Survey of the States*, published by the
National Association of State Budget Officers (NASBO, various years),
the latter half of the 1990s and early 2000s was an unprecedented period of
continuous net tax cuts (Figure 3.4). In the aggregate, the states cut taxes in

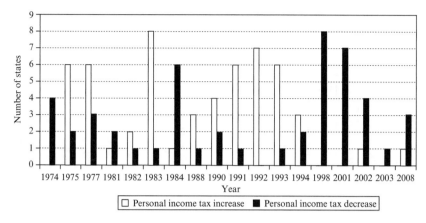

Note: Years with no bars indicate years when states did not enact a change in the tax rate.

Sources: NASBO (various years), Chi (various years) and Prentice-Hall (1984).

Figure 3.1   Number of states enacting changes in the personal income tax rate

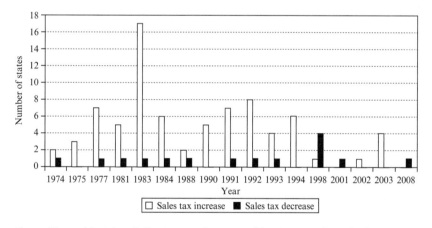

Note: Years with no bars indicate years when states did not enact a change in the tax rate.

Sources: NASBO (various years), Chi (various years) and Prentice-Hall (1984).

Figure 3.2   Number of states enacting changes in the statutory sales tax rate

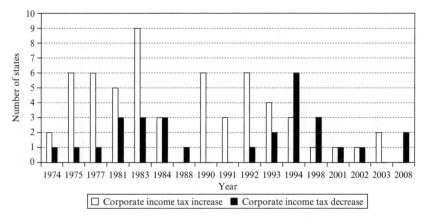

Note: Years with no bars indicate years when states did not enact a change in the tax rate.

Sources: NASBO (various years), Chi (various years) and Prentice-Hall (1984).

Figure 3.3   Number of states enacting changes in the corporate income tax rate

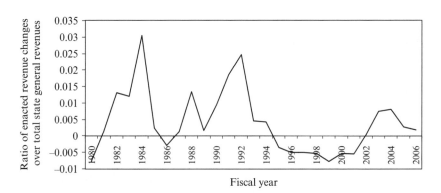

Sources: NASBO (2007) and US Census Bureau (2008).

Figure 3.4   Revenue changes as a percentage of total revenues

the years prior to the recession of 1981–82, but then raised them sharply a few years into the recovery. As a percentage of total state tax receipts they rose to a local peak of 3.1 percent in 1984. After a brief respite in 1986, the states continued to enact net tax increases for the remainder of the decade, even when the economy was expanding at annual rates of between 3.5 percent and 4.5 percent (US Bureau of Economic Analysis, 2008). Modest tax increases continued throughout the 1991–92 recession; without them the states would have faced a massive aggregate deficit. In 1993, state aggregate legislated tax increases as a percentage of state tax receipts rose to 2.5 percent. After one more year of net tax increase, the states then began seven years of consecutive net tax reductions. Modest tax hikes were enacted in 2003–06 (relative to total state tax receipts); the states then resumed their tax-cutting ways in 2007. As of the December 2007 NASBO report, states were not planning tax increases in the aggregate in fiscal year 2008 (FY2008).

TRENDS IN STATE SPENDING AND RESERVES

States' tax-cutting proclivities were not matched by spending cuts. Inflation-adjusted state spending see-sawed in the early 1980s and then grew at an average annualized rate of 3.4 percent from FY1984 through FY1990 (Figure 3.5). Thus, at the same time that inequality widened, state and local spending accelerated. Real state spending did not decline at all during the recession of the early 1990s. Given their low reserves, states chose to tax their way out.

State and local spending also grew sharply relative to other sectors of the economy. After falling from 14.2 percent in 1975 to 12.5 percent in 1984, state and local expenditures as a share of gross domestic product (GDP) jumped sharply over the remainder of the 1980s and the early 1990s, hitting a local peak of 14.4 percent in 1992. The rate of increase in inflation-adjusted state and local spending per capita also slowed in that year (Figure 3.6). Moreover, the composition of state and local expenditures changed in ways that may have further disgruntled taxpayers. Direct purchases as a share of state and local expenditures fell, while transfers as a share of state and local expenditures rose (Figure 3.7).[3]

After the recession in the early 1990s, the states held real growth in spending within the 1-to-3 percent range for a few years, and state and local spending as a share of GDP fell. However, states loosened their purse strings in the late 1990s. For 1994–2000 as a whole, real spending grew at about the same it did from 1984 to 1990. So states heeded the call for tax cuts, but did not pay for them with commensurate spending cuts.

In spite of these trends, states were able to build reserves up from the low levels they had reached at the end of the 1980s. According to NASBO reports, states built up sizeable year-end balances that helped to soften the fiscal blow of the early 1980s recession (9 percent as a percentage of general fund expenditures by the end of FY1980 (Figure 3.8). Still, the states depleted most of these reserves rapidly during the ensuing

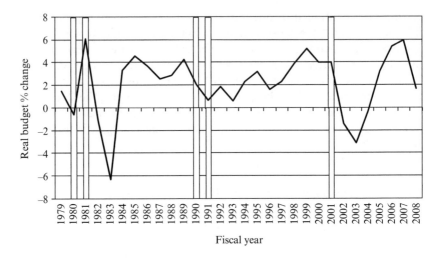

Note: Barred intervals are official NBER recessions.

Source: NASBO (various years).

Figure 3.5   State real annual budget increases, fiscal 1979–2008

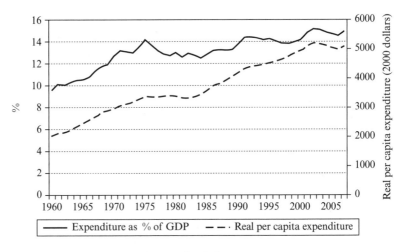

Source: US Bureau of Economic Analysis (2008).

*Figure 3.6   State and local expenditure: real amount per capita and as a
            percentage of GDP*

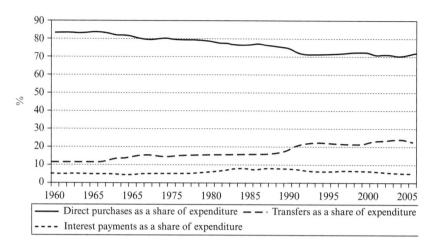

Source: US Bureau of Economic Analysis (2008).

Figure 3.7 Direct purchases, transfers and interest payments as a percentage of state and local expenditures

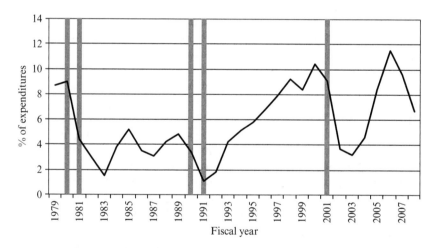

Note: Barred intervals are official NBER recessions.

Sources: NASBO (various years) and US Census Bureau (2008).

Figure 3.8 Total year-end balance as a percentage of expenditures, fiscal 1979–2008

contraction, emerging with a balance-to-spending ratio of only 1.5 percent by the end of FY1983. During the subsequent economic recovery and expansion, states did not replenish their reserves. Balances as a percentage of spending peaked at just over 5 percent in FY1985, remained below that figure for the remainder of the decade, and settled at a low of 3.4 percent in FY1990, just before the next economic downturn. Without much of a cushion to fall back on, the states had to slow growth in spending and to raise taxes. However, during the ensuing recovery, the states were able to build their reserves-to-spending ratio. Over the course of the 1990s, the states saved enough to raise their year-end balances to 10.4 percent of spending by FY2000. As in past recessions, the states spent their reserves down during the early 2000s. However, a combination of stock-market related revenue gains and spending reductions enabled them to build their reserves back up quickly, to a record 11.5 percent of spending in FY2006. Over FY2007 and FY2008, however, the states have increased their spending sharply, and drawn down a large fraction of their reserves, so that as a percentage of spending, reserves now stand at 6.7 percent. A reduction in the ratio of year-end balance to spending of such a magnitude in the latter years of an expansion did not take place in the previous two business cycles. Given current public opinion, state fiscal policy-makers would rather draw down reserves than raise taxes or cut spending.

How did the states manage to build such large balances over the course of the 1990s and again during the mid-2000s? In both periods, accelerating federal aid, especially Medicaid assistance, played an important role. Federal aid to the states was cut sharply during the Reagan era. It recovered partially after this era had passed. Figure 3.9 displays federal aid to state and local governments in constant 2000 dollars from federal fiscal year 1980 (FFY1980) to FFY2007. The aid is broken down into Medicaid and non-Medicaid components. Both components, but especially Medicaid, have risen rapidly, with occasional pauses, since the late 1980s. (The trends are more evident when each component is measured as a percentage of total federal spending and of GDP, as reported in Figure 3.10.) Only since 2004 has this aid leveled off. The acceleration in growth of Medicaid spending during the first half of the 1990s was attributable in part to increasing reliance of state governments on 'Medicaid arrangements', a euphemistic term describing tactics by which many states diverted some Medicaid grants into their general funds without increasing their own spending on medical treatment for eligible patients. The design and implementation of these 'arrangements' displayed a considerable amount of creativity on the part of state governments. The original tactics were devised by a Massachusetts state employee, who won a generous merit award for her ingenuity (*Worcester Telegram and Gazette*, 1991).

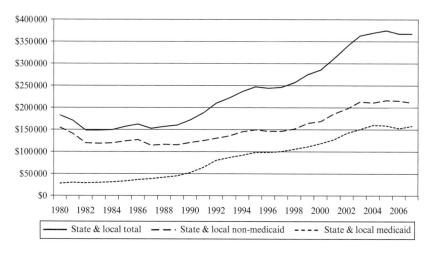

Source: Office of Management and Budget (2008).

Figure 3.9   Federal outlays to state and local governments: constant 2000 dollars (millions)

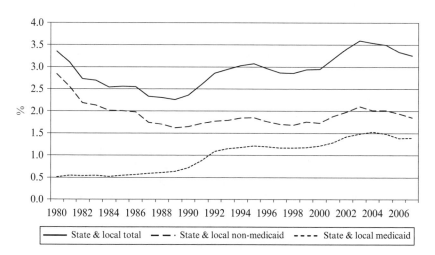

Source: Office of Management and Budget (2008).

Figure 3.10   Federal outlays to state and local governments as share of GDP

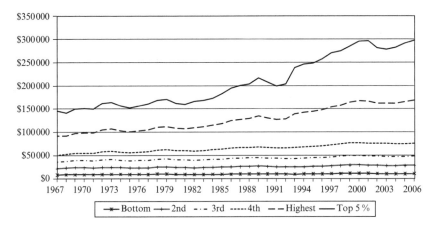

Source: US Census Bureau (2008).

*Figure 3.11   Growth in income inequality, 1967–2006: average real
household income by quintile and for top five percent*

GROWING INEQUALITY AND SLUGGISH GROWTH IN MEDIAN INCOME

By almost any measure, inequality, in both income and wealth, has
widened in the United States since the early 1980s. Furthermore, the
average income of households in the bottom two income quintiles has
been stagnant, despite the rising incidence of two-earner households. The
real median wage of males has fallen.

Consider the trends presented in Figure 3.11, which reports real mean
household income by quintile for the United States from 1967 through
2006. From 1967 through 1973, a period which included a recession, real
incomes grew in all five quintiles nonetheless. The quintile with the fastest-
growing average real income by far was the bottom one (3.4 percent at
an annual rate). The quintile exhibiting the second-fastest income growth
was the second. The average income of the top 5 percent grew more slowly
than that of either of these two quintiles.

The period from 1973 through 1982 was marked by income stagnation.
Over the whole 10 years, average real income declined in the bottom three
quintiles, was flat in the second-highest, and rose only slightly in the top-
earning quintile.

Commencing in 1982, as the nation started to recover from recession,
inequality widened dramatically. From 1982 through 1993, average real

incomes in the bottom two quintiles grew by less 0.5 percent a year. The comparable figures for the top quintile and top 5 percent were 2.2 percent and 3.3 percent, respectively. From 1993 until 2006, inequality continued to widen, albeit at a slightly slower pace. While the average annual rate of growth in the mean real income of the bottom three quintiles ranged from less than 0.6 percent (lowest quintile) to less than 0.8 percent (third quintile), the comparable figures for the top quintile and the top 5 percent were 1.9 percent and 2.8 percent, respectively. For the whole 1967–2006 period, the mean real income of the bottom quintile grew by 38 percent. In the top quintile, it grew by 83 percent. In the top 5 percent, it grew by 105 percent.

If the prototypical household did, in fact, become bitter and disillusioned, leading to a change in state and local fiscal behavior, the seeds of this development were sown between 1973 and 1993. Over this 20-year period, the real incomes of the bottom two quintiles did not budge. Those of the middle quintile rose at an annualized rate of only 0.2 percent per year. The top quintile and top 5 percent enjoyed gains at annualized growth rates of 1.3 percent and 1.9 percent, respectively. Over a 20-year period, disparities of this magnitude mount up.

Trends in the inequality of the distribution of wealth tell a similar story. According to data collected by Mishel et al. (2007), the ratio of the median wealth of the top 1 percent to the median wealth of all US households has risen sharply since the early 1960s. This inequality widened dramatically in the 1980s (Figure 3.12), the period during which, according to our hypothesis, the public's cynicism about state government intensified.

Without women's greater participation in the labor force, median household income might have declined from levels of the late 1970s. The median real average weekly wage of men has declined (Figure 3.13). In 1979 it was $793; by 1990 it had fallen to $743. It bottomed out in 1993–95 at $712, a decline of over 10 percent from its previous peak. It has risen slowly since this trough, but as of 2007 it was still more than 6 percent below its 1979 value. So, the prototypical American household has been treading water only by working harder. For many women, entry into the workforce greatly enhanced the quality of their life. For those compelled to work out of financial necessity, life did not necessarily get better. All the additional costs that often fall on two-earner families – commuting, clothing, daycare and other services – had to be borne, diminishing the gain in household disposable income.

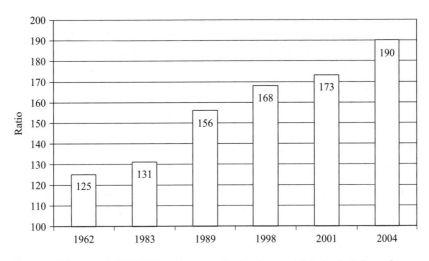

Source: Mishel et al. (2007). The authors specifically cite unpublished calculations of Edward N. Wolfe, performed in 2006, as the source of this figure.

Figure 3.12   The ratio of the wealthiest 1 percent to median wealth in the United States

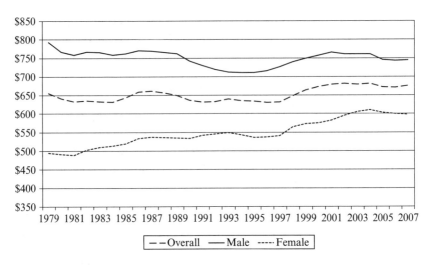

Source: US Bureau of Labor Statistics (2008).

Figure 3.13   Median real weekly earnings per worker by sex, 1979–2007

HAVE CHANGING ATTITUDES TOWARDS GOVERNMENT, STATE GOVERNMENT, OR STATE AND LOCAL TAXES IN PARTICULAR, BEEN EVIDENT IN POLLING DATA OR OPTING BEHAVIOR?

It is all well and good to document growth in government spending during the 1980s and early 1990s, large tax increases in the early 1990s, a subsequent aversion of state policy-makers to tax increases, widening inequality and a lack of significant improvement in the prototypical American's economic well-being. However, is there evidence that these developments are linked, as we have posited, in surveys, election data or econometric studies? We found the evidence to be inconclusive.

Polls: Attitudes Towards Government

If our hypothesis is correct, we would expect to find evidence that public confidence in state government fell in the early and mid-1990s and would be lower than during previous comparable periods in the business cycle (recession and recovery). A few polls have tracked confidence in government over time. Teixeira (1992) conducted a longitudinal study probing changes in a wide range of public attitudes, including the degree of public cynicism towards government in general. He did not distinguish among levels of government. Among the many questions he posed were: (1) 'Can government be trusted?' (2) 'Does government waste tax money?' and (3) 'Is government run by big interests?' His observations run in four-year intervals, from 1964 through 1988. He found large increases between 1964 and 1980 in the percentage of respondents who felt that government: (1) can never be trusted or trusted only some of the time; (2) wastes tax money; and (3) is run by big interests (as opposed to run for the benefit of all). Contrary to our expectation, these percentages then fell (although to nowhere near their levels of 1964), over the course of the 1980s, the period when inequality increased markedly. Unfortunately, Teixeira provides no data on attitudes towards government after 1988.

The US Advisory Commission on Intergovernmental Relations (ACIR, various years) and Cole and Kincaid (2006) conducted a poll over several years investigating the level of confidence of the American public in the various levels of government. Results are reported since 1987 (Figure 3.14). Between 1987 and 1992, the percentage of respondents reporting 'a great deal or a fair amount' of trust in state governments plummeted from 73 percent to 51 percent; the percentage expressing little confidence or none at all skyrocketed from 23 percent to 44 percent. Confidence in the federal

State and local fiscal policy

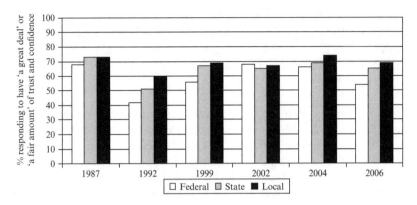

Note: Surveys included separate questions for the three types of government.

Sources: Cole and Kincaid (2006). Data for 1987 and 1992 from surveys conducted by ACIR and reported by authors.

Figure 3.14   *Trust and confidence in governments: federal, state and local*

and local levels experienced a similar pattern. Confidence in all levels of government recovered partially over the remainder of the 1990s. Unlike in the early 1990s, no level of government suffered a marked erosion of confidence during the recession of the early 2000s. Cole and Kincaid found a sharp decline in confidence in the federal government in 2006.

The ACIR and Cole and Kincaid surveys also asked: 'From which level of government do you believe that you get the most for your money?' Results are available from most years since the early 1970s (Figure 3.15). During this period, state government is almost always chosen as the level of government that provides the least value for money. State government's rating was near record lows in 1993, then shot up to a record high by 1999. It is not clear whether this change in sentiment reflected approval of state governments' growing fiscal conservatism during the mid- and late-1990s. Since 1999, the public's rating of the state governments' relative budgetary efficiency has declined to a level close to its all-time low. These low ratings might be a factor inhibiting states from basic tax rate increases and inducing more creative thinking about how to raise revenues.

One poll, conducted by The Gallup Organization and Hart & Teeter Research and reported by Shaw and Reinhart (2001), has periodically posed the following question: 'I am going to read you a list of institutions in American Society, and I'd like you to tell me how much confidence you

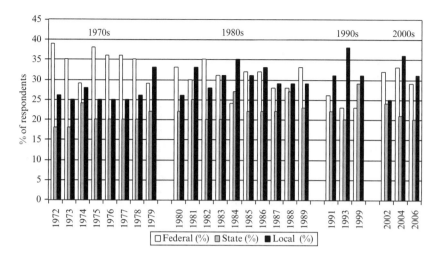

Sources: Cole and Kincaid (2006). Data through 1993 from surveys conducted by ACIR and reported by authors.

Figure 3.15   *'From which level of government do you feel that you get the most for your money?'*

have in each one – a great deal, quite a lot, some, or very little.' One of the institutions on the list was 'state government' (Figure 3.16). Unfortunately, this poll did not include a question probing confidence in state and local government between May 1975 and April 1994. In that period, the percentage of respondents who answered either 'a great deal' of confidence or 'quite a lot' of confidence plummeted from 47 percent to 20 percent, and that responding 'very little' rose from 16 percent to 31 percent. By 1998, confidence in the states had improved, so that the percentage expressing 'a great deal' or 'quite a lot' of confidence had risen back to 36 percent, and the percentage expressing 'very little' confidence had fallen back to 17 percent. This partial restoration of confidence may reflect public support for the belt-tightening and tax-cutting that states undertook, or a trend typically found during economic recovery and expansion. Because of the 19-year gap in polling results, one cannot determine precisely whether the precipitous drop in confidence between 1975 and 1994 is typical of years during and/or immediately following a recession, or represents significant secular erosion.

A similarly worded question used by The Gallup Organization (various years a) elicited different results from those of Shaw and Reinhart. In this poll, The Gallup Organization asked respondents: 'How much trust and confidence do you have in the government of the state where you live

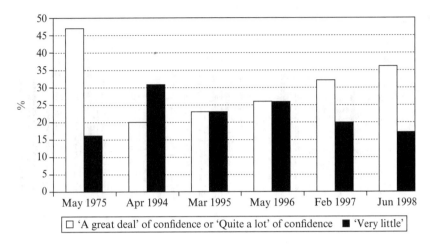

Source: Shaw and Reinhart (2001).

Figure 3.16   Confidence in state government

when it comes to handling state problems?' Again a long gap in the data
– this time from 1976 to 1997 – severely limits its relevance to the issues
addressed in this chapter. The percentage of the respondents who reported
'a great deal' or 'a fair amount' of confidence in state government is displayed in Figure 3.17. No clear-cut pattern emerges, other than a marked
erosion of confidence in 2001 and 2003. Again, these are years during and
immediately following a recession. (The high relative confidence level in
1998 may reflect the fact that the poll, unlike in other years, was taken
between Christmas and New Years Day.)

   Another piece of polling data that may be relevant is the question posed
by the US Advisory Commission on Intergovernmental Relations (various
years) and Cole and Kincaid (2006): 'Which do you think is the worst tax
– that is, the least fair?' Taxes listed in this question included the federal
income tax, the state income tax, the state sales tax and the local property
tax (Figure 3.18). Since the early 1970s, when the question was first posed,
the two state taxes have routinely received far lower relative 'unfairness'
ratings than the federal or local tax. Since the late 1990s, the relative
unfairness of the local property tax has risen sharply, to levels not seen
since the days of the 'property tax revolt', in the early 1970s. By contrast
the state income and sales taxes have continued to be rated as relatively
fair. One might interpret these results as a window for state governments to
raise state tax rates, if coupled with property tax relief. However, given the
widespread concern about the fiscal condition of municipal governments,

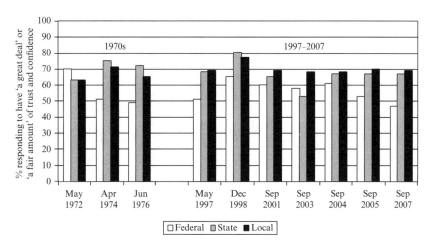

Notes: Respondents asked about each sphere of government separately. September 2001 results reported from survey administrated prior to September 11 attacks.

Source: The Gallup Organization (various years [a]).

Figure 3.17 *Trust and confidence in governments: federal, state and local*
(Gallup)

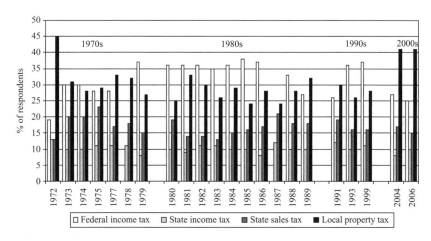

Sources: Cole and Kincaid (2006). Data through 1993 from surveys conducted by ACIR and reported by authors.

Figure 3.18 *'Which do you think is the worst tax – that is, the least fair?'*

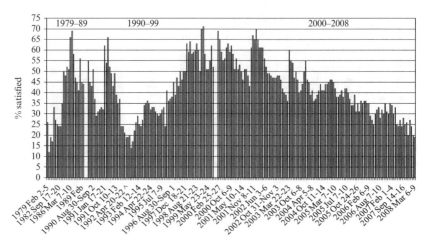

Source: The Gallup Organization (various years [b]).

Figure 3.19   *'In general, are you satisfied or dissatisfied with the way
things are going in the United States at this time?'*

any such arrangement would be difficult to sell politically unless accompanied by substantial increases in state aid to cities and towns. Under such a policy package, states would still need to figure out ways to raise revenues to finance state programs.

Polls: The General Mood of the Country

A deterioration in the general mood of Americans during the 1980s and early 1990s could have led to decreased tolerance for taxation in subsequent years.

Gallup polls (The Gallup Organization, various years b) did, indeed, detect a spreading generalized dissatisfaction among Americans in the 1980s (Figure 3.19). The percentage of respondents registering dissatisfaction with 'the way things are going in the United States at this time' fell sharply in the vicinity of the cyclical trough of both the 1981–82 and 1991–92 recessions. The incidence of general optimism rose sharply after the former contraction, perhaps as the second of the oil shocks absorbed by the national economy finally receded into the distance. Note, however, the gradual deterioration in mood after 1986, even as the economy continued to expand at a rate above potential. The recession of 1991–92 precipitated dissatisfaction ratings rivaling those of the oil-shock days of the late 1970s (in June 1992, 84 percent of those polled expressed dissatisfaction with the direction the country was taking). Dissatisfaction dominated the national mood for several more years, as the economy experienced the first of its 'jobless' recoveries. Satisfaction levels rose only gradually, not surpassing 50 percent until early 1998. Satisfaction began to decline with the economy in mid-2001, received a boost from the trauma and patriotic reaction to 9/11, and has fallen steadily since, regardless of the economy's performance.

The aborted recovery of optimism in the last half of the 1980s, the pronounced pessimism of the early 1990s, and its persistence throughout most of the remainder of the decade, may have been related to the stagnation of the weekly male median wage, discussed earlier in this chapter. After falling sharply from 1979 to 1981, it bounced around during the ensuing five years. However, it fell steadily from 1987 through 1995. Only after it started to rebound steadily, in 1996, did satisfaction levels rebound. Perhaps these collective mood swings, especially the depressed mood of the later 1980s to mid-1990s, inhibited the enactment of visible increases in state tax rates in subsequent years.

Change in Propensity to Oust Incumbents or Candidates of Incumbent's Political Party in State Elections

We uncovered little empirical evidence of a high propensity of voters to oust incumbents in gubernatorial elections during or after the recession of the early 1990s (Figure 3.20). In years when approximately two-thirds of governors have been up for re-election ('mid years' in the national electoral cycle), usually 30 percent to 40 percent of candidates run by the incumbent party lose. The highest 'ouster rate' in mid-year elections between 1970 and 1996 was registered in 1970 when, among 35 elections, the party in power changed in 15 of them (43 percent). In 1990 and 1994, the ouster rates were 42 percent and 39 percent, respectively. In 1994, Republicans picked up 12 of 36 gubernatorial offices, or 33 percent, that they had not held before. The comparable number for Democrats was one. According to Moore (1995) the Republican candidates who ousted Democrats ran on aggressive tax-cutting platforms; after the election, according to Moore, 70 percent of the population lived in a state with a Republican governor. He also reports that a large percentage of Democratic state legislators went down to defeat at the hands of Republican candidates (he did not supply numbers).

Econometric evidence linking economic conditions with voters' propensity to oust incumbent political parties is largely absent. While Chubb (1988) found a positive relationship between growth in national and state personal income and the success of the incumbent party in gubernatorial

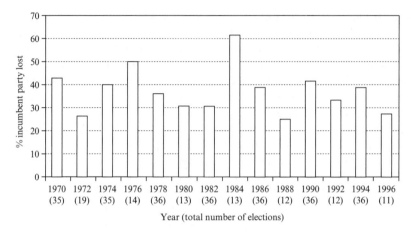

Note: Chart only includes years in which there were at least ten gubernatorial elections.

Source: Congressional Quarterly (1998). *Gubernatorial Elections 1787–1997*. Washington, DC: Congressional Quarterly, Inc.

Figure 3.20   *Gubernatorial elections in which incumbent party lost, 1970–96*

elections, most other studies find an insignificant or even negative impact (for example, Peltzman, 1987; Adams and Kenny, 1989; Simon et al., 1991; Levernier, 1993; Mitchell and Willett, 2006).

Econometric evidence investigating the impact of increases in state taxes on voting behavior, and how this impact might have changed over time, is also inconclusive. Kone and Winters (1993), looked at 407 gubernatorial elections from all 50 states from 1957 to 1985. They found evidence that incumbents are slightly more likely to be thrown out of office after having raised sales taxes, but found no negative consequences for raising other state taxes. They found no electoral reward for lowering state taxes.

However, a sharp increase in voters' aversion to tax increases may still have affected tax policy, even if it did not increase the likelihood that tax-raising incumbents would fail in re-election bids. Some incumbents who raised taxes may have been deterred from running for another term. Also, since the sample examined by Kone and Winters encompassed 28 years, and ended in 1985, one should be cautious in drawing conclusions from their study about the political implications of tax increases since the early 1990s.

Niemi et al. (1995) attempted to estimate the impact of increases in state taxes on subsequent support for the political parties of gubernatorial incumbents by examining the determinants of voters' actual behavior. For data they used ABC/*Washington Post* exit polls taken during 34 gubernatorial elections in 1986. They found that raising the rate of the general sales tax, personal income tax or one of the 'sin' taxes (alcohol, tobacco, cigarettes) decreased the probability that a voter would support the incumbent's party by 13 percent. They also found a statistically significant negative correlation between the number of such taxes raised during an incumbent's tenure and the probability that a voter would support the incumbent's party. However, since these results pertain to one year, they provide no insight into trends over time in the impact of tax increases on voters' choices.

THE OBSOLESCENCE HYPOTHESIS[4]

Many scholars and observers of subnational taxation have alleged that state and local revenue systems are becoming increasingly 'out of sync' with the economy's changing structure (see, for example, Boyd, 2000; Tannenwald, 2001, 2004; Brunori, 1998). The economic stocks and flows that these systems are designed to 'meter' comprise a shrinking fraction of the nation's wealth and economic activity. Four trends, in particular, have been cited as threats to the long-term viability of state and local tax systems as we know them:

1. The intensification of interjurisdictional competition.
2. The shift in the nation's mix of production and consumption from goods to services.
3. The proliferation of electronic commerce.
4. The tendency of state courts to invalidate the local property tax as the principal means of financing public primary and secondary education.

The Intensification of Interjurisdictional Competition

States and municipalities have engaged in fiscal competition since the founding of the republic. Indeed, to some observers, the persistence and ubiquity of such competition imply its inevitability among fiscally autonomous subnational governments. As long as businesses, shoppers and vacationers are mobile, states and municipalities will continue to design their revenue systems in part to attract and to retain firms, residents and consumers (Tiebout, 1956).

While it can be beneficial, according to Alice Rivlin (1996), tax competition 'has escalated into a bidding crescendo that is injuring the winners as well as the losers' (Rivlin, 1996). Burstein and Rolnick (1996) have characterized it as a 'negative sum game', in which jurisdictions short-change themselves on critical public goods (such as education and infrastructure) to finance incentives for prospective employers. Any attempts to raise taxes in a direct and transparent way – say by raising corporate statutory rates – is effectively undercut by employers' threats to pull up stakes and to move to a jurisdiction with a more 'favorable' tax climate.

Fiscal competition has intensified for a variety of reasons. During the late 1970s and early 1980s, the combination of soaring energy costs and persistently high rates of unemployment galvanized states and municipalities to do something to attract and to maintain jobs for their constituents. The shift to services has also been partially responsible. Industries requiring proximity to primary resources (such as steel) or central locations (such as autos) have declined in importance in the United States, while sectors that are growing, such as services, are more footloose. Even within an industry, new communications technology has enhanced mobility. Stiffer competition from overseas has also played a role in motivating jurisdictions to offer whatever inducements are necessary to attract and to retain businesses.

The damper that competition places on subnational corporate income taxation is partially reflected in the declining ratio of state and local corporate income tax collections to corporate profits since the late 1970s (Figure 3.21). This ratio peaked in 1980 at 8.8 percent. By 2004, it had sunk to 4.1. (By 2007, it had risen back to 5.1 percent.) Some of the lost revenue has been recouped through the personal income tax because competitive pressures and desire to conform to federal tax law have led to state legislation permitting the formation of limited liability partnerships (LLPs) and limited liability corporations (LLCs).

Apart from competitive pressures to keep taxes low, state revenue officials have faced an increasingly broad and sophisticated campaign by large multijurisdictional corporations to reduce their taxes through tax avoidance (Brunori, 2006; Pomp, 1998; Fox et al., 2007; Sullivan, 2007). A number of factors are responsible, such as the increasingly global scope and concomitant organizational complexity of multijurisdictional entities, and the greater attention paid by tax planners to state and local corporate taxation as its burden rose over the course of the 1970s and 1980s. As alluded to above, these perfectly legal and largely successful tax avoidance schemes have given state governments an opportunity to gain back some lost revenue through 'loophole-closing'. It is one thing to raise taxes on business simply to augment revenue, even at the peril of undermining

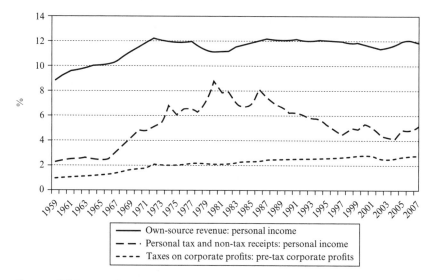

Source: US Bureau of Economic Analysis (2008).

Figure 3.21   Trends in state and local tax burdens, 1959–2007

competitiveness. It is another thing to enact reforms that 'level the playing field' as well as raise revenue, that close the door on tax provisions inserted in the law largely at the behest of lobbyists, provisions that were not explicitly designed to promote socially or economically desirable behavior (such as investment tax credits). However, the erosion of the bases of state corporate income taxes and similar taxes (such as Texas's former franchise tax) has been one of the strongest inducements to consideration of alternative business tax regimes (such as Ohio's Commercial Activities Tax, Michigan's Business Tax, New Hampshire's Business Enterprise Tax, and Texas's Margin Tax).

Erosion of State and Local Sales Tax Bases

Much has been written about the implications for sales taxes of the nationwide decline in the proportion of both production and consumption accounted for by goods, and the rise in the proportion accounted for by services. In 1960, 42 percent of US wages and salaries were earned in the goods-producing sector (manufacturing, mining, construction and agriculture). Forty-seven years later, the share attributed to goods production had fallen to 19 percent. By contrast, the share of US wages and salaries generated by the delivery of private services rose over this period from 16 percent to 38 percent. As for the change in the mix of personal consumption, in 1960, American households allocated 41 percent of their consumption dollars to services. By 2007, this percentage had risen to 64 percent (Bureau of Economic Analysis, 2008). These trends, along with the rise of electronic commerce (discussed in the next section), have allegedly eroded the sales tax base because the taxation of services is so difficult politically and administratively. Russo (2005) has presented evidence that the ratio of taxable sales to personal income and/or gross domestic product has trended downward in recent decades, despite an obscuring idiosyncratic spike in the consumption of consumer goods during the late 1990s and early 2000s. When in need of additional revenues, therefore, states have occasionally turned to increases in state statutory sales tax rates. However, as noted above, states have been more reluctant to raise statutory sales tax rates in recent years. Many states have reached the point where further increases in sales tax rates are neither politically feasible nor economically beneficial. Hence, a further impetus to 'tax creativity'.

Tannenwald (2001, 2004) wonders if the switch from a 'goods' to a 'services' economy has eroded the base of the sales tax as much as has been generally assumed. True, the rapid rise in services as a percentage of consumption has taken its toll on taxable sales. However, on the production side of the ledger, goods-producing industries have generally enjoyed protection from sales taxation since its inception – so their declining share of production has not had as much of an impact on sales tax productivity as some argue. State and local governments had never taxed such intermediate purchases that much in the first place. Conversely, as the production of services has expanded, sectors that have not historically enjoyed sales tax protection have grown, and the taxation of their intermediate purchases has offset reduction in the sales tax base elsewhere. At the same time, the intermediate purchases of all businesses, regardless of sector, are shifting away from goods to services (contracting out, telecommunications and computer systems development and maintenance, specialized consultants in other fields, and so forth). This third trend has diminished sales tax productivity. So two factors – the change in mix of consumption, and the increasing share of intermediate purchases accounted for by services – have reduced sales tax productivity. A third factor, the growing share of production accounted for by services, has boosted sales tax productivity. What has been the net impact on taxable sales? A moderate decline, according to Tannenwald.

Nevertheless, the growing importance of services in the mix of intermediate purchases has strengthened the reluctance of states to tax services. If states impose taxes on services consumed by households, they cannot easily exempt services purchased by businesses. Apart from administrative difficulties, the resulting pyramiding from taxing intermediate purchases of services would cause considerable distortions. Only radical reform, involving the substitution of a gross receipts tax or value added tax for the sales tax, and perhaps other levies, with a broadly defined base and a low statutory rate to mitigate distortions, might enable state and local governments to 'meter' and tax these swelling economic flows. This, perhaps, is why such novel taxes are getting an increasing amount of attention.

The Spread of Electronic Commerce

A great deal has also been written about the spread of electronic commerce and the constitutional and administrative impediments to taxing these transactions. According to the US Census Bureau, the total value of electronic commerce in the US in calendar year 2006, the latest year for which data are available, was $2.9 trillion. In 2004, Bruce and Fox projected that state and local sales tax revenues foregone in FY 2008 because of the spread of electronic commerce would range from $11.8 to $17.9 billion, or between 1.5 percent and 3.9 percent of state and local sales and gross receipts tax in that fiscal year.[5]

Revenue losses from the inability of state and local governments to tax electronic commerce have given new life to the Streamlined Sales Tax Agreement, a multistate compact that its architects believe, if implemented, would give state and local governments the constitutional authority to tax all remote sales at their source.[6] A confluence of factors, in addition to the potential long-run revenue gain, is gradually building support for this agreement and inducing states to ratify it. This is true despite the considerable amount of alteration in their sales tax bases (with attendant political creativity) and some short-term revenue loss that some states have sustained in order to conform to the agreement. 'Bricks and mortar' retailers are on board because they do not want their electronic competitors to be at a tax advantage. Large multistate businesses like the greater ease of compliance under a more uniform system of sales taxation. It would minimize exposure to lawsuits when they accidentally collect too much, and uncover tax payments they must pay to governments when they collect too little.

Tax Creativity Induced by School Funding Court Cases

Since the 1970s, many state courts have ruled that funding public primary and secondary education through a local property tax violates provisions of state constitutions requiring the state to provide an adequate education, state constitutional equal protection clauses, and/or an assortment of other state constitutional requirements (Enrich, 1995; Minorini and Sugarman, 1999). In some cases, such court rulings, or the threat of one, have helped to precipitate the enactment or at least consideration of substantial and novel tax reform at the state level. Sullivan (2008) attributes the enactment of Texas's Margin tax (a variant of a value added tax or VAT) in part to the threat of such a court case. New Hampshire has gone through tax contortions worthy of an Olympic gymnast in order to comply with the school finance decisions rendered by its Supreme Court in order to avoid a broad-based personal income or sales tax. For example, it enacted a state property tax which, for the most part, simply replaced a large chunk of the local property tax, the proceeds of which were distributed right back to the localities from which the tax was collected. School court cases in Vermont have sparked serious consideration of local option income taxes and a state gross receipts tax.

CONCLUDING THOUGHTS: TAX CREATIVITY AND 'THE PERFECT STORM'

The title of Part I of this volume for which this chapter was written is 'The perfect storm?' Of late, state tax pundits have used this term to describe a potentially devastating state and local revenue scenario in the short- to intermediate run, in which economic developments conspire to attack the bases of all the major state and local taxes: the sales, personal income, property and corporate income taxes. Under this scenario, extreme ubiquitous weakness in residential real estate markets will narrow the bases of property taxes; fully offsetting increases in statutory rates, while feasible in theory, will be politically impossible in practice. Housing woes, compounded with high oil prices and the onset of a recession, will continue to weaken consumption and the sale of construction materials, crimping sales tax bases. After dizzying rates of growth, corporate profits have been shrinking since 2007 and will likely continue to do so for at least several more quarters. A retreat in the stock market, a development that caused a sharp, unexpected shrinkage in taxable personal income in FY2001 and FY2002, will inflict similar damage in the current downturn. Meanwhile, still-uncontrolled increases in the costs of health care, needs for infrastructure maintenance and repair that have been postponed once too often, the unceasing demand for improvements in public education, pension funding requirements, recent cuts in federal aid and a host of other factors will limit options for cuts in spending. Reserves are being rapidly depleted. Some early reports on the new alternative state business taxes have been negative (see, for example, Sullivan, 2008).

Given this likely scenario, it is not clear that tax creativity is going to be sufficient. With a change in political party controlling the White House in 2009, federal proclivities to cut taxes might weaken. It might be time to get less creative and go back to the basics – increases in state and local tax rates.

NOTES

1. The views expressed in this chapter do not necessarily represent those of the Federal Reserve Bank of Boston or the Board of Governors of the Federal Reserve System. We would also like to thank Mary Pierotti for her able assistance in editing. Many thanks to Elena Papoulias, intern (from Simmons College), at the New England Public Policy Center, for her excellent research assistance.
2. http://www.reaganfoundation.org/reagan/speeches/first.asp.
3. Figures 3.6 and 3.7 are updated versions of those originally displayed in Fisher (1994).
4. This section relies heavily on Tannenwald (2004), with updated statistics and exhibits.
5. For FY2008, total state and local sales and gross receipts taxes totaled an estimated $304 billion, according to the US Census Bureau (http://ftp2.census.gov/govs/qtax/table1).
6. Courts have ruled that such taxation would impose an unconstitutionally prohibitive compliance burden on vendors given the complexity and variety of the myriad state and local sales tax bases currently in existence. The Streamlined Sales Tax Agreement is designed to make this compliance burden sufficiently low that taxation of remote sales at the source would pass constitutional muster. For more on this subject, see Hellerstein and Swain (2006) and Bruce et al. (2003).

REFERENCES

Adams, J.D. and Kenny, L.W. (1989). The retention of state governors. *Public Choice* 62 (1): 1–13.

Advisory Commission on Intergovernmental Relations (ACIR) (various years). *Changing Public Attitudes towards Government and Taxes*. Washington, DC: ACIR.

Boyd, D.J. (2000). *State Fiscal Issues and Risks at the Start of a New Century*. Albany, NY: Nelson A Rockefeller Institute of Government.

Bruce, D. and Fox, W.F. (2004). State and local sales tax revenue losses from e-commerce: estimates as of July 2004. Working Paper. Knoxville, TN: Center for Business and Economic Research, University of Tennessee.

Bruce, D., Fox, W.F. and Murray, M.N (2003). To tax or not to tax? The case of electronic commerce. *Journal of Contemporary Economic Policy* 21 (1): 25–40.

Brunori, D. (ed.), (1998). *The Future of State Taxation*. Washington, DC: Urban Institute Press.

Brunori, D. (2006). *State Tax policy: A Political Perspective*. 2nd edition. Washington, DC: Urban Institute Press.

Burstein, M.L. and Rolnick, A.J. (1996). Congress should end the economic war for sports and other businesses. *Region* (Federal Reserve Bank of Minneapolis) 10 (2): 35–6.

Butterfield, F. (2005). As gambling grows, states depend on their cut. *New York Times*, 31 May.

Chi, K. (ed.). (various years). *The Book of the States*. Lexington, KY: Council of State Governments.

Chubb, J.E. (1988). Institutions, the economy, and the dynamics of state elections. *American Political Science Review* 82 (1): 133–54.

Cole, R.L. and Kincaid J. (2006). Public opinion on US federal and intergovernmental issues in 2006. *Publius: The Journal of Federalism* 36 (3): 443–59.

Enrich, P.D. (1995). Leaving equality behind: new directions in school finance reform. *Vanderbilt Law Review* 48 (1): 101–94.

Fisher, R.C. (1994). Trends in state–local finances: toward a fiscal agenda for the next five years. *Proceedings of the Eighty-Sixth Annual Conference of the National Tax Association*. Charleston, SC: National Tax Association.

Fox, W.F., Luna, L. and Murray, M.N. (2007). Emerging state business tax policy: more of the same, or fundamental change? *State Tax Notes* 44 (6): 393–405.

Greenhouse, S. (2008a). *The Big Squeeze: Tough Times for the American Worker*. New York: Knopf.

Greenhouse, S. (2008b). Worked over and overworked. *New York Times*, 20 April.

Hellerstein, W. and Swain, J. A. (2006). *Streamlined Sales and Use Tax*. Boston, MA: Warren, Gorham & Lamont.

Kone, S.L. and Winters, R.F. (1993). Taxes and voting: electoral retribution in the American states. *Journal of Politics*, 55 (1): 22–40.

Levernier, W. (1993). Election outcomes and economic conditions: an application of a logit model. *Journal of Economics and Finance* 17 (1): 115–25.

Minorini, P.A. and Sugarman, S.D. (1999). School finance litigation in the name of educational equity: its evolution, impact, and future. In H.F. Ladd, R. Chalk and J.S. Hansen (eds), *Equity and Adequacy in Education Finance: Issues and Perspectives*. Washington, DC: National Academies Press.

Mishel, L., Bernstein, J. and Allegretto, S. (2007). *The State of Working America 2006/2007*. An Economic Policy Institute Book. Ithaca, NY: ILR Press, an imprint of Cornell University Press.

Mitchell, D.M. and Willett, K. (2006). Local economic performance and election outcomes. *Atlantic Economic Journal* 34 (2): 219–32.

Moore, S. (1995). In the states, everything's coming up supply side. Prepared for A.B. Laffer, V.A. Cantor & Associates. Reprinted, with permission, in *State Tax Notes* 9: 1063.

National Association of State Budget Officers (NASBO) (various years). *Fiscal Survey of the States*. Washington, DC: NASBO.

Niemi, R.G., Stanley, H.W. and Vogel, R.L. (1995). State economies and state taxes: do voters hold governors accountable? *American Journal of Political Science* 39 (4): 936–57.

Office of Management and Budget (2008). Budget of the United States government. Historical tables, fiscal year 2009. Washington, DC: OMB.

Peltzman (1987). Economic conditions and gubernatorial elections. *The American Economic Review* 77 (May): 293–97.

Peterson, K. (2006). 48 states raking in gambling proceeds. Stateline.org. Posted 23 May. http://www.stateline.org/live/ViewPage.action?siteNodeId=136&languageId=1&contentId=114503.

Pomp, R.D. (1998). The future of the state corporate income tax: reflections (and confessions) of a tax lawyer. In D. Brunori (ed.), *The Future of State Taxation*, Washington, DC: Urban Institute.

Prah, P.M. (2004). States turn to gambling to fix budget woes. Stateline.org. Posted 18 May. http://www.stateline.org/live/ViewPage.action?siteNodeId=13 6&languageId =1&contentId=15650.

Prah, P.M. (2007). States scramble for gambling jackpot. Stateline.org. Posted 12 September. http://www.stateline.org/live/details/story?contentId=239294.

Prah, P.M. (2008). Proliferation of gambling sets off an 'arms race' among the states. *State of the State Report 2008*. http://archive.stateline.org/flash-data/ StateOfThe States2008.pdf.

Prentice-Hall (ed.) (1984). State tax guide. Englewood Cliffs, NJ: Prentice-Hall.

Rivlin, A. (1996). An economic war. *Region* (the Federal Reserve Bank of Minneapolis) 10 (2): 20–6.

Russo, B. (2005). Will the state sales tax future be like its past? *State Tax Notes* 35 (2): 115–23.

Shaw, G.M. and Reinhart S.L. (2001). Trends: devolution and confidence in government. *Public Opinion Quarterly* 63 (3): 369–88.

Simon, D.M., Ostrom, Jr, C.W. and Marra, R.F. (1991). The president, referendum voting, and subnational elections in the United States. *American Political Science Review* 85 (4): 1177–92.

Sullivan, M.A. (2007). State corporate tax leakage: $14.5 billion in 2006. *State Tax Notes* 46 (9): 601–15.

Sullivan, M.A. (2008). Business tax reform: lessons from Texas. *State Tax Notes* 48 (5): 347–52.

Tannenwald, R. (2001). Are state and local revenue systems becoming obsolete? *New England Economic Review* (Federal Reserve Bank of Boston) 4 (July/ August): 27–43.

Tannenwald, R. (2004). Are state and local revenue systems becoming obsolete? Brookings Institution Metropolitan Studies Program. Washington, DC: National League of Cities. http://www.brookings.edu/reports/2004/10metropoli tanpolicy_ tannenwald.aspx.

Teixeira, R.A. (1992). *The Disappearing American Voter*. Washington, DC: Brookings Institution.

The Gallup Organization (various years a). Trust in government poll data. http:// www.gallup.com/poll/5392/Trust-Government.aspx

The Gallup Organization (various years b). Trust in government poll data. http:// www.gallup.com/poll/5392/Trust-government.aspx

Tiebout, C. (1956). A pure theory of local expenditure. *Journal of Political Economy* 64 (3): 416–24.

US Bureau of Economic Analysis (2008). National income and product accounts. http://www.bea.gov/national/index.htm#gdp.

US Census Bureau (2008). State government finances. http://www.census.gov/ govs/www/state.html.

Worcester Telegram and Gazette (1991). Medicaid loophole plugged\budget hero Betts looks back at fame. 16 September, p. A1.

Comments on 'Major state–local policy challenges: outside-the-box solutions needed'

Mary Mathewes Kassis

'Major state–local policy challenges: outside-the-box solutions needed' by Ronald C. Fisher reviews six key fiscal policy challenges currently facing state and local governments in the United States. In choosing his key issues, the author focused on long-run issues that have been relatively intractable from a policy perspective and that have a broad impact on society over and above just their fiscal impact on state and local governments. The six issues the author identified were health care costs and provision; assessment, productivity and accountability in education; privatization of higher education and related issues of access; corrections and public safety; resurgence of the property tax revolt; and the expectation that economic development is a primary objective or responsibility of state–local government. In discussing these issues, the author emphasized the need for economists not just to research and analyze the issues but also to become active in designing solutions to these problems.

The chapter does a good job defining these six issues and demonstrating that each one meets the author's criteria of a key or fundamental fiscal policy challenge facing state–local governments. Each of these issues is not only important from a fiscal policy perspective, but is also an important social issue in its own right. Any attempt to define the six most fundamental issues will always create some controversy – there are clearly important issues that will not make this finite list. However, the author clearly tried to think 'outside the box' in developing his list, emphasizing spending and programmatic issues more than the traditionally heavily researched tax issues. In general, public finance economists really need to put more emphasis on expenditure programs. Clearly, efficient use of our public resources is as important to society as efficient taxation. It is important for policy-makers to consider the opportunity cost of government expenditures in areas such as economic development. If there is little social benefit to be gained from the bidding wars between states to attract new firms, the resources focused on state and local economic development programs may be better used in other areas. Policy-makers also have a tendency to throw money at problem areas such as education and public safety without giving much thought to how effectively the money is being used. Public finance economists could help guide policy-makers with more research aimed at evaluating the effectiveness of programs and by helping to engineer new programs.

Although the emphasis on expenditure programs is good, the list of key issues may have put too little emphasis on the revenue side. All of the expenditure programs discussed – health care, education, corrections, state and local economic development – require a consistent revenue source. The goals of expenditure programs can be derailed by the budget problems associated with an economic downturn. Although the downturn itself may be a short-run problem, the impact of the business cycle on state and local budgets is a long-term problem as almost all states have some type of balanced budget requirement. The impact of recessions on state and local governments can jeopardize the goals and delivery of important state programs such as education and health care, and policy-makers clearly have difficulty in dealing with these fiscal crises, as the 2001 recession illustrates (Sheffrin, 2004). In addition, many states continue to rely on sales taxes on goods even though the tax base continues to shrink as the United States becomes more of a service economy. As of 2007, services accounted for almost 60 percent of consumption expenditures (US Department of Commerce, 2007). Although there may be more emphasis on tax policy than on expenditures in public finance research, tax reform is still a fundamental fiscal policy challenge for state and local governments. Strategies also need to be developed to help states cope with the revenue declines associated with economic downturns without jeopardizing the goals of critical government programs such as health care, corrections and education. Individual tax reform issues may not seem to meet the broad societal impact requirement of this chapter. However, developing effective tax policy for the twenty-first century does have a broad impact on society through its impact on all government expenditure programs as well as overall economic efficiency. Clearly, society needs well-engineered tax policy as much as it needs well-engineered expenditure programs.

REFERENCES

Sheffrin, S.M. (2004). State budget deficit dynamics and the California debacle. *Journal of Economic Perspectives* 18 (Spring): 205–26.
US Department of Commerce, Bureau of Economic Analysis. National Income and Product Accounts (2007). Table 2.3.5: Personal consumption expenditures by major type of product.

Comments on 'Genesis of state–local creativity'

Jason S. Seligman

Robert Tannenwald et al. have presented a chapter here that is about the conditions that foster 'creativity', or really innovation – right in line with the spirit of this volume. Tannenwald, Jennifer Weiner and Igor Popov have generated many observations and support them with data which underscore the idea that necessity motivates creativity. By Tannenwald et al.'s account there is ample necessity to drive innovation. Stuck between declines in economic activity, and voter resistance to rate increases, Tannenwald et al. argue that state and local government revenue creativity must be less incremental than in the past.

To give an example which may help strengthen the understanding of the Tannenwald et al. thesis, I offer an anecdote from my drive to Atlanta to discuss this paper with its authors. In fact I now believe that the chapter informed my perspective on what at first appeared to be a trivial event. Traffic was moving much slower than usual. (Traffic in Atlanta is usually quite speedy.) No accidents were apparent, or reported ahead on the radio. What was on the radio, though, was informative in its own right. Atlanta Mayor Shirley Franklin was discussing two issues: first, a budgetary shortfall; and second, increases in enforcement of traffic regulations. She tied the recent growth slowdown to the revenue shortfall, and the shortfall to the plan to increase citations. Now this represents a traditional incremental approach to revenue creativity that addresses voter resistance to direct tax increases. When I placed the Mayor's message in the context of my slow commute, I realized that I might just be witnessing evidence of what Tannenwald et al. are getting at; the Mayor's incremental plan is underwhelming, due to behavioral responses. Thus incremental policy innovations may be insufficient as Tannenwald, Weiner and Popov posit. In such a case further revenue innovation is necessary.

To know what kind of innovation might suit our situation, the authors address two hypotheses, 'tax obsolescence' and 'alienation', focusing much of their attention on the latter. In that spirit, we can start with the premise: It would seem expedient simply to increase one or more tax rates to increase revenue. Indeed, the chapter does a great job of documenting voter response to the more transparent state tax increases of the early 1990s.[1] However, Tannenwald et al. note that the electoral outcomes which followed make rate increases seem politically infeasible. Lest we believe that we are about to witness a large number of tax rate increases, Tannenwald et al. further provide evidence in the form of real earnings and voter sentiment data which argues against this belief, and in support of their 'alienation' hypothesis.[2] So to summarize, with direct tax increases unpopular and indirect revenue enhancements being of limited use, Tannenwald et al. argue that more wholesale revenue mechanism innovation is required. By this genesis we are being forced 'out of the box'.

I concede that 'forced' may seem a bit too strong, as generally federal outlays to state and local governments have increased, and additionally state savings policies have been bolstered since the early 1990s. (Regarding savings policies, many states have set up or expanded 'rainy-day' programs which mandate savings be held to act as a buffer stock to meet cyclical revenue shortfalls.) I think it useful to go though Tannenwald et al.'s arguments regarding both phenomena.

Starting first with revenue sharing, Tannenwald et al. provide evidence that while real outlays have more or less consistently increased since the early 1980s, most of the increases since the 1990s are related to one program, Medicaid. Additionally, we observe a significant break in trend beginning in 2002.[3] Outlays have essentially been flat since.[4] Moving on to the second possible opportunity for relief, buffer savings stocks, the authors provide very thorough information on this stock in their chapter. Focusing on recessions, we can see that total year-end balances as a percentage of state expenditures are reported to have averaged 9 percent in 1980, just ahead of the early 1980s recessions, and roughly 5 percent ahead of the early 1990s episode. By comparison they averaged a bit more than 10 percent ahead of the 2001 recession, and grew to more than 11 percent at their most recent maximum in 2005.[5]

Indeed, Tannenwald et al.'s data are very useful because patterns of use of balances can be observed therein. At a nadir, average balances appear to have been less than 2 percent of expenditures in 1983, closer to 1 percent of expenditures in 1991, and a bit over 3 percent in 2003; thus one can calculate that states on average drew down roughly 75 percent of their buffer in the early 1980s, about 80 percent of their buffer in the early 1990s, and about 70 percent of their buffer in the early 2000s. By comparison, buffers have declined from over 11 to just over 6 percent of expenditures since FY2006, a decline in the buffer of roughly 45 percent (five-elevenths). If we were to consider the average draw down in the early 1980s, early 1990s, and early 2000s, that amounts to 75 percent, we would estimate that a little over 3 percent of expenditures is left to be drawn from. If instead we considered funds as available to the average of the previous nadirs, say to a level of 2 percent, then we would estimate that approximately 4 percent remain. In either case, by Tannenwald et al.'s work we see that, historically, not a lot of buffer remains, and so 'forced out of the box' may indeed be closer to true. Another bad year or two seems likely to exacerbate state and local finances. Tannenwald et al. thus rather convincingly argue that there is mounting economic and political pressure for more significant innovation.

Having laid out the general arc of the Tannenwald et al. thesis as I read it, the question becomes: where might future revenue capacity come from? Tannenwald et al. offer a few ideas based on observation of current discussion. These include state-managed value added taxes (VAT), increased interstate coordination of sales tax assessment though mechanisms like the Streamlined Sales Tax Project (SSTP) / Streamlined Sales Tax Agreement (SSTA), and tax simplification (specifically the removal of loopholes). To these I might add a speculation that we might see increased use of financial markets (borrowing, and the securitization of assets). My speculation regarding borrowing is based on the idea that we have seen increased borrowing at both the federal and household level, and innovations to support this use.[6] I suspect that a few yet-unrealized opportunities of this sort exist for states and local governments as well, and that in managing 'rainy-day' enhanced surpluses, communication with financial intermediaries may have increased in such a way as to facilitate this sort of innovation. Less speculative is the notion of securitization. In the past decade we have seen states securitize and thereby realize state tobacco settlement funds originally structured for payout over a 30-year period. I add the observation that other conversations on potential asset sales are emerging: for example, recently there has been reported interest in 'privatizing' (that is, realizing the present value of the expected future stream of profits, or selling) the Massachusetts State Lottery.[7] Similar interest has been reported in Illinois, and I imagine that discussion is not limited to these two instances.[8] Finally, bringing the discussion back to my commute, the state of Georgia has considered various toll road conversions of existing roadways, some of which incorporated an asset sale of the road. These have not proved too popular to date, but may yet.

To end my comments I will ask rhetorically: will borrowing and securitization adequately address the current 'genesis' for creativity as predicted by the Tannenwald et al. thesis? I expect the answer is 'no', inasmuch as asset sales and new borrowing have their limits. This chapter, then, is provocative. As it addresses the factors motivating creativity it provokes me to ask: given these factors, what should state and local tax portfolios consist of? I think this is an excellent frame from which to consider other chapters in volume.

NOTES

1. Tannenwald et al.'s Figure 3.1, 'Number of states enacting changes in the personal income tax rate', shows that there have been relatively few such rate increases across all 50 states since 1992, for example.
2. Tannenwald et al.'s Figures 3.13, 'Median real weekly earnings per worker by sex, 1979–2007', and 3.19, 'In general, are you satisfied or dissatisfied with the way things are going in the United States at this time?' document wage stagnation, and dissatisfaction, respectively.
3. The sort of block grant innovation that we have seen in other areas of finance are not as popular at present, even as Medicaid-related fiscal pressures on states are large.
4. Tannenwald et al.'s Figure 3.9, 'Federal outlays to state and local governments'.
5. As reported in Figure 3.8, 'Total year-end balance as a percentage of expenditures, fiscal 1979–2008'.
6. Specifically at the federal level the Treasury has increased issuance along the yield curve since 2000, whereas households have made increased use of household equity.
7. 'Massachusetts Republican senators to file bill to privatize state lottery', *Boston Globe*, 22 October 2007.
8. 'Illinois seeks to privatize its state lottery', *New York Times*, 22 January 2007.

PART II

How states cope with alternative structures

4. Going without an income tax: how do states do it?

David L. Sjoquist[1]

INTRODUCTION

There are seven states that do not impose a state income tax: Alaska, Florida, Nevada, South Dakota, Texas, Washington and Wyoming. In addition, New Hampshire and Tennessee have very limited personal income taxes, taxing only interest and dividend income. For purposes of this chapter, I consider these nine states 'no-income tax' states. A question that arises is: how do these states finance government in the absence of an income tax? At one level the answer to the question of how these states are able to get along without an income tax is simple: these states must either spend less or rely more heavily on other revenue sources. But in this chapter I attempt to explore this question in a bit more depth.

Income taxes are an important source of revenue to the other 41 states. For example, in fiscal year 2008 (FY2008), income tax revenue (personal and corporate) is expected to account for 48.9 percent of Georgia's state revenue. In FY2007, for all 50 states, income tax revenue was 42.6 percent of total tax revenue. Given the relative importance of income taxes, it would appear to be a challenge for a state to go without an income tax. Yet, occasionally, proposals are made to eliminate state income taxes. For example, in 2007 and 2008, suggestions have been made that Georgia should eliminate its income tax. So, a related question is: how would a state finance government in the absence of an income tax? One approach to this question is to consider the states without an income tax and study how these states are able to get along without this source of revenue. The experiences of the states without income taxes might be instructive as states consider diversification of their sources of revenue.

This chapter compares the level, on a per capita basis, and the composition of revenue for the states without an income tax with a sample of ten other 'income tax' states. There are a host of issues that should be considered in making the decision regarding the elimination of a state income tax, including equity, federal tax offset and economic incentive effects.

However, this report focuses on just one aspect of the decision to eliminate the income tax, the funding of public services. The data used in all of the tables are from US Bureau of the Census (2004 a; b).

DIFFERENCES IN STATE AND LOCAL GOVERNMENT REVENUE

There are several possible explanations for how states are able to get along without an income tax, including:

- the states might raise less revenue, that is, spend less on public services;
- the states might rely more heavily on federal grants;
- the states might rely more heavily on local government;
- the states might rely more heavily on a specific non-income tax revenue source such as a sales tax;
- the states might be able to rely on the existence of unique situations such as oil extraction.

To explore these possibilities I compare the nine states listed above to other states.

One way to survive without an income tax is to simply raise less revenue. Table 4.1 shows total state and local general revenue per capita in each of the seven states without an income tax and the two states with limited income taxes, along with the US average.

Only two of the nine states, Wyoming and Alaska, have larger state plus local general revenue per capita than the average for the United States. The average general revenue per capita for the nine no-income tax states is $5869, while the average for the US is $6447. Six of the nine states (66.7 percent) have general revenue per capita of less than $6000, while only 15 of the other 41 states (36.6 percent) have general revenue per capita of less than $6000. Thus, with two exceptions, states without income taxes have less general revenue per capita than other states. As I note below, Alaska is a unique case. Thus, we can conclude that states without an income tax do collect less revenue than most other states.

To explore the other explanations, I selected ten states for comparison. I first identified states that had state plus local general revenue per capita between $5300 and $6400, which is the range of seven of the nine states with no income tax. Twenty-two states fell within that range. I picked ten of these 22 states to ensure a good geographic distribution of the comparison states and a sample that was representative of the range

Table 4.1 State and local general revenue per capita, 2004

State	State & local general revenue per capita ($)
United States	6447
Alaska	12962
Florida	5908
Nevada	5686
New Hampshire	5727
South Dakota	5658
Tennessee	5372
Texas	5519
Washington	6405
Wyoming	10120

Source: US Bureau of the Census, 2004a.

of general revenue per capita. The comparison states are: Alabama, Colorado, Georgia, Indiana, Kansas, Kentucky, Ohio, Oklahoma, Oregon and Utah.

Comparisons with Alaska seem pointless given the uniqueness of its revenues. Alaska not only has no personal income tax, but it also has no sales tax. As compared to other states, Alaska has much larger revenue per capita from severance taxes, which are taxes on the extraction of natural resources, corporate taxes and miscellaneous revenue sources. Nearly all of these revenues are from oil; in fact, over 50 percent of the state revenue is from oil. Most of Alaska's tax revenue is raised through severance taxes on oil and fishing, and corporate income taxes. But in addition, other taxes are entirely or substantially from oil. For example, all of the property tax revenue is from oil-related property, and nearly all of the corporate income tax revenue is from oil-related businesses. Miscellaneous revenue, which accounts for 61.2 percent of total revenue, comes largely from investments of the state, including royalty income. Only about 12 percent of Alaska's own-source revenue is from sources other than oil and investments. Given Alaska's reliance on revenue from oil, Alaska is not a good model for other states to look to for how to replace their income tax revenue, and I exclude Alaska from further comparisons.

Table 4.2 shows general revenue per capita for the ten comparison states and the eight no-income tax states. As expected given the selection criteria, with the exception of Wyoming, the two sets of states have similar general revenue per capita. For the ten comparison states, income tax revenue (personal and corporate) was $804 per capita, while for the

Table 4.2   State and local general revenue per capita, 2004

State	States without income tax		State	Comparison states	
	State & local general revenue per capita ($)	State & local general expenditures per capita ($)		State & local general revenue per capita ($)	State & local general expenditures per capita ($)
Weighted average	5784	5776	Weighted average	5813	5932
Florida	5908	5782	Alabama	5643	5987
Nevada	5686	5791	Colorado	6112	6173
New Hampshire	5727	5722	Georgia	5308	5630
South Dakota	5658	5422	Indiana	5732	5726
Tennessee	5372	5391	Kansas	5953	5957
Texas	5519	5512	Kentucky	5549	5624
Washington	6405	6863	Ohio	6311	6486
Wyoming	10120	8955	Oklahoma	5453	5122
			Oregon	6062	6157
			Utah	5714	5744
			United States	6447	5932

Source: US Bureau of the Census, 2004a.

eight no-income tax states, income tax revenue was $49. This gives a frame of reference for considering the magnitude of revenue that has to be accounted for in the absence of an income tax.

Besides spending less, a second way that a state could get along without an income tax is if the federal government provided substantial grant revenue. Of course states have little control over this source of revenue, but the receipt of substantial federal grant revenue could allow a state to go without an income tax. Table 4.3 shows federal grants per capita and federal grants as a percentage of total general revenue. Wyoming had federal grants per capita of $2844, which is roughly twice that of the comparison states. The weighted average of grants per capita for the eight states with no income tax is smaller than for the ten comparison states, although the difference is slight. The weighted average of federal grants as a percentage of general revenue is also slightly smaller for the states without an income tax than for the comparison states. The reliance on federal grants among the no-income tax states is somewhat bifurcated, with three of the eight states having a reliance on grants that surpasses the comparison states, and three that have less reliance than the comparison states. On average, however, states without an income tax do not seem to rely on the federal government more than do the comparison states.

A third way a state could get along without an income tax is by imposing greater responsibilities for funding services on local governments. For example, the state could provide less money for schools, requiring local school systems to raise more revenue. This of course would mean that the state has shifted the burden of the income tax to the property tax or local sales tax. Table 4.4 shows local government own-source revenue per capita and local government own-source revenue as a percentage of state and local own-source revenue.

On average, the eight no-income tax states had greater local own-source revenue, both in dollars and as a percentage of state plus local own-source revenue. While Wyoming has the largest local own-source revenue per capita, the local share of total own-source revenue is small. It appears that the no-income tax states have shifted some of the financing responsibility to local governments, but not an extraordinary amount.

Table 4.5 presents total general revenues per capita, state-level own-source revenue per capita, and state-level own-source revenue as a percentage of total (state plus local) general revenue. The total effect of federal grants and greater reliance on local governments to finance public services can be seen by comparing the first two columns for each group of states. The difference between state own-source revenue and general revenue represents the contribution of federal grants and local revenues to total state and local revenue. State own-source revenue divided by total general

Table 4.3   Federal grant revenue per capita, 2004

State	States without income tax		State	Comparison states	
	Federal grant revenue per capita ($)	Grants as % of general revenue		Federal grant revenue per capita ($)	Grants as % of general revenue
Weighted average	1248	21.6	Weighted average	1303	22.4
Florida	1103	18.7	Alabama	1507	26.7
Nevada	823	14.5	Colorado	1131	18.5
New Hampshire	1210	21.1	Georgia	1110	20.9
South Dakota	1764	31.0	Indiana	1178	20.6
Tennessee	1616	30.1	Kansas	1147	19.3
Texas	1231	22.3	Kentucky	1507	27.2
Washington	1246	19.5	Ohio	1425	22.6
Wyoming	2844	28.1	Oklahoma	1368	25.1
			Oregon	1375	22.7
			Utah	1331	23.3
			United States	1452	22.5

Source: US Bureau of the Census, 2004a.

Table 4.4 Local government share of own-source revenue, 2004

State	States without income tax		State	Comparison states	
	Local OSR per capita ($)	Local OSR as % of total OSR		Local OSR per capita ($)	Local OSR as % of total OSR
Weighted average	2272	50.1	Weighted average	1990	44.1
Florida	2508	52.2	Alabama	1762	42.6
Nevada	2433	50.0	Colorado	2730	54.8
New Hampshire	1940	42.9	Georgia	2055	49.0
South Dakota	1758	44.8	Indiana	1919	42.1
Tennessee	1739	46.3	Kansas	2294	47.7
Texas	2244	52.3	Kentucky	1244	30.8
Washington	2218	43.0	Ohio	2191	44.8
Wyoming	3156	43.3	Oklahoma	1493	36.5
			Oregon	2012	42.9
			Utah	1623	52.3
			United States	2268	45.3

Source: US Bureau of the Census, 2004a.

Table 4.5 General revenue and state own-source revenue per capita 2004

State	States without income tax			State	Comparison states		
	State & local general revenue per capita ($)	State own-source revenue per capita ($)	Own-source/ general revenue %		State & local general revenue per capita ($)	State own-source revenue per capita ($)	Own-source/ general revenue (%)
Weighted average	5784	2264	39.1	Weighted average	5813	2520	43.3
Florida	5908	2297	38.9	Alabama	5643	2375	42.1
Nevada	5686	2430	42.7	Colorado	6112	2252	36.8
New Hampshire	5727	2577	45.0	Georgia	5308	2143	40.4
South Dakota	5658	2163	38.0	Indiana	5732	2635	46.0
Tennessee	5372	2017	37.5	Kansas	5953	2512	42.2
Texas	5519	2044	37.0	Kentucky	5549	2797	50.4
Washington	6405	2941	45.9	Ohio	6311	2695	42.7
Wyoming	10120	4120	40.7	Oklahoma	5453	2592	47.5
				Oregon	6062	2675	44.1
				Utah	5714	2760	48.3
				United States	6447	2733	42.4

Source: US Bureau of the Census 2004a.

revenue also reflects the extent to which federal grants and local revenues account for total general revenues.

On average, state own-source revenue makes up a smaller percentage of total general revenue for the eight no-income tax states than for the ten comparison states. For only one of the ten comparison states is state own-source revenue as a percentage of total general revenue less than the smallest percentage for the eight no-income tax states. Four of the comparison states have percentages that exceed the largest percentage for the no-income tax states. Thus, it appears that states without an income tax rely more on the federal and local governments than the comparison states, but the magnitude of the difference in reliance is not large.

STATE-OWN SOURCE REVENUE

The analysis above suggests that seven of the states with no income tax or a limited personal income tax have lower total general revenue per capita than the average state, and that compared to states with similar total general revenue per capita, they rely more heavily on federal grants and local governments to make up some of the revenue forgone by not having an income tax. But the analysis also suggests that federal grants and reliance on local governments do not account for a large share of the revenue that might come from an income tax. Thus, I turn to a discussion of how these states raise their own-source revenue. Table 4.6 presents the average per capita revenue and the average share of revenue derived for major revenue categories, including various taxes, licenses and fees, for all states the eight no-income tax states, and the ten comparison states.

Table 4.6 shows that the eight no-income tax states as a group rely more heavily on every source of revenue than the ten comparison states, except for charges and income taxes. The largest difference is for sales and gross receipts revenue: $327 per capita. This amounts to 43.3 percent of the difference in per capita income tax revenue between the no-income tax states and the comparison states. Excise taxes and other taxes account for an additional $251 in revenue per capita, or 33.2 percent of the difference in per capita income tax revenue. Thus, the eight no-income tax states do not simply rely on one source of revenue to replace the revenue that might be generated by an income tax.

Tables 4.7–4.10 present the same information as contained in Table 4.6, but for each of the eight no-income tax states and comparison states. The pattern found in Table 4.6 is generally consistent for each of the states, with a couple of notable exceptions. First, note that New Hampshire, contrary to the heavy reliance on sales taxes by the other no-income tax states, does not have a sales tax. However, it does collect a substantial amount of

Table 4.6   State own-source revenue by major categories, 2004

	Revenue per capita ($)			Revenue share (%)		
	United States	No-income tax states	Compar-ison	United States	No-income tax states	Compar-ison
Sales and gross receipts	675	882	555	24.7	38.9	22.0
Income Taxes	773	49	804	28.3	2.2	31.9
Excise Taxes	325	387	264	11.9	17.1	10.5
Other Taxes	108	183	55	4.0	8.1	2.2
Licenses	136	152	117	5.0	6.7	4.6
Charges	392	295	444	14.4	13.0	17.6
Misc. revenue	321	316	281	11.8	14.0	11.2
Total	2730	2264	2520	100.0	100.0	100.0

Source: US Bureau of the Census, 2004a.

revenue from its limited income tax and relies heavily on charges. Second, the share of revenue from sales and gross receipts taxes for Wyoming is about the same for most of the comparison states, but Wyoming is much more reliant on other taxes, and in particular severance taxes. For the comparison states, Oregon is somewhat unique in that it does not have a sales tax, but it relies more heavily on its income tax than the other states.

Table 4.11 presents the average per capita revenue and the average share of revenue derived for a detailed list of revenue sources for all states, the eight no-income tax states, and the ten comparison states. The Appendix contains the tables with these data for the individual states. Several of the no-income tax states rely heavily on state property taxes, particularly New Hampshire, Washington and Wyoming. While these states either do not have an income tax or have a limited income tax, Texas and Tennessee do impose significant corporate licenses.

To simplify the comparisons I compare Georgia's revenue structure to each of the eight states in order to identify what revenue sources the eight states rely on to make up for the absence of an income tax. I chose Georgia because it was convenient and it is a reasonable proxy for the average of the comparison states.

Florida

Florida's own-source revenue per capita is about 7 percent larger than Georgia's. The state sales tax in Florida raises nearly 1.8 times the revenue

Table 4.7   State own-source revenue by major categories, 2004 ($)

	FL	NV	NH	SD	TN	TX	WA	WY
Sales and gross receipts	985	961	0	761	992	688	1357	915
Income taxes	83	0	356	61	142	0	0	0
Excise taxes	361	669	519	362	254	408	393	220
Other taxes	225	125	515	15	52	91	378	1638
Licenses	102	267	153	180	177	182	111	201
Charges	212	259	557	272	261	313	465	241
Misc. revenue	329	150	476	513	139	363	236	905
Total	2297	2431	2577	2163	2017	2044	2940	4120

Source: US Bureau of the Census, 2004a.

Table 4.8 State own-source revenue by major categories, 2004 ($)

	AL	CO	GA	IN	KS	KY	OH	OK	OR	UT
Sales and gross receipts	418	415	552	764	707	595	688	452	0	645
Income taxes	560	794	821	715	762	773	853	696	1278	759
Excise taxes	394	214	174	345	289	372	253	211	209	240
Other taxes	91	36	18	24	75	172	10	226	31	25
Licenses	88	73	69	72	100	131	158	238	181	65
Charges	590	403	268	429	328	458	446	478	597	766
Misc. revenue	234	316	241	285	251	296	287	290	378	261
Total	2375	2252	2143	2635	2512	2797	2695	2592	2675	2760

Source: US Bureau of the Census, 2004a.

Table 4.9   State own-source revenue by major categories, 2004 (%)

	FL	NV	NH	SD	TN	TX	WA	WY
Sales and gross receipts	42.9	39.5	0.0	35.2	49.2	33.7	46.2	22.2
Income taxes	3.6	0.0	13.8	2.8	7.0	0.0	0.0	0.0
Excise taxes	15.7	27.5	20.1	16.7	12.6	19.9	13.4	5.3
Other taxes	9.8	5.1	20.0	0.7	2.6	4.5	12.8	39.8
Licenses	4.4	11.0	6.0	8.3	8.8	8.9	3.8	4.9
Charges	9.2	10.7	21.6	12.6	12.9	15.3	15.8	5.9
Misc. revenue	14.3	6.2	18.5	23.7	6.9	17.7	8.0	22.0
Total	100.0	100.0	100.0	100.0	100.0	100.0	100.0	100.0

Source: US Bureau of the Census, 2004a.

Table 4.10 State own-source revenue by major categories, 2004 (%)

	AL	CO	GA	IN	KS	KY	OH	OK	OR	UT
Sales and gross receipts	17.6	18.4	25.8	29.0	28.1	21.3	25.5	17.5	0.0	23.4
Income taxes	23.6	35.3	38.3	27.1	30.3	27.6	31.6	26.8	47.8	27.5
Excise taxes	16.6	9.5	8.1	13.1	11.5	13.3	9.4	8.2	7.8	8.7
Other taxes	3.8	1.6	0.8	0.9	3.0	6.2	0.4	8.7	1.2	0.9
Licenses	3.7	3.3	3.2	2.7	4.0	4.7	5.9	9.2	6.8	2.3
Charges	24.8	17.9	12.5	16.3	13.1	16.4	16.5	18.5	22.3	27.7
Misc. revenue	9.9	14.1	11.3	10.8	10.0	10.6	10.6	11.2	14.1	9.5
Total	100.0	100.0	100.0	100.0	100.0	100.0	100.0	100.0	100.0	100.0

Source: US Bureau of the Census, 2004a.

Table 4.11 State own-source revenue by detailed source, 2004

	Revenue per capita ($)			Revenue share (%)		
	United States	No-Income Tax States	Comparison	United States	No-Income Tax States	Comparison
Property tax	38.98	45.18	16.59	1.4	2.0	0.7
General sales & gross receipts tax	675.36	881.88	554.69	24.7	39.0	22.0
Alcoholic Beverages	15.67	27.05	13.85	0.6	1.2	0.6
Amusements	17.03	15.59	16.71	0.6	0.7	0.7
Insurance premiums	47.51	50.74	40.26	1.7	2.2	1.6
Motor fuels	115.19	128.69	120.84	4.2	5.7	4.8
Pari-mutuels	1.03	0.80	1.02	0.0	0.0	0.0
Public utilities	36.21	51.76	18.08	1.3	2.3	0.7
Tobacco products	41.98	30.44	34.87	1.5	1.3	1.4
Other selective sales taxes	50.65	81.92	18.50	1.9	3.6	0.7
Alcoholic beverages licenses	1.33	1.82	1.27	0.0	0.1	0.1
Amusements licenses	0.79	1.91	0.28	0.0	0.1	0.0
Corporation licenses	21.63	46.58	14.01	0.8	2.1	0.6
Hunting & fishing licenses	4.23	3.80	5.26	0.2	0.2	0.2
Motor vehicle licenses	59.15	57.39	56.56	2.2	2.5	2.2
Motor vehicle operators licenses	6.80	6.49	8.22	0.2	0.3	0.3

81

Table 4.11 (continued)

	Revenue per capita ($)			Revenue share (%)		
	United States	No-Income-Tax States	Comparison	United States	No-Income-Tax States	Comparison
Public utilities licenses	1.74	1.29	0.74	0.1	0.1	0.0
Occupation & business licenses	37.23	31.20	27.78	1.4	1.4	1.1
Other licenses tax	2.62	1.69	2.51	0.1	0.1	0.1
Individual income tax	671.97	3.42	729.23	24.6	0.2	29.0
Corporation net income tax	103.13	45.56	74.39	3.8	2.0	3.0
Death & gift taxes	19.56	14.85	12.66	0.7	0.7	0.5
Documentary & stock transfer taxes	26.92	74.79	1.29	1.0	3.3	0.1
Severance taxes	21.71	47.59	23.88	0.8	2.1	0.9
Taxes, not elsewhere classified	0.78	-	-	0.0	0.0	0.0
Charges	391.82	295.26	444.32	14.3	13.0	17.6
Miscellaneous revenue	321.34	316.13	281.04	11.8	14.0	11.2
Total	2732.36	2263.84	2518.86	100.0	100.0	100.0

Source: US Bureau of the Census, 2004a.

Table 4.12   State sales tax rates and number of services taxed

State	State sales tax rate, 2006 (%)	Number of services included in sales tax base, 2004
Florida	6.0	62
Georgia	4.0	36
Nevada	6.5	15
New Hampshire	NA	NA
South Dakota	4.0	146
Tennessee	7.0	67
Texas	6.25	81
Washington	6.5	157
Wyoming	4.0	62

Notes: NA: not applicable.

Source: Federation of Tax Administrators (2004; 2006).

per capita as does the sales tax in Georgia. Florida has a 6 percent state sales tax rate as compared to Georgia's 4 percent rate (Table 4.12). If the per capita sales tax bases were the same in the two states, this rate differential would imply that Florida should raise 1.5 times as much revenue as Georgia. But in addition, Florida's per capita income is 9.6 percent greater than Georgia's, and this should translate into a larger sales tax base. The combined higher sales tax rate and larger income suggests that Florida's sales tax revenue per capita should be 1.64 percent larger.

Furthermore, Florida has a broader sales tax base than Georgia. For example, out of 168 services that at least one state includes in its sales tax base, Georgia taxes 36 while Florida taxes 62 (Table 4.12).

Florida also has more visitors from out of state than does Georgia, and thus Florida has a larger sales tax base and generates a much larger percentage of its sales tax revenue from tourists. In 2002, estimated visitor spending in Florida was 3.57 times larger than in Georgia, $54.5 billion compared to $15.3 billion.[2] On a per capita basis, Florida's visitor spending was 1.83 times larger than Georgia's.

While Florida does not have an individual income tax, it does have a corporate income tax and raises nearly 50 percent more corporate tax revenue per capita then does Georgia. Florida also raises substantially more revenue from its document and stock transfer tax, in part due to a tax rate that is seven times larger than Georgia's 0.1 percent rate; in Georgia revenue from the transfer tax goes mostly to local governments.

Nevada

Nevada also collects more in sales tax revenue than Georgia, about 1.74 times what Georgia collects. Nevada's sales tax rate is 6.5 percent, which suggests that Nevada should collect 1.63 times as much revenue as Georgia, given Georgia's 4 percent sales tax rate. But Nevada only taxes 15 services, so its tax base may not be as broad as Georgia's. On the other hand, Nevada has more tourists than Georgia. In 2002, estimated visitor spending in Nevada was 1.33 times larger than in Georgia, $20.2 billion compared to $15.3 billion.[3] On a per capita basis Nevada visitor spending was five times larger.

Nevada raises substantial revenue from gambling. For example, amusement tax revenue per capita was $369.27 for Nevada, compared to zero for Georgia. And, while Nevada does not have an income tax, it collects a substantial amount of revenue from occupational taxes.

New Hampshire

New Hampshire has a limited personal income tax and no sales tax. The state relies instead on property taxes, transfer taxes, corporate taxes, fees and charges, and a set of miscellaneous taxes and revenues sources. In addition to an 8.5 percent corporate income tax, New Hampshire levies a 0.75 percent tax on a firm's payroll, interest payments and dividends paid. Its transfer tax is 1.5 percent compared to Georgia's 0.1 percent (the revenue from which goes mostly to Georgia's local governments).

South Dakota

South Dakota relies on its sales tax and miscellaneous revenue sources to make up for the absence of a personal income tax. South Dakota raises about 1.38 times more revenue from its sales tax than Georgia does. The sales tax rate is 4 percent in both states, but South Dakota's sales tax base is much broader than Georgia's. South Dakota taxes food for home consumption and includes 146 of the 168 identified services in its sales tax base.

Tennessee

Tennessee also relies heavily on its sales tax, and generates revenue that is 1.8 times Georgia's sales tax revenue per capita. Tennessee sales tax rate is 7 percent, which implies that Tennessee should generate 1.75 times the revenue Georgia raises. Tennessee taxes food for home consumption (but at a 6 percent rate) and taxes 67 of the 168 identified services, both of which suggest Tennessee should collect more revenue per capita per penny sales tax than Georgia does. Per capita incomes are essentially the same for Tennessee and Georgia, so that should not be a factor. Tennessee does have a corporate income tax with a top rate of 6.5 percent. On a per capita basis, estimated expenditures by tourists in Tennessee are essentially the same as in Georgia.[4]

Texas

On a per capita basis, Texas collects only about 25 percent more revenue from its sales tax than does Georgia, even though the sales tax rate in Texas is 6.25 percent. Texas taxes 81 services compared to Georgia's 36, and has a slightly higher per capita income than does Georgia. These factors suggest that Texas's per capita sales tax revenue should be substantially greater than Georgia's. I cannot explain why per capita sales tax revenue is not higher in Texas. Texas relies more heavily on miscellaneous excise taxes and other revenue sources than does Georgia. Texas generates more severance tax revenue than Georgia, but nothing close to what Alaska collects on a per capita basis.

Washington

Washington relies heavily on sales and gross receipts taxes. Unlike the other states listed in Table 4.7, Washington imposes a gross receipts tax, which is levied on the gross receipts of all businesses in Washington. Most firms pay a rate of 0.43 percent, but service businesses pay a rate of 1.5 percent. About 26 percent of the sales and gross receipts revenue reported in Table 4.7 is generated from the gross receipts tax. This implies that per capita sales tax revenue in Washington is about $1000, or 1.81 times Georgia's sales tax revenue per capita. Washington has a sales tax rate of 6.5 percent and has a per capita income that is 17 percent larger than Georgia's, which suggests that Washington should collect 1.73 times what Georgia collects. In addition, Washington taxes 157 services, which explains at least some of the remaining difference in sales tax revenue.

Washington also collects about 74 percent more in charges than does Georgia, and Washington has a state transfer tax rate of 1.33 percent and imposes numerous selective sales taxes. Washington also relies more heavily on the property tax at the state level as compared to Georgia.

Wyoming

A third of Wyoming revenue comes from severance taxes. It also collects 66 percent more sales and gross receipts tax revenue per capita than Georgia.

However, part of that revenue is collected for local governments, and thus does not reflect the amount of revenue collected through Wyoming's state sales tax rate of 4 percent. Making an adjustment for this, based on information from the annual report of the State of Wyoming Department of Revenue (2004), suggests that state sales tax revenue per person in Wyoming is about $593, which is about 7.6 percent more than in Georgia. This larger amount is due in part to the fact that Wyoming taxes food for home consumption and includes 62 services in its tax base. Wyoming's miscellaneous revenue is $904 as compared to $241 for Georgia.

Summary

Wyoming (and Alaska) rely heavily on severance taxes. But these are the only two states that are able to employ such a state-specific tax base to largely replace the revenue from not having an income tax. The other unique state-specific tax bases are visitors to Florida, legalized gambling in Nevada and oil in Texas.

Other than these unique state-specific sources of revenue, the states without an income tax or a limited income tax generally rely more heavily on the sales tax by imposing a higher tax rate and/or using a broader base than does our comparison state, Georgia. But in addition, all of these states collect more revenue per capita than Georgia from nearly all other revenue sources listed in Table 4.7.

REQUIRED CHANGE IN REVENUE STRUCTURE

We can also consider how a state's revenue structure would change if it eliminated its personal income tax and modeled its tax structure to match one of the states without a personal income tax or a limited income tax. Given Alaska's and Wyoming's reliance on severance taxes, these two states are clearly not models that a state might follow. But there is no obvious reason why the other seven states could not be a model for a state's tax structure if it were to replace the revenue from its income tax, although Florida and Nevada have greater tourism and Texas can rely on severance tax revenue. However, Washington seems to be the most likely candidate on which to 'model' a state's own-source revenue structure if it were to eliminate its income taxes and replace the revenue. I use the revenue structure of the average for the ten comparison states as the base and show how that tax structure would change if Washington's revenue structure was adopted.

To investigate how the average comparison state's structure of state own-source revenue would have to change to match Washington's, I start with the per capita revenues by the sources listed in Tables 4.11 and 4.A1. I adjusted each revenue line for Washington by the same percentage so that the adjusted total revenue per capita equaled total revenue per capita (including its personal and corporate income tax revenue) for the comparison state average. I calculated the required revenue change for each revenue source by subtracting the actual revenue for the average comparison state from the adjusted Washington revenue structure. I also calculated the percentage change required for each revenue source.

Table 4.13 shows the dollar and percentage change that would be necessary for each revenue source in order for the average comparison state to make up the revenue that would be lost from eliminating both its corporate and personal income taxes, and to have a revenue structure like Washington. The column total equals the per capita revenue generated from the corporate and personal income taxes for the average comparison state. To illustrate, the average comparison state would have to impose state property taxes of $210.72 per capita to match the adjusted Washington state property tax revenue. However, the current state property tax revenue per capita for the average comparison state is $16.59, and thus the required increase would be $194.13, which implies an increase of 1170 percent. The biggest dollar change that would be required would be a significant increase in general sales and gross receipts taxes.

SUMMARY AND CONCLUSIONS

There are seven states that do not impose a personal income tax and two other states that have limited personal income taxes. I have considered how these states are able to finance government without an income tax and how a state's revenue structure might change if it eliminated its income tax and adopted the revenue structure of one of those states. These states do raise slightly less revenue per capita than does the average US state.

I compared the revenue structure of the states without an income tax to a sample of comparison states whose general revenues per capita are about the same as most of the no-income tax states. Excluding Alaska, which is unique, I found that the no-income tax states do, on average, receive more grants from the Federal government and rely more heavily on local governments than do the comparison states. But mostly, these states rely on own-source revenue, and rely on a variety of own-source revenue sources rather than one source. Alaska and Wyoming rely heavily on severance taxes, but the other states rely more heavily on most non-income tax

Table 4.13   Required net change in average state's own-source revenue structure

	Required change	
	$ per capita	% change in revenue per capita
Property taxes	194.13	1170.0
General sales and gross receipts	607.99	109.6
Alcoholic beverages	12.73	91.9
Amusements	−16.70	−100.0
Insurance premiums	7.44	18.5
Motor fuels	6.94	5.7
Pari-mutuels	−0.77	−76.0
Public utilities	30.66	169.6
Tobacco products	13.80	39.6
Other selective sales	18.77	101.5
Alcoholic beverages	0.11	8.7
Amusements	−0.27	−96.2
Corporation	−11.44	−81.7
Hunting and fishing	−1.07	−20.3
Motor vehicle	−10.42	−18.4
Motor vehicle operators	−1.62	−19.7
Public utility	1.31	176.6
Occupation and business, NEC	−1.48	−5.3
Other licenses	3.02	120.1
Individual income	−729.23	−100.0
Corporation net income	−74.39	−100.0
Death and gift	6.64	52.5
Documentary and stock transfer	87.06	6746.9
Severance	−18.69	−78.3
Other	0.00	
Charges	−45.80	−10.3
Miscellaneous revenue	−78.72	−28.0
Total	803.62	

Note: NEC: 'not elsewhere classified'.

Source: Author's calculations.

revenue sources than do the comparison states. However, the general sales and gross receipt taxes are the principal revenue source in the absence of an income tax.

Excluding Alaska and Wyoming, which rely heavily on special taxes such as severance taxes, there are five states that finance state government without a personal income tax, and three states that do so without a corporate or personal income tax. Other than Washington, these five states do have some unique characteristics relative to Georgia. But nonetheless, each of the states other than Alaska and Wyoming could be used to illustrate how another state's revenue structure would look if it eliminated the personal and/or the corporate income tax. I have shown how the own-source revenue structure for the average comparison state would have to change if it adopted Washington's revenue structure. The changes would be significant.

NOTES

1. I thank Don Bruce for his comments on an earlier version of this chapter. This chapter is a modification of 'Revenue structures of states without an income tax', which appeared in the 18 June 2007 issue of *State Tax Notes*.
2. Travel Industry Association of America, http://www.tia.org.
3. Travel Industry Association of America, http://www.tia.org.
4. Travel Industry Association of America, http://www.tia.org.

REFERENCES

Federation of Tax Administrators (2004). Sales taxation of services. http://www.taxadmin.org/fta/pub/services/services.html

Federation of Tax Administrators (2006). Sales tax rates and vendor discounts. http://www.taxadmin.org/fta/rate/sale/sale_vdr.html

State of Wyoming, Department of Revenue (2004). *2004 Annual Report*. http://revenue.state.wy.us/PortalVBVS/uploads/2004AnuualReport.pdf

US Bureau of the Census (2004a). State and local government finances: 2003–04. http://www.census.gov.govs/www/estimate04.htm

US Bureau of the Census (2004b). 2004 state government tax collections. http://www.census.gov/govs/www/statetax04.html

APPENDIX

Table 4.A1   Per capita state own-source revenue by source for no-income tax states, 2004

	FL	NV	NH	SD	TN	TX	WA	WY
Property tax	15.92	56.78	379.98	-	-	-	245.95	276.30
General sales & gross receipts tax	985.25	961.22	-	760.56	991.89	687.98	1,357.04	914.71
Alcoholic beverages	34.03	14.52	9.42	16.13	15.62	26.78	31.03	2.63
Amusements	-	369.27	1.37	0.03	-	1.03	0.01	-
Insurance premiums	40.91	83.25	61.16	71.78	59.58	50.31	55.68	35.64
Motor fuels	116.29	125.84	100.01	163.45	141.21	129.89	149.14	138.29
Pari-mutuels	1.54	-	3.17	1.14	-	0.52	0.29	0.45
Public utilities	98.50	4.14	50.49	2.53	0.81	35.29	56.89	5.96
Tobacco products	25.85	55.32	76.99	35.85	20.28	23.79	56.80	36.72
Other selective sales taxes	44.17	16.26	216.52	70.80	16.95	140.03	43.50	-
Alcoholic beverages licenses	1.98	-	13.48	0.38	0.41	1.71	1.62	0.01
Amusements licenses	0.26	41.01	0.27	0.17	0.13	0.31	0.01	-
Corporation licenses	9.29	22.61	3.11	3.53	86.00	84.38	3.00	12.50
Hunting & fishing licenses	0.84	3.07	6.95	28.70	4.24	3.56	4.90	54.94
Motor vehicle licenses	64.70	59.78	65.00	54.69	43.29	54.85	53.85	100.36
Motor vehicle operators licenses	8.73	6.23	10.05	2.43	7.08	4.28	7.70	3.77

Public utilities licenses	1.59	-	5.01	1.16	1.06	0.77	2.39	-
Occupation & business licenses	14.70	132.38	47.42	75.22	34.49	30.33	30.69	29.42
Other licenses tax	0.00	2.12	2.03	13.84	0.73	1.50	6.45	-
Individual income tax	-	-	42.16	-	23.76	-	-	-
Corporation net income tax	82.91	-	313.78	61.10	117.90	-	-	-
Death & gift taxes	22.25	10.52	23.51	12.09	16.38	6.73	22.53	11.94
Documentary & stock transfer taxes	183.86	41.45	111.91	0.18	29.56	-	103.12	-
Severance taxes	2.80	15.93	-	2.61	0.18	84.41	6.06	1350.21
Taxes, not elsewhere classified	-	-	-	-	5.47	-	-	-
Charges	212.00	259.00	557.00	272.00	261.00	313.00	465.00	241.00
Miscellaneous revenue	329.00	150.00	476.00	513.00	139.00	363.00	236.00	905.00
Total	2297.17	2430.71	2576.78	2162.90	2016.73	2043.80	2939.94	4119.63

Source: US Bureau of the Census, 2004b.

Table 4.A2   Per capita state own-source revenue by source for comparison states, 2004

	AL	CO	GA	IN	KS	KY	OH	OK	OR	UT
Property tax	48.94	-	7.30	1.43	21.05	109.96	3.55	-	4.42	-
General sales & gross receipts tax	418.25	414.87	551.84	764.32	707.00	595.37	688.34	452.40	-	644.73
Alcoholic beverages	30.33	6.81	16.80	6.18	32.05	19.10	7.71	19.42	3.71	11.85
Amusements	0.02	21.54	-	122.97	0.24	0.06	-	1.52	0.02	-
Insurance premiums	54.27	38.63	35.60	28.63	44.56	80.13	36.95	40.92	14.53	44.10
Motor fuels	118.34	129.85	84.77	128.82	156.91	115.07	134.60	117.85	112.66	141.22
Pari-mutuels	0.71	0.98	-	0.76	1.29	3.73	1.39	0.80	0.81	5.72
Public utilities	132.72	2.03	-	1.70	0.27	-	24.09	6.01	2.93	25.47
Tobacco products	20.61	14.16	25.49	54.39	45.57	4.98	48.70	17.99	73.89	11.76
Other selective sales taxes	37.03	-	10.86	1.41	8.14	148.80	-	6.84	-	0.47
Alcoholic beverages licenses	0.55	1.22	0.26	1.55	0.90	1.23	2.61	1.48	0.73	-
Amusements licenses	-	0.16	-	0.65	0.08	0.92	-	1.34	0.22	1.09
Corporation licenses	16.17	1.57	5.97	0.85	17.25	47.86	25.94	11.91	1.19	8.54
Hunting & fishing licenses	3.25	14.36	2.69	2.75	6.67	5.15	2.69	6.12	11.11	38.33
Motor vehicle licenses	38.19	41.92	31.40	25.46	59.07	49.57	62.28	156.87	116.65	3.81
Motor vehicle operators licenses	3.69	3.11	4.14	34.05	5.43	2.71	5.90	3.98	8.84	3.81

Public utilities licenses	2.29	-	0.00	-	1.80	1.98	0.28	0.00	3.34	-
Occupation & business licenses	23.69	10.93	13.16	6.47	8.23	20.62	58.21	56.67	36.64	11.25
Other licenses tax	0.00	0.15	11.64	0.23	1.01	0.92	0.48	0.11	2.57	1.36
Individual income tax	495.81	741.83	765.92	611.51	700.63	680.68	760.28	658.09	1189.29	698.90
Corporation net income tax	64.54	52.06	55.47	103.55	60.94	92.11	92.63	37.83	89.13	59.89
Death & gift taxes	6.51	10.90	7.40	22.48	17.58	16.34	5.61	31.54	20.50	4.00
Documentary & stock transfer taxes	9.96	-	0.05	-	-	0.83	-	3.42	1.75	-
Severance taxes	25.12	25.18	-	0.09	35.90	45.17	0.71	185.88	4.62	20.66
Taxes not elsewhere classified	-	-	3.07	-	-	-	-	4.71	-	-
Charges	590.00	403.00	268.00	429.00	328.00	458.00	446.00	478.00	597.00	766.00
Miscellaneous revenue	234.00	316.00	241.00	285.00	251.00	296.00	287.00	290.00	378.00	261.00
Total	2374.53	2251.64	2142.73	2634.89	2512.41	2797.32	2695.37	2592.07	2674.80	2760.09

Source: US Bureau of the Census, 2004b.

Table 4.A3   *Share of state own-source revenue for no-income tax states, 2004 (%)*

	FL	NV	NH	SD	TN	TX	WA	WY
Property tax	0.7	2.3	14.7	0.0	0.0	0.0	8.4	6.7
General sales & gross receipts tax	42.9	39.5	0.0	35.2	49.2	33.7	46.2	22.2
Alcoholic beverages	1.5	0.6	0.4	0.7	0.8	1.3	1.1	0.1
Amusements	0.0	15.2	0.1	0.0	0.0	0.1	0.0	0.0
Insurance premiums	1.8	3.4	2.4	3.3	3.0	2.5	1.9	0.9
Motor fuels	5.1	5.2	3.9	7.6	7.0	6.4	5.1	3.4
Pari-mutuels	0.1	0.0	0.1	0.1	0.0	0.0	0.0	0.0
Public utilities	4.3	0.2	2.0	0.1	0.0	1.7	1.9	0.1
Tobacco products	1.1	2.3	3.0	1.7	1.0	1.2	1.9	0.9
Other selective sales taxes	1.9	0.7	8.4	3.3	0.8	6.9	1.5	0.0
Alcoholic beverages licenses	0.1	0.0	0.5	0.0	0.0	0.1	0.1	0.0
Amusements licenses	0.0	1.7	0.0	0.0	0.0	0.0	0.0	0.0
Corporation licenses	0.4	0.9	0.1	0.2	4.3	4.1	0.1	0.3
Hunting & fishing licenses	0.0	0.1	0.3	1.3	0.2	0.2	0.2	1.3
Motor vehicle licenses	2.8	2.5	2.5	2.5	2.1	2.7	1.8	2.4
Motor vehicle operators licenses	0.4	0.3	0.4	0.1	0.4	0.2	0.3	0.1

Public utilities licenses	0.1	0.0	0.2	0.1	0.1	0.0	0.1	0.0
Occupation & business licenses	0.6	5.4	1.8	3.5	1.7	1.5	1.0	0.7
Other licenses tax	0.0	0.1	0.1	0.6	0.0	0.1	0.2	0.0
Individual income tax	0.0	0.0	1.6	0.0	1.2	0.0	0.0	0.0
Corporation net income tax	3.6	0.0	12.2	2.8	5.8	0.0	0.0	0.0
Death & gift taxes	1.0	0.4	0.9	0.6	0.8	0.3	0.8	0.3
Documentary & stock transfer taxes	8.0	1.7	4.3	0.0	1.5	0.0	3.5	0.0
Severance taxes	0.1	0.7	0.0	0.1	0.0	4.1	0.2	32.8
Taxes, not elsewhere classified	0.0	0.0	0.0	0.0	0.3	0.0	0.0	0.0
Charges	9.2	10.7	21.6	12.6	12.9	15.3	15.8	5.9
Miscellaneous revenue	14.3	6.2	18.5	23.7	6.9	17.7	8.0	22.0
Total	100.0	100.0	100.0	100.0	100.0	100.0	100.0	100.0

Source: US Bureau of the Census, 2004b.

95

Table 4.A4 Share of state own-source revenue for comparison states, 2004 (%)

	AL	CO	GA	IN	KS	KY	OH	OK	OR	UT
Property tax	2.1	0.0	0.3	0.1	0.8	3.9	0.1	0.0	0.2	0.0
General sales & gross receipts tax	17.6	18.4	25.8	29.0	28.1	21.3	25.5	17.5	0.0	23.4
Alcoholic beverages	1.3	0.3	0.8	0.2	1.3	0.7	0.3	0.7	0.1	0.4
Amusements	0.0	1.0	0.0	4.7	0.0	0.0	0.0	0.1	0.0	0.0
Insurance premiums	2.3	1.7	1.7	1.1	1.8	2.9	1.4	1.6	0.5	1.6
Motor fuels	5.0	5.8	4.0	4.9	6.2	4.1	5.0	4.5	4.2	5.1
Pari-mutuels	0.0	0.0	0.0	0.0	0.1	0.1	0.1	0.0	0.0	0.0
Public utilities	5.6	0.1	0.0	0.1	0.0	0.0	0.9	0.2	0.1	0.2
Tobacco products	0.9	0.6	1.2	2.1	1.8	0.2	1.8	0.7	2.8	0.9
Other selective sales taxes	1.6	0.0	0.5	0.1	0.3	5.3	0.0	0.3	0.0	0.4
Alcoholic beverages licenses	0.0	0.1	0.0	0.1	0.0	0.0	0.1	0.1	0.0	0.0
Amusements licenses	0.0	0.0	0.0	0.0	0.0	0.0	0.0	0.1	0.0	0.0
Corporation licenses	0.7	0.1	0.3	0.0	0.7	1.7	1.0	0.5	0.0	0.0
Hunting & fishing licenses	0.1	0.6	0.1	0.1	0.3	0.2	0.1	0.2	0.4	0.3
Motor vehicle licenses	1.6	1.9	1.5	1.0	2.4	1.8	2.3	6.1	4.4	1.4
Motor vehicle operators licenses	0.2	0.1	0.2	1.3	0.2	0.1	0.2	0.2	0.3	0.1

Public utilities licenses	0.1	0.0	0.0	0.0	0.1	0.1	0.0	0.0	0.1	0.0
Occupation & business licenses	1.0	0.5	0.6	0.2	0.3	0.7	2.2	2.2	1.4	0.4
Other licenses tax	0.0	0.0	0.5	0.0	0.0	0.0	0.0	0.0	0.1	0.0
Individual income tax	20.9	32.9	35.7	23.2	27.9	24.3	28.2	25.4	44.5	25.3
Corporation net income tax	2.7	2.3	2.6	3.9	2.4	3.3	3.4	1.5	3.3	2.2
Death & gift taxes	0.3	0.5	0.3	0.9	0.7	0.6	0.2	1.2	0.8	0.1
Documentary & stock transfer taxes	0.4	0.0	0.0	0.0	0.0	0.0	0.0	0.1	0.1	0.0
Severance taxes	1.1	1.1	0.0	0.0	1.4	1.6	0.0	7.2	0.2	0.7
Taxes, not elsewhere classified	0.0	0.0	0.1	0.0	0.0	0.0	0.0	0.2	0.0	0.0
Charges	24.8	17.9	12.5	16.3	13.1	16.4	16.5	18.5	22.3	27.7
Miscellaneous revenue	9.9	14.1	11.3	10.8	10.0	10.6	10.6	11.2	14.1	9.5
Total	100.0	100.0	100.0	100.0	100.0	100.0	100.0	100.0	100.0	100.0

Source: US Bureau of the Census, 2004b.

97

5. California's state and local revenue structure after Proposition 13: is denial the appropriate way to cope?

Robert W. Wassmer

INTRODUCTION

California's path on a state and local government revenue structure that is different from that observed in most of the United States began with its citizens' 1978 approval of the Proposition 13 ballot initiative in 1978. This initiative placed in California's Constitution the requirement that the *ad valorem* rate of property taxation anywhere in the state should not exceed 1 percent of a property's acquisition value. Acquisition value is set at the time of an arm's-length sale and increases annually from the time of sale at a rate that cannot exceed the higher of 2 percent or inflation. The result of Proposition 13's nearly 60 percent cut in California's local property taxes is illustrated in Figure 5.1. In 1977–78, the last fiscal year before the imposition of Proposition 13, nearly 28 percent of state and local general revenue generated in the state came from property taxation. California's property tax reliance was 26 percent greater than the reliance exhibited in all states in 1977–78.[1] By 2005–06, the most recent fiscal year for which data are available, California's reliance on property taxation as a source of state and local general revenue had fallen to less than 13 percent. This was 24 percent below the property tax reliance occurring throughout the rest of the United States in 2005–06.

The purpose of this chapter is to describe how California has coped with its choice to reduce its reliance on property taxation. As the title implies, much of this coping has come through a denial of the existence of a structural deficit and/or a denial of the need to eliminate it. California merits this examination for two reasons: (1) its relative size within the United States: the gross domestic product (GDP) of California is nearly 14 percent of that of the nation, New York's GDP – the next closest – is just 60 percent of California's; and (2) as a cautionary tale to other states that if they adopt California-style revenue reliance, and experience similar

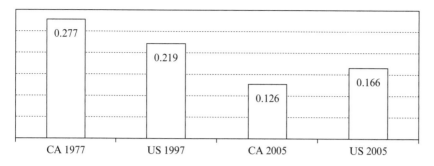

Source: State and Local Finance Data Query System, Urban Institute – Brookings Institute Tax Policy Center, www.taxpolicycenter.org.

Figure 5.1   State and local property taxes as a fraction of general revenue

economic and demographic changes, they too will experience the fiscal instability described here.

The next section of this chapter examines how California's state and local revenue reliance has changed since Proposition 13. In this section, I also describe the state and local revenue instruments in the state for which reliance has increased, and the additional ballot measures that have amended the state's Constitution to deal with the repercussions of Proposition 13, *Serrano* v. *Priest* and a supermajority budget vote. The third section offers a description of outcomes attributable to California's reduction in property tax reliance. In the fourth section of this chapter, I continue with a summary of suggestions that have been offered on how better to deal with California's current fiscal situation, and include an 'out-of-the-box' idea.

CALIFORNIA'S STATE AND LOCAL REVENUE AFTER PROPOSITION 13

Before looking at some specifics on how California's state and local revenue reliance has changed since Proposition 13, it is appropriate to first look for any changes in overall revenue raised. In Figures 5.2 and 5.3, this is done for real per capita revenue and for revenue as a percentage of personal income. California's real per capita state and local revenue increased by just over $4000 between 1977–78 and 2005–06, or by about 65 percent. Nevertheless, over the same period, this figure also rose for the entire United States. California's real per capita state and local revenue was 29 percent above that observed in the entire United States in 1977–78;

State and local fiscal policy

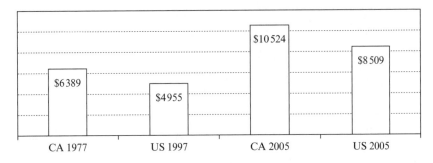

Source: State and Local Finance Data Query System, Urban Institute – Brookings
Institute Tax Policy Center, www.taxpolicycenter.org.

Figure 5.2   Real per capita state and local total revenue

by 2005–06 it had fallen to 11 percent above the United States. However,
California is a relatively affluent state and it is thus appropriate to
compare its state and local revenue to the rest of the country by weighing
it by personal income. As shown in Figure 5.3, at 23 percent of the state's
personal income, California's state and local revenue in 1977–78 was 11
percent above the same figure calculated for the rest of the United States.
In 2005–06, the percentage difference in revenue as a percent of personal
income between California and the United States had risen to 15 percent.
The amount of state and local revenue in California has increased after the
passage of Proposition 13, but so has it in the entire United States. Using
personal income terms, in 2005–06 California had further distanced itself
from the rest of the United States. Using per capita terms, California's
distance above the rest of the United States had shrunk.

   If California has not significantly reduced the revenue its state and local
governments raise, how has it made up for lost property tax revenue? Part
of this answer is found in Figures 5.4–5.6. As shown in Figure 5.4, both
California and the entire United States in 1977–78 raised about 10 percent
of their state and local revenue from personal income taxes. By 2005–06,
California's reliance had increased to 16 percent and the rest of the United
States to only 12 percent.

   As shown in Figure 5.5, California's reliance on the corporate income
tax had fallen in 2005–06 to the United States' average in 1997–78, but
was still above the country's average in 2005–06. Prior to Proposition
13, California's state and local governments relied on general charges as
a source of revenue less than the rest of the United States. As Figure 5.6
illustrates, in 2005–06 reliance on this revenue instrument is now greater.

   The 1978 passage of Proposition 13 did more than just reduce

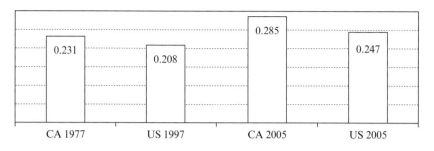

Source: State and Local Finance Data Query System, Urban Institute – Brookings
Institute Tax Policy Center, www.taxpolicycenter.org.

Figure 5.3   State and local total revenue as a fraction of personal income

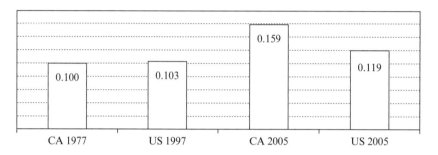

Source: State and Local Finance Data Query System, Urban Institute – Brookings
Institute Tax Policy Center, www.taxpolicycenter.org.

*Figure 5.4   State and local individual income taxes as a fraction of general
revenue*

California's reliance on local property taxation, it added to the state's
constitution a two-thirds vote requirement for any changes in state and
local taxes within California for increasing revenues. In 2007, 11 states
required such a supermajority. This requirement is compounded by the
fact that California's Constitution has always required a two-thirds vote
by the legislature to pass a budget. Only Arkansas and Rhode Island
impose similar requirements.

A consideration of California's revenue structure after Proposition 13
would not be complete without a mention of the *Serrano* v. *Priest* court
decisions in 1971 and 1976. California's Supreme Court found the state's
reliance on local property taxes to fund local schools in violation of the
equal protection clause in the state Constitution. The legislative remedy
(AB 65) was a state-based funding scheme that intended to equalize

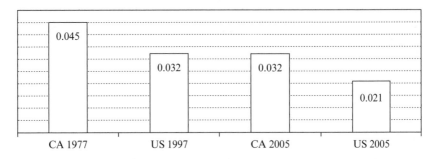

Source: State and Local Finance Data Query System, Urban Institute – Brookings Institute Tax Policy Center, www.taxpolicycenter.org.

Figure 5.5   *State and local corporate income tax as a fraction of general revenue*

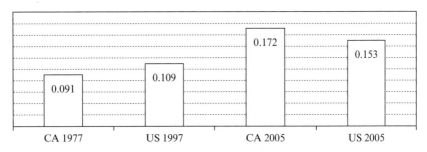

Source: State and Local Finance Data Query System, Urban Institute – Brookings Institute Tax Policy Center, www.taxpolicycenter.org.

Figure 5.6   *State and local total current charges as a fraction of general revenue*

general-purpose spending per student across the state's school districts by offering financial support to low-spending districts and capping this value for previously high-spending districts. More than thirty years after the *Serrano* v. *Priest* court decisions, the results are that over 95 percent of California school districts are within $350 of each other in terms of general-purpose spending, but California's total per-pupil spending has fallen from being among the top five states before 1977–78, to 33rd in 2004–05 (Education Data Partnership, 2008). Fischel (1989) and others have attributed the separation of local finances from local school spending that resulted from *Serrano* v. *Priest* as one causal explanation for voter support of Proposition 13 and the general dislike of taxes that it spawned in California.

Supermajority vote requirements, and the anti-tax sentiment generated by *Serrano* v. *Priest* and Proposition 13, have further encouraged Californians to use the ballot box to make and constrain state and local revenue choices. Table 5.1 describes the California ballot measures, passed since Proposition 13, that the Legislative Analyst's Office note as having major state and local fiscal implications (LAO, 2006a, pp. 14–15). Further restrictions on the power of local entities beyond Proposition 13 to levy taxes for the provision of local services (Props. 62 and 218) make it more likely that state revenue is used to fund previously locally funded services. Requiring the state to devote a minimum amount of general fund expenditure to K–14 education (Prop. 98) reduces what is available for other needed state expenditures. Raising state taxes, but then directing them to only one category of expenditure (as in Props. 99, 172, 10, 42, 49 and 63) makes it difficult to exercise the budget flexibility needed to reallocate existing revenues when spending priorities change. Finally, California's Constitution now prohibits the state from shifting property tax revenue from the county and city governments in a county to the school districts in the county (Prop. 1A). In times of statewide fiscal stress, this restriction increases the likelihood that California spends beyond its means to meet its mandated Prop. 98 school funding obligations.

THE LEGACY OF CALIFORNIA'S POST-PROPOSITION 13 REVENUE STRUCTURE

Figures 5.7 and 5.8 illustrate how the overall state and local revenue structure in California is different from the average in all of the United States. Notably, in 2005–06 California generated a smaller proportion of its revenue in property taxes and greater proportions of its revenue in the forms of individual and corporate income taxes. The result is a greater reliance on revenue sources that are markedly less stable over the business cycle.

California's personal income tax is highly progressive. For 2007–08, the upper marginal tax rate of 9.3 percent began at a taxable income of $89,628 for a married household. There is an additional 1 percent surcharge levied on taxable income greater than $1 million that is earmarked for the provision of mental health services in the state. For 2007–08, the state's corporate net income tax rate was 8.84 percent, with bank and financial corporations paying 10.84 percent. The California Budget Project (2007, p. 2) notes that the 1.7 percent of corporations with net income greater than $1 million paid 84 percent of these taxes. The LAO (2006a, p. 26) reports that in 2004–05, taxable household incomes above

State and local fiscal policy

Table 5.1   California propositions with major state–local fiscal implications

Measure / election	Provisions
Proposition 4 (Gann Amendment) November 1979	Limits spending by state and local governments to prior-year amount adjusted for population growth and per-capita income. If exceeded, state must return surplus to taxpayers in two years. Only reached in 1987 and weakened over the years through the exemption of certain appropriations. Many believe that it is now a meaningless constraint.
Proposition 6 June 1982	Prohibits state gift and inheritance taxes.
Proposition 62 November 1986	New local general taxes require two-thirds approval of governing body and a majority of local voters.
Proposition 218 November 1996	Further limits authority of local governments to impose taxes, assessments and fees. Two-thirds of voters must approve any new local non-general taxes.
Proposition 98 November 1988	Guarantees a minimum level of state general fund revenues be devoted to funding K–14 public education. Guaranteed amount is calculated based upon greater of three tests: (1) % received equal to % received in FY1986–87 (approx. 40%); (2) as much as received previous year adjusted for enrollment, or (3) same as (2) except growth factor is equal to growth in per capita general fund revenues plus 0.5%. Intended to act as a floor, in practice worked as a ceiling typically equal to 40–45% of state's general fund revenue going to K–14.
Proposition 99 November 1988	Imposes an additional $0.25 tax on cigarette packs and limits revenue to health-related uses.
Proposition 172 November 1993	Increases state general sales tax by 0.5% and dedicates revenue to public safety programs.
Proposition 10 November 1998	Imposes an additional $0.25 tax on cigarette packs and limits revenue to childhood development programs.
Proposition 42 March 2002	Selective sales taxes collected on gasoline are permanently earmarked for transportation uses only.
Proposition 49 November 2002	Increases state grants to K–12 schools for before- and after-school programs. No additional funding source prescribed; currently close to $0.5 billion of state spending devoted to it.
Proposition 63 November 2004	Imposes a 1% additional tax on personal income earned in the state over $1 million; revenue used to fund mental health services and expected to raise $0.8 billion in FY2006–07.

Table 5.1   (continued)

Measure / election	Provisions
Proposition 1A November 2004	After the passage of Proposition 13, local property taxes paid to California counties and the state had the constitutional right to distribute those revenues to cities and school districts in the county, and the county government in a manner they chose. During times of statewide fiscal stress, this often resulted in the state reducing payments to counties and cities and shifting them to school districts to meet constitutionally imposed Proposition 98 funding requirements. This constitutional amendment freezes the current allocation in a county in place unless the governor declares a fiscal emergency and agrees to repay imposed transfers after three years. Also requires the state to fund local mandates.

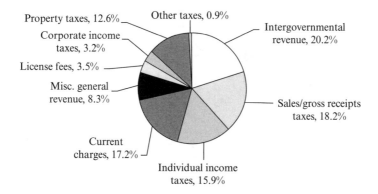

Source: State and Local Finance Data Query System, Urban Institute – Brookings Institute Tax Policy Center, www.taxpolicycenter.org.

Figure 5.7   General fund state and local revenue reliance for State of California, FY2005–06

$500 000 accounted for only 1 percent of returns, but 39 percent of personal income tax revenue collected in California. These high-income taxpayers are more likely to record stock options and capital gains as part of their taxable income. As Figure 5.9 shows, since the realization of these components of taxable income fluctuate widely over the business cycle, so does the revenue collected from all taxes. California's tax revenue during the previous recession declined from $76 billion in 2000–01, to $63 billion

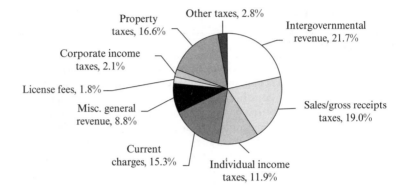

Source: State and Local Finance Data Query System, Urban Institute – Brookings Institute Tax Policy Center, www.taxpolicycenter.org.

Figure 5.8   General fund state and local revenue reliance for United States, FY2005–06

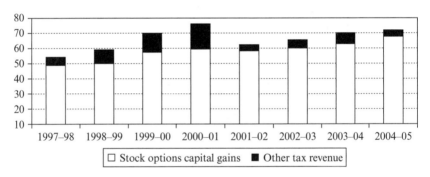

Source: LAO (2004) Table 8.

Figure 5.9   California tax revenue (billions real $) by fiscal year

in the following fiscal year. This 17 percent loss in tax revenue was almost entirely composed of a loss in personal income tax revenue due to a reduction in realized stock options and capital gains. Even in 2004–05, almost three years after the last recession officially ended, income tax revenues from these two volatile sources were $2 billion less than their peak in 2000–01.

The variability of tax revenue from stock options and capital gains, as a driver of California's yearly operating deficits, finds further support through the observed relationship between the changes in state revenue

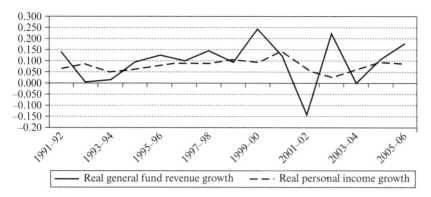

Source: LAO (2002) Table 3.

Figure 5.10 *California growth in real general fund revenue and personal income (billions $)*

and personal income drawn in Figure 5.10. Notice that growth in state revenue is above growth in personal income from 1993–94 to 2000–01. It is only when the growth in personal income is on a general downward trend, and stock options and capital gains less likely to be realized, that growth in revenue falls below growth in personal income (that is, before 1993–94 and after 2000–01). Referring to Figure 5.11, these are the same periods when California exhibited negative values for its budget stabilization fund.

For a given fiscal year, Figure 5.11 shows the ratio of the budget stabilization fund to general fund expenditures for both California (solid line) and aggregated for all states (dashed line). When these measures fall below the middle line, the yearly operating budget has gone negative enough that the budget stabilization fund cannot cover it and it turns negative. Notice that deficits of this magnitude are not all that unusual in California, while they have never occurred in the aggregate measure calculated for all states.

The volatility that California's general revenue stream has experienced in this decade is the same as observed in the state from the late 1970s to early 1990s. The only thing that spares California's state budgets from an operating deficit large enough to cause the budget stabilization fund to turn negative (as occurred in 1982–83, 1991–92 to 1992–93 and 2000–01) is a persistent period of growth in the state's economy (as occurred between 1994–95 and 2000–01 and 2002–03 to 2006–07). To appreciate this claim, I offer next a summary of California's fiscal experiences throughout the 1990s.

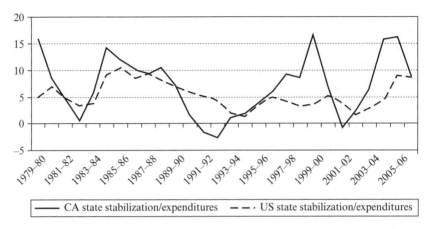

Sources: California Department of Finance (2006), and NASBO (2005), Table 9.

Figure 5.11 *State(s) budget stabilization fund as a percentage of general fund revenue*

Beginning in the mid-1990s, California's economy boomed along with its 'dot-com' industries. There was $50 billion in taxable income from exercised stock options and realized capital gains in the state in 1996. By 2000, these had quadrupled to $200 billion and the annual personal income tax revenue collected from these sources doubled to nearly $8 billion (Hill, 2002). In 1998, after campaigning and winning re-election on a platform based on the need to fund public education better, Governor Davis, with the support of the California Legislature, began spending a larger portion of these revenue windfalls on education, health and human service programs. Included were: (1) K–12 (Kindergarten to grade 12) teacher salary increases; (2) Kindergarten to third grade class size reduction (which began in 1996 and continues to offer $800 per student annually to districts that reduce these level class sizes to 20 per teacher); (3) additional spending in the state's higher education systems to forestall fee increases; (4) covering county trial court expenses which were previously funded locally; and (5) a tax expenditure in the form of a nearly $4 billion annual cut in vehicle license fees. Many have since questioned the wisdom of funding ongoing expenditure commitments with tax revenue that most understood at the time as transitory in nature. But as Tim Gage, then Director of California's Department of Finance points out, the choice was motivated by the politics of the situation: '[t]he fundamental driver is simply, you've got constituents and it's nice to do things for them' (Murray, 2006). This logic is truly the reason why highly procyclical state revenue sources put a state on a fiscal roller-coaster. Revenue surpluses in a boom period are committed to ongoing expenditures that remain after the loss of the boom period's windfall revenue.

By late 2002, the bottom had fallen out of California's economic boom and revenue from the state's personal income tax fell by nearly 25 percent in that year. The 2002–03 operating budget for the state ended up $11 billion in the red, and because there were no specific plans to cut spending or increase revenues by any significant amount, the projected deficit for the following year was $27 billion. These cumulative deficits became the basis for the figure cited by Governor Davis that the 2003 operating deficit for California was $38 billion. In the setting of these immense fiscal problems, Davis ran for re-election in November 2002 and won. However, only months after re-election, his popularity plummeted as he faced the prospect of constructing a state budget to deal with a deficit projected to be nearly one-third of that year's operating budget. In October 2003 Governor Davis directed the Department of Finance to institute an increase in California's vehicle license fees (VLF) through a 'trigger' present in earlier legislation that allowed such an increase if the governor judges that the state is no longer able to pay its bills. This increase became the major point of contention in the historic recall election that occurred in the same month and swept Governor Schwarzenegger into office.

Fulfilling a campaign promise, Schwarzenegger's first act as Governor was to repeal the VLF tax increase and place the State of California's budget an additional $3.5 billion in the red. As noted by Zuckerman (2004), Schwarzenegger dealt with this huge budget shortfall by: (1) proposing to seek future voter approval to borrow nearly $11 billion (which was later approved by voters at $15 billion); (2) instituting loans and borrowing from state funds that amounted to about $5.5 billion, and state program changes that led to $9.2 billion in savings (largely through an accounting change in Medi-Cal); (3) California State University and University of California tuition increases of nearly 30 percent; (4) state employee lay-offs or non-replacements, reductions in judiciary and criminal justice spending; and (5) not fully funding the Proposition 98 guarantee for state funding of K–14 education. The result of these changes, and an unexpected rebound in state tax revenues, allowed California in 2004–05 to report a positive operating balance of over $3 billion and a surplus in its reserve fund of over $9 billion.

Between 2005 and early 2007, the California economy remained strong. The Legislative Analyst's Office (LAO) (2006a) reported that state revenues had grown over the past three fiscal years by over $11 billion. Perhaps not surprisingly, the governor and legislature used this additional revenue to increase further the state's spending on K–12 education and to fund an

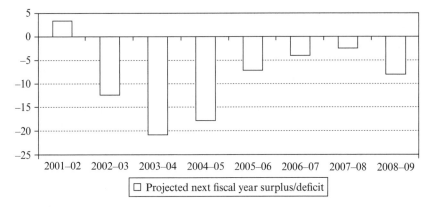

Source: LAO (2006b), Table 23.

Figure 5.12   Projected next fiscal year surplus/deficit

early pay-off of debt taken on to cover previous deficits. However, this improvement in the state's economy only served to decrease the operating deficit predicted by the LAO in November of each year. As shown in Figure 5.12, only after the large personal income tax windfalls gained from high capital gains realizations in 2001–02, has this prediction included an expected surplus in the state budget. What this indicates, and what many observers have repeatedly pointed out, is that the change in California's revenue structure that began with Proposition 13 has resulted in a persistent structural deficit in the twenty-first century that, despite repeated calls to do otherwise, was not dealt with during the economic recovery that the state experienced between 2003 and mid-2007.

   The meaning of a state's finances exhibiting a 'structural deficit' is that in 'normal' times (normal meaning that the economy is not in recession nor is it in an abnormal boom), given the state's revenue structure and expenditure commitments, the state is expected to bring in less revenue than it spends. Observers have pegged this annual structural deficit as in the range of $3 billion to $8 billion dollars. Even with an annual revenue base of around $100 billion, this is a significant shortfall. The obvious solution to cope with a structural deficit is either to raise revenues or to cut expenditures. The political difficulty in implementing the obvious, especially in a state that requires a two-thirds majority to raise taxes and to approve its annual state budget, comes in the form of first deciding whether the problem is primarily revenue- or expenditure-based, and then determining what revenue instruments to increase or what expenditure program to cut. Because of this, many of California's policy-makers have decided to cope with its structural deficit by denying that it exists and/or that there is a need for an imminent solution.

The California Department of Finance predicted that the 2007–08 state budget would be around $4 billion in surplus (Governor's Budget, 2008). Due to an unforeseen rise in oil prices, the subprime mortgage crisis and declines in residential construction and real estate values, by mid-2007 it was apparent that California's economy was slowing and that this surplus would not materialize. In November 2007, Governor Schwarzenegger's proposed budget for the upcoming fiscal year identified an expected revenue gap of $14.5 billion for 2007–08. His proposal to deal with it was a 10 percent cut in all state expenditures. Many, including the LAO, thought this simplistic approach inappropriate. In an unprecedented action, the LAO (2008a) chose not just to offer an analysis of the Governor's proposed budget, but also to propose its own 'alternative budget' that identified $17 billion in possible expenditure cuts – chosen based upon the necessity of service provided and equity considerations – and close to $3 billion in increased revenue through a list of potential reduced tax expenditures to business. Notably, the LAO's alternative budget contained no new taxes or increases in existing tax rates.

After a further weakening of the economy, in February 2008 the LAO (2008b) raised its prediction of the expected two-year budget shortfall to greater than $16 billion. This prompted California's Legislature to enter into special session and the approval of over $3.3 billion in additional approved, but never issued deficit bonds; and the suspension, delay and shift of other expenditure programs that yielded an additional $4.2 billion in savings. More than $7 billion of these changes are one-time and do nothing to deal with the state's structural deficit.

California's economic situation continued to decline in March and April of 2008. Given the state's heavy reliance on personal income taxes, analysts expected the two-year deficit value to rise. By mid-April, many said it was back to an amount similar to what it was before the one-time cuts made in the special session of the Legislature. In late April of 2008, Governor Schwarzenegger shocked many by publicly stating that he believed the current two-year deficit figure to be over $20 billion. The 2008–09 budget passed into law on 23 September 2008 accounted for a $24 billion dollar two-year deficit: $7.1 billion rolled over from 2007–08 and an additional $16.9 billion in projected deficit for 2008–09 if nothing changed from the previous year (California Budget Project, 2008).

A California Legislature and Governor dealing with a deficit that is one-fifth of the state's own-source revenue brings this story back to 2002 and the state's last recession, when Governor Davis forecast an even greater deficit. In less than ten years, Californians have ridden the fiscal roller-coaster of going from boom to bust, back to relative boom, and in the fall of 2008 heading toward a bust whose trough is not in sight. Budget experts, analysts and observers are well aware of the tendency for California's post-Proposition 13 system of state and local revenue reliance to produce such a pattern, and have offered the solutions discussed next.

IDEAS ON HOW TO COPE BETTER

The suggestions put forth to reduce the instability currently inherent in balancing the yearly operating budget of California can be broken down into two categories. The first is reforms targeted at changes in the institutions and rules surrounding the budget process itself. The second deals with altering the way California raises revenue for its state and local governments. For each of these categories, I provide summaries of some suggested reforms. The items contained below are from reviews put together by Simmons (2002) and the Institute for Government Studies (2003).

Budget Process Reforms

Reduce two-thirds voting requirements
Many of the commissions, studies and individuals that have explored ways to reform California's budget process have come to the conclusion that change is required in its two-thirds vote requirements. The California Constitution Revision Commission in 1996 and the California Citizens Budget Commission in 1998 recommended amending the Constitution to require a simple majority to enact a budget. The California Commission on Tax Policy in the New Economy in 2003 concluded that the vote threshold for approval of local special taxes be reduced to 55 percent. The California Budget Project in 1999 (whose purpose is to represent the well-being of low- and middle-income Californians) suggested the elimination of all supermajority vote requirements across the state, while the California Business Roundtable in 1995 favored the elimination of a supermajority vote requirement for the passage of a state budget, but not for new taxes. The League of Women Voters of California in 1995 believed that if two-thirds vote requirements exist for taxes, they should also for the approval of tax expenditures.

Create greater fiscal discipline
Analysts who have previously studied California's fiscal situation believe that greater discipline could be instilled in the budget process through a

better accounting of, and public information campaign on, the magnitude of tax expenditures by the state, a loosening of revenue and spending restrictions currently locked into California's Constitution, a curtailment on future propositions, and the establishment of a truly 'reasonable and necessary' prudent state budget reserve fund that is required by the Constitution. For instance, the Speaker's Commission on the California Initiative Process in 1992, the California Constitution Revision Commission and the California Business Roundtable all suggested that voter-approved propositions be subject to allowed modification by the Legislature after various periods to remedy the unintended fiscal consequences wrought by their simple majority passage.

Move to multiyear budgeting

With the hope of allowing policy-makers more time to evaluate program effectiveness and adjust proposed and current legislation for economic and caseload changes, some have suggested that California move to multi-year budgeting. The California Citizens Budget Commission suggested a three-year perspective, while the Little Hoover Commission in 1995, the California Business Roundtable and the California League of Women Voters have recommended a two-year budget cycle.

Improve the public's and legislators' understanding of the budget

Governor Schwarzenegger's proposed budget summary for California in 2008 is nearly 350 pages long and highly technical.[2] Previous observers of the state's budget process contend that a budget described in this form does not promote public, or even legislative, scrutiny of spending choices, economic forecasts and program performance. Though state organizations like the LAO, Department of Finance and private organizations like the California Budget Project offer summaries and analyses of the state budget that are easier to digest, the suggestion here is for even more public dissemination of the constraints, trade-offs and choices necessary in a state budget.[3]

Revenue Reliance Reforms

Another list of suggested reforms to improve the outcome observed in California state budgeting relate to changing the way that general fund revenue is raised. Since state finances are so closely tied to local finances in post-Proposition 13 California, some have also suggested that the only way to improve budget outcomes is through reforms to the state's entire system of state and local finance.

Increase state revenue reliance on tax bases more stable over the business cycle
As the previous discussion has made clear, much of the fiscal strife experienced by California is attributable to: (1) approximately a quarter of California's general fund revenue coming from personal income taxes; (2) the high top marginal income rate; (3) the large percentage of households that fall into the top bracket and contribute a large percentage of the income tax revenue raised; and (4) the variability of this revenue due to much of it being in the form of stock options and capital gains. So any reduction in reliance on this tax instrument funded by greater reliance on a more stable tax instrument would make the state's general revenue flow more predictable and less prone to generating negative operating balances during an economic downturn. Obvious suggestions to do this have been raising the vehicle license fee, raising or instituting other fees and charges, expanding the general sales tax base to include services and/or instituting a statewide property tax.

Raise more state revenue
If it is not politically possible to raise a more stable stream of general fund revenue in California, some have suggested that a reasonable alternative to reducing the reoccurring pattern of operating deficits in California is raising more revenue. Often suggested is a reinstatement of the higher top marginal income tax rates of 10 and 11 percent that existed throughout much of the 1990s. Also proposed is the idea of expanding the state's sales tax base to include services and/or allowing a split role property tax in which business property would move back to market value-based assessment.

Reduce local government reliance on state revenue by shifting to greater local tax reliance
Nearly every commission and expert that has studied California's overall system of financing state and local government has come to the conclusion that it is in need of major reform. The California Citizens Budget Commission concluded that local governments need greater fiscal independence. The California Governance Consensus Project in 2002, California Budget Project, California Constitution Revision Commission and California Business Roundtable all agree, and further suggest a significant realignment of state–county public service responsibilities.

FEASIBILITY OF REFORMS

Any of the previously suggested reforms, if adopted in California, would likely offer some relief to the boom–bust tendency exhibited in the state's fiscal situation after Proposition 13. Objective analyses based in the disciplines of political science and/or public administration broadly support the budget process reforms described above, while the same forms of analyses based in the economics of public finance throw their support (to various degrees) behind the suggested reforms to California's revenue reliance. But the reality in California is that the policy reforms suggested by these analyses would require amending the Constitution, and hence approval by a majority of voters. Thus it is essential that the political feasibility of these reforms be assessed to determine their real-world viability as a solution. It is for this reason that I next turn to the results of recent elections that featured initiatives that contained some of the elements of reform just suggested.

Californians were asked in March of 2004 to vote on Proposition 56. If passed, this proposition would have enacted many of the budget process reforms suggested above, including: (1) the requirement that budget and budget-related tax and appropriation bills may be enacted by a 55 percent legislative majority rather than the two-thirds vote currently required; (2) the production of a budget summary for all state ballot pamphlets sent to voters; and (3) the requirement that 25 percent of certain state revenue increases are deposited into a reserve fund. Only about a third of voters approved of this budget reform package and it failed. What passed on this same ballot, by respective margins of 63 percent and 71 percent, were Propositions 57 and 58. If the second proposition also passed, the first proposition allowed the issue of up to $15 billion dollars in general obligation bonds to pay off the accumulated general fund deficit. The second proposition required the enactment of a balanced general fund budget (which previously was never a constitutional requirement) and a formula for calculating yearly deposits into a budget reserve that was smaller in magnitude and less binding than what was proposed in Proposition 56. The passage of Proposition 58 was a movement in the right direction of the suggested budget process reforms, but most experts would have preferred the passage of Proposition 56.

Since March 2004, there has only been one initiative on California's statewide ballot whose roots are in satisfying the budget process reforms suggested above, while there have been two whose end results are likely to be quite the opposite. Proposition 1A, which barely gained majority support on the November 2004 ballot, has raised the state's level of fiscal stress by constitutionally prohibiting: (1) unfunded mandates by the state to local governments; (2) any reduction of the 1 percent statewide sales tax that goes to the local government site of a sale; and (3) the future shift of property tax revenues raised in a county from the county and local governments in the county, to state-funded K–12 schools in the county. On the same ballot in November 2004, the voters continued their favored path of locking into California's Constitution the earmarking of specific revenue streams. With an approval rate of 54 percent, Proposition 63 constitutionally requires that the revenue (about $800 million in FY2006–07) from an additional 1 percent tax on taxable personal income above $1 million fund the expansion of mental health services and programs. Alternatively, Proposition 76, which failed with a 62 percent majority in November 2005, would have limited state spending to the prior year's level plus three previous years' average revenue growth, reduced the degree that Proposition 98 binds the state's funding of K–14 (Kindergarten to community college) education to a specific percentage of general fund expenditure, and under specified 'fiscal emergencies' allowed the Governor to reduce budget appropriations within a fiscal year.

The political feasibility of enacting the budget process reforms suggested above has historically been small. Perhaps the greatest opportunity for major reform of this type occurred with the March 2004 ballot when citizens seemed willing to listen to Governor Schwarzenegger (whose job approval rating was above 60 percent) for suggestions on how to get the state out of its fiscal crisis. First, to qualify for this ballot was the citizen-initiated Proposition 56 that contained the widely suggested reduction of the two-thirds legislative vote requirement for approval of a state budget and new taxes to the smaller supermajority of 55 percent. Propositions 57 ($15 billion in deficit bonds) and 58 (which gave the impression of achieving budget process reform) were placed on the same ballot by the Legislature. This forced Schwarzenegger to choose between endorsing the stricter Proposition 56, or Proposition 57 that many in his Republican Party favored because of the populist view that the two-thirds vote requirements hold state government spending and taxes down in California.[4] He chose to endorse Proposition 57 (which helped convince some Republicans to endorse the deficit bond proposal that he needed to make his fiscal recovery plan work) and remained mute on Proposition 56. Perhaps if he had chosen otherwise, California voters would have followed their 'Governator' and the state would have achieved the reduction in the two-thirds vote requirement that many experts point to as the cornerstone of true budget process reform.

California's budget formulation for 2008–09 resulted in a legislative stand-off that took 85 days beyond the date that it was required by the state's Constitution. The historic amount of time it took to craft this budget, and the fact that many believe it is still not balanced and relies upon direct and indirect ways of borrowing future revenues, resulted in an increased outcry by some to try again to alter the institutions blamed for the inability to reach a balanced-budget compromise between ideologically driven Republicans (no new taxes) and Democrats (no spending cuts).

Governor Schwarzenegger wasted little time after signing the flawed 2008–09 budget to use it as a concrete example of why legislative districts need to be redrawn in California. Districts have been gerrymandered to result in extremely safe legislative seats for either a Democrat or a Republican. The political parties use this fact to elect strongly ideological candidates that support the party line. A redistricting effort that was designed to yield districts that were far less safe for either party would likely result in a more moderate and willing-to-compromise group of assembly-persons and senators to craft future California budgets. Alternatively, a group of Democrats have argued that the 2008–09 round of budget deliberations in the state, and the flawed budget it produced, points to the need to reduce the two-thirds vote requirement to pass a budget. They have vowed to campaign to place a proposed constitutional amendment to that effect on an upcoming state ballot.

What about the political feasibility of instituting any of the revenue reliance changes suggested earlier? To assess this possibility, one must first consider that California's Constitution still requires a two-thirds vote of both houses of the Legislature to pass any increase in state taxes. Given that Democrats do not possess this majority, and Republicans in California remain strongly opposed to any new taxes (even if tied to a tax decrease in a current tax instrument), the option of steadying California's revenue stream through greater reliance on more stable taxes is limited.

The revenue reliance reform favored by many academics and policy analysts, but still disliked by a majority of California's voting populace, is a reduction in government dependence on state revenue by shifting to greater local tax reliance. This would be best achieved through a loosening of the Proposition 13 restriction that property taxation in the state never exceeds 1 percent. Unfortunately, the current populist support for such a proposal is nearly non-existent. Political folklore widely recognizes Proposition 13 as the 'third rail' of California politics: touch it as a politician and your political life dies. Or, as Governor Schwarzenegger is paraphrased as telling his elder political advisor Warren Buffet: 'Mention changing Prop. 13 one more time and you will do 500 pushups'.

With the downside that it is likely a regressive tax (see California Budget Project, 2002b), the choice of raising the vehicle license fee (VLF) tax back to its historic rate of 2 percent seems a viable way of providing California with a more stable revenue structure. In 1998, the California Legislature lowered this tax from 2 percent of the market value of the vehicle – where it had been for most of the 60 years it was in place in the state – to 1.5 percent. Subsequent legislation in 2000 lowered it to the 1.3 percent where it stands today. One of the last acts of Governor Davis was triggering a provision in the legislation that allowed an increase in the VLF rate back to 2 percent during the time of a state budget 'emergency'.[5] As the recalled Governor found out, voting Californians dislike the visibility and burden of taxing their second most valuable piece of property. Governor Schwarzenegger won the recall election based upon promising to roll back the VLF to 1.3 percent. Thus, while he remains in office, additional revenue is unlikely to come from this source.

A second potential stable revenue source could come from maintaining the 1 percent *ad valorem* rate of property taxation specified by Proposition 13, but eliminating the acquisition value of assessment for non-residential property. Many politicians dismiss such a 'split-role' property tax because of the 'third-rail' impression they have toward changing anything about Proposition 13. As of the summer of 2009, with California facing a two-year projected budget deficit of $25 billion and a budget agreement still not in sight a month after it was due, the subject of raising additional revenue through property taxation barred by Proposition 13 is still not widely discussed.

In addition, there is now documented discussion in California policy-making circles that expanding the state's current 6.25 percent rate of sales taxation to exempted service items needs to be on the table as a possible revenue source. A recent study by the State's Board of Equalization places the revenue potential of doing such at close to $2.7 billion. Not all services are being considered – notably not mentioned are legal and medical services – but the suggested base expansion does include automobile repairs and services, entertainment and recreation, household repair and maintenance, and personal services like dry cleaning.

A final way of closing the state's structural deficit through increased revenues would be a reinstatement of the 10 and 11 percent upper rates of marginal income taxation that were last used by Republican Governor Pete Wilson to counteract budget shortfalls during the early 1990s. If a 10 percent rate was added for single (married) taxpayers making $130,000 ($260,000) in 2002 dollars, and an 11 percent rate for those making $260,000 ($520,000), the California Budget Project (2002a) estimates that it would have raised $3.5 billion in 2004. But with strong Republican opposition to tax increases, and particularly ones that fall upon the state's highest earners, the supermajority vote requirement makes the adoption of this (or a higher VLF, split property tax role, or expanded sales tax base) politically difficult. In addition, if one of these were the only fiscal reform adopted, an argument could be made that it could make the volatility of the state's operating deficits worse if the surpluses it generated in good years produces even greater commitments to ongoing spending that cannot be met in the bad years.

Governor Schwarzenegger's proposed 2008–09 state budget included a suggestion for a 'Budget Stabilization Act' that would amend the Constitution in a manner designed to save revenues in order to amass a revenue stabilization fund. The initial 2008–09 budget passed by the California Legislature drastically diluted Schwarzenegger's budget stabilization proposal. Subsequently, the Governor chose to veto this initial budget and the legislature responded by sending him a second budget that included most of the elements of his original proposal. The establishment of such a fund requires the passage of a constitutional amendment that will be put before California's voters in early 2009. The amendment placed on the ballot by the second budget deal requires that in each fiscal year the state contribute 3 percent of its general fund revenue to a Budget Stabilization Fund (BSF) until it reaches 12.5 percent of estimated general fund revenues for the current fiscal year. Transfers out of the BSF could only occur through the passage of a bill that contains no other provisions. The governor's ability to suspend the required transfers into the BSF is severely limited and the use of BSF funds is constrained. In addition, the proposed Act would allow the governor to make mid-year reductions in expenditures and suspend cost-of-living-adjustments when the state's finance director determines that the current fiscal year's budget is in deficit. The maximum cut in yearly state appropriations is set at 7 percent (see California Budget Project, 2008). Some (including the LAO) have already expressed their disapproval of such a constitutional amendment because of the shift in expenditure power it entails to the executive branch.

McNichols and Lav (2008) reports that California was not alone in facing a budget shortfall for the 2008–09 fiscal year; at least 25 states were in the same situation. As a percentage of the fiscal year's expenditure, California's budget gap was expected to be the second largest at 15.4 percent, with Arizona's larger at 17.8, and Florida's at 11, Nevada's at 13.5, New Jersey's at a maximum of 10.6 and Rhode Island's at 11.2 percent. The usual solutions of expenditure cuts and/or tax increases are always problematic during an economic recession and the use of a reserve fund to fill gaps during an economic downturn makes sense. The problem is that many states do not possess a significant reserve to fill the expected gap. In the final section of this chapter, I explore a possible revenue option that could be used by California, or any state using cap-and-trade to reduce greenhouse gas emissions, to raise revenue to create such a reserve.

AN 'OUT-OF-THE-BOX' REVENUE IDEA

In July 2005, Governor Schwarzenegger signed Executive Order S-3-05 that declared climate change a reality and emphatically stated that it was time for California, the 12th-largest emitter (in terms of government-based entities) of greenhouses gases (GHGs) in the world, to take action to reduce these emissions. The executive order directed the state by 2010 to reduce GHG emissions to 2000 levels; by 2020 to reduce GHG emissions to 1990 levels and by 2050 to reduce GHG emissions to 80 percent below 1990 levels. In September 2006, Governor Schwarzenegger proceeded to sign the Global Warming Solutions Act (AB 32) that codified the GHG reduction targets previously specified in EOS-3-05 into law and required, by the start of 2009, mandatory reporting rules for significant sources of greenhouse gases and a specific plan to achieve the required GHG emissions through regulations, market mechanisms and/or other actions. AB 32 also required the creation of an Economic and Technology Advancement Advisory Committee (ETAAC) to advise California's Air Resource Board on the specific implementation of the law. In late February 2008, in anticipation of the year-end deadline imposed by AB 32 for an implementation plan, the ETAAC (2008) released its final report. The recommendations of the Market Advisory Committee of the ETAAC are contained in Chapter 9 of this report.

Policy analysts remain divided on whether cap-and-trade or carbon taxes are the better policy instruments to achieve a desired reduction in GHGs (see Green et al., 2007; or EconoSpeak, 2007). Basically the trade-off between the two comes down to greater certainty in the amount of GHGs reduced, and less certainty in the cost of companies complying with this reduction, when choosing a cap-and-trade system as opposed to a carbon tax. The ETAAC's Market Advisory Committee came out in favor of a system of cap-and-trade as the 'best' solution to reduce GHGs in California.

An important item to consider in designing a cap-and-trade system for California is how to price the initial allocation of GHG allowances. The choices are: (1) free allocations of GHG allowances based on historical emission levels; (2) free allocations based on previous economic output; or (3) revenue-generating allowance auctions. The ETAAC report concluded that some level of auctioning is preferred for the clear and early price signal it will send on a unit of GHG emission under the specified cap. Furthermore, they recommend that productive and appropriate uses of these auction revenues include making direct investments in low-carbon technologies, allocating dollars to California universities for research and development surrounding GHG reduction, and investment in technologies that could improve air quality in low-income neighborhoods disproportionately affected by the trade portion of the program (an important objective explicit in AB 32). Most importantly for the purpose of this chapter, the ETAAC's Market Advisory Committee (2008) recommends that the:

California Air Resources Board may wish to convene an advisory group involving persons with budgetary experience and a wide knowledge of energy, environmental, tax and budgetary policy and including representatives of both the Department of Finance and Legislature, to prepare a study outlining several sensible options for recycling revenues to businesses or individuals. (p. 56)

My 'out-of-the-box' suggestion is that California employ only a system of cap-and-trade to reach its stringent GHG goals, that initial allocations be fully auctioned off and a portion of the earned revenue be used to establish a rainy-day fund that is built up to a maximum of a predetermined percentage of the state's general fund expenditure (say 10 percent). Additional auction revenues reduce the rates of existing distortionary taxes only after this rainy-day fund is established. Rules for drawing down this fund could be the same as those proposed for the Budget Stabilization Fund.

An anticipated difficulty in this suggestion is that California's courts are very likely to interpret auction revenues as a fee, and based upon the earlier Sinclair Paint Decision require a nexus between the purpose of the fee and the use of its corresponding revenues.[6] As pointed out by the advocacy group Carbon Share: 'Because the sky belongs to all of us', what has been auctioned off is publicly owned California air.[7] A nexus possibly exists if the revenue from selling this public good supplements the state's general fund revenue with the intention of providing public goods and services that confer public benefits to those who owned the state's air. If this argument does not pass legal muster, the auction revenues are from a tax and a two-thirds vote of the California Legislature would be required for their use for any purpose not related to further GHG reduction.

The revenue raised from the proposed auction depends negatively on the number of GHG units available for auction and if it is an annual auction to price GHGs emitted in the upcoming year (as opposed to a one-time auction that sells the right to emit GHGs forever). An annual auction best suits California's desire to reduce over time the allowed GHGs emitted annually, and its desire for companies to invest in the latest GHG reduction technologies. If this is the case, a yearly revenue estimate for California in 2007 dollars ranges from $2 billion to $8 billion a year depending on a price per ton between $5 and $20.[8] A reasonable expectation must be that even if such a plan was used in California (or any other state), the auction revenue gained from it would only last as long as a similar cap-and-trade plan was not adopted at the federal level. At the time of a federal plan, California would need to abandon its own and become part of that. In the meantime, this out-of-the-box idea would yield the double dividend of getting California closer to the GHG reductions required by AB 32 and establishing an initial rainy-day fund that may be substantial enough to offset the fiscal cyclicality built into California's current revenue reliance. Like in the proposed Budget Stabilization Fund, state revenue growth over a long-term trend would need to replenish this fund once the California GHG auctions went away. But the use of this cap-and-trade revenue would forestall the annual 3 percent transfers from annual general fund revenue required if the BSF is placed into California's Constitution.

NOTES

1. In Figures 5.1–5.6 and Figure 5.11, a year refers to the fiscal year that begins with the year listed.
2. The full text of Governor's proposed 2008 budget for California is at http://www.ebudget.ca.gov/pdf/BudgetSummary/FullBudgetSummary.pdf.
3. The LAO's, California Department of Finance's and California Budget Project's descriptions of the proposed state budget can, respectively, be found at: http://www.lao.ca.gov/main.aspx?type=3&CatID=10, http://www.ebudget.ca.gov/BudgetSummary/BSS/BSS. html and http://www.cbp.org/pdfs/2008/080116_govbudget.pdf. An example of one way that trade-offs inherent to crafting a state budget are being shared with the public is a computer-based simulation called Eureka (created by the Center for California Studies at Sacramento State University) that asks the user to craft a balanced California state budget using real-world data (http://www.csus.edu/calst/civic_education/eureka.html). A second is the recent work of Gordon et al. (2007) at the Public Policy Institute of California.
4. The California Budget Project (2004, p. 5) notes: '[T]here is very little research on the impact of supermajority vote requirements on state fiscal policymaking. The research that is available suggests that supermajority vote requirements may serve to increase, rather than decrease, spending and do not necessarily result in lower taxes.'
5. Later, Governor Schwarzenegger would argue that the state's budget situation had not reached the required degree of emergency that the legislation intended before the VLF tax increase could be put in place.
6. 'When is a fee really a tax?' an article in *Alert*, a newsletter put out by the California Business Chamber of Commerce, offers a good summary of this interpretation. Available at http://www.lumberassociation.org/Weekly%20E-Update/CalChamber_TaxvFee_Article_2-15-08.pdf.
7. The Carbon Share website can be found at www.carbonshare.org.
8. See www.carbonshare.org/june22event.htm.

REFERENCES

California Budget Project (2002a). What would be the impact of reinstating the 10 and 11 percent personal income tax rates? *Budget Brief.* www.cbp.org/2002/qh020531.pdf.

California Budget Project (2002b). Options for balancing the budget: reinstating the vehicle license fee rate. *Budget Brief.* www.cbp.org/2002/qh020508.html.

California Budget Project (2004). What would Proposition 56 mean for the state's budget process? *Budget Brief.* Sacramento, CA. www.cbp.org/2004/0402prop56.pdf.

California Budget Project (2007). Who pays taxes in California? www.cbp.org/ pdfs/2007/0704_pp_taxes.pdf.

California Budget Project (2008). Governor signs 2008–09 budget. www.cbp.org/ pdfs/2007/082407govsigns.pdf.

California Department of Finance (2006). Chart B: historical data budget expenditures. http://www.dof.ca.gov/Budget/BudgetCharts/chart-b.pdf.

Economic and Technology Advancement Advisory Committee (ETAAC) (2008). *Technologies and Policies to Consider for Reducing Greenhouse Gas Emissions in California.* Sacramento, CA: California Air Resources Board. www.arb.ca.gov/ cc/etaac/ETAACFinalReport2-11-08.pdf.

EconoSpeak (2007). Mankiw on carbon taxes. econospeak.blogspot.com/2007/09/ mankiw-on-carbon-taxes.html.

Education Data Partnership (2008). Comparing California. www.ed-data.k12. ca.us/Articles/article.asp?title=California%20comparison.

Fischel, W.A. (1989). Did *Serrano* cause Proposition 13? *National Tax Journal* 42: 465–74.

Gordon, T.M., Alderate, J.C., Murphy, P.J., Sonstelle, J. and Zhang, P. (2007). *Fiscal Realities: Budget Tradeoffs in California Government.* San Francisco, CA: Public Policy Institute of California. www.ppic.org/main/publications.asp?i=578.

Governor's Budget (2008). Proposed budget summary. www.ebudget.ca.gov/ BudgetSummary/INT/32270934.html.

Green, K.P., Hayward, S.F. and Hassett, K.A. (2007). Climate change: Caps vs taxes. *Environmental Policy Outlook.* Washington, DC: American Enterprise Institute for Public Policy Research. www.aei.org/publications/pubID.26286/ pub_detail.asp.

Hill, J. (2002). Boom and bust. *Sacramento Bee.* www.caltax.org/Hill-BoomBust12-30-02.pdf.

Institute for Government Studies (2003). Constitutional reform and the California budget process. Berkeley, CA. www.igs.berkeley.edu/library/htConstReform 2003.html.

Legislative Analyst's Office (LAO) (2002). *Cal Facts.* www.lao.ca.gov/2002/cal_ facts/2002_calfacts_toc.html.

Legislative Analyst's Office (LAO) (2004). *Cal Facts.* www.lao.ca.gov/2004/cal_ facts/2004_calfacts_toc.htm.

Legislative Analyst's Office (LAO) (2006a). Analysis of the 2006–07 budget bill. www.lao.ca.gov/laoapp/analysis.aspx?year=2006&chap=0&toc=0.

Legislative Analyst's Office (LAO) (2006b). *Cal Facts.* www.lao.ca.gov/2006/ cal_facts/2006_calfacts_toc.htm.

Legislative Analyst's Office (LAO) (2008a). Analysis of the 2008–09 budget bill. www.lao.ca.gov/laoapp/Analysis.aspx?year=2008&chap=0&toc=0.

Legislative Analyst's Office (LAO) (2008b). A budget update. www.lao.ca.gov/ handouts/state_admin/2008/Budget_Update_04_24_08.pdf.

McNichols, E.C. and Lav, I. (2008). *25 States Face Total Budget Shortfall of at Least $40 billion in 2009.* Washington, DC: Center on Budget and Policy Priorities. www.cbpp.org/1-15-08sfp.htm.

Murray, B. (2006). Covering the California state budget and the budget crisis. (FACSNET: Reporting Tools.) www.facsnet.org/tools/biz_econ/gage.php.

National Association of State Budget Officers (December 2005). The fiscal survey of the states, Washington, DC. http://www.nasbo.org/Publications/fiscalsurvey/ fsfall2005.pdf.

Simmons, C.W. (2002). *A Summary of Recommendations for Reforms to the State Budget Process*, Sacramento, CA: California Research Bureau. www.library. ca.gov/crb/02/notes/v9n1.pdf.
Zuckerman, S. (2004). *State Responses to Budget Crises in 2004: California*. Washington, DC: Urban Institute. www.urban.org/UploadedPDF/410948_CA_ budget_crisis.pdf.

Comments on 'Going without an income tax: how do states do it?'

Don Bruce

State revenue systems are under enormous strain, the current economic recession notwithstanding. For starters, sales tax bases continue to erode as a result of our shift in consumption toward services (and away from goods) and the continuing growth in remote sales, namely electronic commerce. Corporate income taxes are a declining revenue source thanks to aggressive tax planning activities alongside state efforts to use tax breaks to attract business activity. The siege on property taxes, which picked up significant steam with the passage of California's Proposition 13, continues today. One might wonder, then, how nine of the 50 US states have been able to operate without the relative stability of a tax on personal income. Sjoquist's chapter asks this important question by comparing states without personal income taxes to those with personal income taxes.

The major problem with prior discussion along these lines is that consideration of adding a tax on personal income is often viewed by the voting public as an effort to increase taxes. This inability to separate the structure of the revenue system from the size of the revenue pie has seriously impeded productive reform efforts in many states. Sjoquist dispenses with this issue by comparing states without personal income taxes to a relatively more comparable group of ten income-taxing states.

The obvious answer to how these states survive is that they either depend more heavily on other sources of revenue, or they spend less. Sjoquist finds that they tend to spend less in general than states with personal income taxes. Moreover, compared to income-taxing states with similar spending levels, they tend to rely more heavily on other revenue sources. And while the sales taxes carries much of that burden, non-income-taxing states also tend to rely more heavily on most other sources of revenue (especially federal grants and local revenue sources).

Perhaps most importantly for this discussion, however, is the fact that states without income taxes are generally quite different from income-taxing states in other ways. Several of them are extremely rich in natural resources such as oil, coal or natural gas, with revenue streams based on resource extraction permitting the luxury of not having a personal income tax. Others have significant amounts of tourism activity, allowing the exporting of tax burden through such things as the sales tax or through state-sponsored gambling activities. These unique features are not easily replicated in income-taxing states, so care must be taken in deriving lessons from the fiscal structures in many of the states without personal income taxes. Sjoquist is wise to remove Alaska from the comparisons for this reason.

On a similar note, it is nice to see the separate narratives that are provided for each of the non-income-taxing states. While Sjoquist's major point is to compare each of those states with Georgia, the detail included in those paragraphs is useful in a more general sense. For example, it is important to determine whether increased reliance on the sales tax among non-income-taxing states tends to take the form of higher rates on similar bases, similar rates applied to broader bases, or some combination of the two. Also, it would have been nice to see a table comparing sales tax rates and bases across the two broad categories of non-income-taxing states and income-taxing states.

Sjoquist does an admirable job of addressing the question of how states without personal income taxes have managed to fund public services. His analysis raises two additional questions that are worthy of further study. First, why do states forego the opportunity to tax personal income? This is an especially relevant question in states that do not have access to significant resource-based revenue, tourism or gambling. Is the lack of an income tax simply a means to constrain the size and growth of the public sector? Are there fundamental objections to (or constitutional constraints on) the taxation of personal income in those states?

A second interesting question is: what are the consequences of not having a tax on personal income? Are state revenues more or less volatile as a result? Are revenue shortfalls more significant in times of economic recession? Are more frequent tax rate adjustments required in order to maintain revenue adequacy over the business cycle? Additionally, how does the distribution of tax burden differ between states with and without personal income taxes? Is the tax system more regressive in non-income-taxing states? Finally, is there any evidence of statistically different public service quality across the two groups of states? For example, are education and health outcomes better or worse on average in non-income-taxing states? These issues will be important components of the ongoing discussion of state revenue structures.

Comments on 'California's state and local revenue structure after Proposition 13: is denial the appropriate way to cope?'

Don Bruce

In keeping with California's long tradition of providing the world's best movie and television drama, Robert Wassmer's chapter provides all of the juicy narrative on California's state tax history that any interested reader could want. The focus in this chapter is on how California has changed as a result of the enactment of Proposition 13 (Prop. 13) in 1978, and how the state might make much-needed changes to address the significant fiscal stresses that have plagued California since that time.

With a tax limitation such as Prop. 13, the two major options are to either reduce state and local spending or to increase reliance on other revenue sources. The California experience has certainly been more of the latter variety, with the share of revenues from personal and corporate income taxes (and indeed, the state share of state and local revenue) increasing relative to national averages since 1978. In short, Prop. 13 has done nothing at all to constrain the size or growth of state and local spending in California. In fact, per capita spending has grown in California since 1978. The main impacts of Prop. 13 have been on the structure and uses of tax revenues.

More discussion of the shift over time in the state–local division of taxes and spending is certainly warranted. It would be useful to consider not only whether and how the state share has changed, but also the implications of that change on the flexibility, adequacy, and quality of public service delivery.

I appreciate Wassmer's focus on instability and volatility, but I disagree with a few of the suppositions in the chapter. First, instability and volatility are only bad when they are not adequately managed, or when they are ignored by the forecasters and planners. California has enough experience with this to know better, but political and legal constraints always seem to get in the way of meaningful reform. Second, Bruce et al. (2006) show that the personal income tax is not necessarily the most volatile tax in the portfolio, so revising the tax mix away from the income tax will not necessarily reduce volatility at times when we dislike it the most (during recessions).

Third, California's problem is not necessarily a revenue problem, and the solution is not necessarily a revenue-side solution. To be sure, some recent actions on the revenue side have made the problem worse, but the real problem appears to be the usual lack of planning and spending discipline. In short, volatility with discipline can be exactly what is needed in California. California has tried to institutionalize some variations of this with the various propositions, but spending is still huge and inflexible.

What is really missing from this analysis is a defense of the massive per capita state and local spending in California. Two thousand dollars above the US average is a lot of money. Could additional strategic spending cuts be part of the longer-term solution? Wassmer's proposed cap-and-trade system certainly has its merits, especially given the current green wave in America, but it does not really address the underlying situation that he spent so many pages describing in such wonderful detail. The cap-and-trade system would essentially amount to throwing new money at the same structural deficit, but using environmental advantages to sell it to the politicians and voters. The notion that this new tax and revenue stream would solve California's structural deficit is a bit far-fetched, especially if it would be viewed as a new tax by the voting public. Given the state's history, it seems that the new revenue would have to be earmarked for environmental causes if the proposal were to have any chance of passage. This, of course, would doom the new cap-and-trade system's ability to address the old revenue system's problems.

REFERENCE

Bruce, D., Fox, W.F. and Tuttle, M.H. (2006). Tax base elasticities: a multi-state analysis of long-run and short-run dynamics. *Southern Economic Journal* 73 (2): 315.

PART III

New forms of taxation

6. An exploration of various corporate tax structures in Georgia: some effects of moving from three-factor apportionment of corporate income to a gross receipts tax

Jonathan Rork and Laura Wheeler

INTRODUCTION

In 2004, the major tax on corporations in 40 of the 50 states of the USA was some form of a business tax. These taxes are often placed on corporate income as defined at the federal level with various modifications at the state level. Since 2002, however, four states have joined Washington in using some form of a gross receipts tax (GRT) as an alternative form of corporate taxation (Pogue, 2007).

A GRT, often referred to as a turnover tax, is a tax placed on the value of goods and services sold. It makes no allowances for costs incurred by a firm and there are often no exemptions for type of sale. The GRT reached its heyday in the 1930s (Mikesell, 2007) and had seemed to fade away as a viable tax option. With the GRT's recent reincarnation, discussions concerning the pros and cons of such a tax have become more frequent. Missing from these discussions, however, are any empirical exercises that can help shed light on these issues.

By utilizing eight years of corporate tax return data in Georgia, we are able to estimate the winners and losers from switching to a GRT. In Georgia, all corporate filers who apportion their corporate earnings have to include their gross receipts; thus we have reliable estimates of gross receipts for over 200,000 filers during this time frame. By creating a revenue-neutral GRT, we are able to compare tax bills under Georgia's corporate tax system with this hypothetical GRT. We demonstrate that while the tax is more evenly distributed across firms when a GRT is imposed, the corporate tax is not as unbalanced as one may first think.

We proceed by outlining the details of how a GRT operates. We then outline the argument for and against the GRT, highlighting the parts of the argument we are able to investigate with our data. We then show the impacts of switching from Georgia's corporate tax system to the GRT. Because Georgia's corporate tax system during our time-frame used a three-factor apportionment formula, such a switch involves changing both the apportionment rules (from three-factor to single-factor) and the tax base (from corporate income to gross receipts). To shed light on each component of the change, we also perform our analysis on the two intermediate steps of going from three-factor apportionment to single-factor apportionment, and then from single-factor apportionment to a GRT.

THE GROSS RECEIPTS TAX

Mechanics

A gross receipts tax, sometimes referred to as a turnover tax, is levied on the value of products sold, the gross proceeds of sale (or total revenue), or the gross income of the business. The specific definition of a gross receipts tax base is decided by the state in designing the tax. In Washington, the base includes all revenue to the firm, including interest income, sales of assets, dividend income, rental and royalty income and capital gains (both long- and short-term). Ohio's base includes gross receipts from the sale or operation of the business as well as rental and royalty income but excludes from the base interest earnings, dividends received and capital gains. Thus, while Washington's tax includes all forms of corporate income and is a traditional GRT, Ohio's version resembles a business sales tax or consumption tax since it excludes the cost of capital from the base.

The Various States

In this section, we discuss the experiences of four states (Washington, Ohio, Texas and Delaware) with their forays into using some variant of a GRT.

Washington's business and occupation tax

In Washington, the gross receipts tax is referred to as the business and occupation (B&O) tax and is calculated on gross income or gross receipts derived from business activities conducted within the state of Washington.[1] Businesses report gross income under one of eight tax classifications with varying tax rates. Rates vary from 0.471 percent for retailing to 1.5 percent for service activities.

According to the Washington State Department of Revenue, B&O tax collections in fiscal year 2004 (FY04) totaled just over $2 billion, representing almost 16 percent of state tax revenues.[2] Almost all businesses, including corporations, limited liability companies (LLCs), partnerships, sole proprietors and non-profit organizations, are subject to the state B&O tax. Businesses with annual gross income of $28,000 or less do not have to file. In addition, many small firms have their liability reduced through a tax credit for small businesses.

There are generally no deductions from the B&O tax for labor costs, materials, taxes, and/or any other costs of doing business.[3] Businesses can reduce their taxable incomes by taking advantage of deductions not related to the costs of doing business, including bad debts and inter-state and foreign sales. The most common B&O exemptions include incomes from farming, the sale and rental of real estate, certain non-profit and social service organizations,[4] government and credit unions. Some businesses also qualify for tax credits based on the size (payroll), nature (high-technology) and the location (distressed area) of the business. Further, businesses that perform more than one taxable activity for the same product can take advantage of the Multiple Activities Tax Credit (MATC) to reduce the occurrence of multiple layers of taxation. For instance, manufacturers who also sell finished products as whole-salers are required to report each activity under the appropriate B&O classification.

Ohio's commercial activity tax
In June 2005, Ohio enacted a gross receipts tax referred to as the commercial activity tax (CAT). This tax is imposed on the taxable gross receipts of almost all commercial activities and business entities in Ohio, including C corporations, S corporations, partnerships and LLCs.[5] The initial top rate of the CAT is 0.06 percent and is scheduled to increase to 0.26 percent when the tax is fully implemented. The tax is being phased in over a five-year period starting in 2005. Once fully phased in, the CAT will exclude gross receipts of up to $1 million annually from taxation. Businesses with at least $150,000 in Ohio taxable gross receipts in a calendar year must register for the CAT and pay a minimum $75 fee included on the CAT form.[6] Only a few deductions are associated with the CAT, including cash discounts, bad debts, and returns and allowances. On the other hand, several forms and sources of income are excluded from the base. These include, among others, interest and dividend income and capital gains, and compensation, including benefits, for services for an employer. In addition, non-profit organizations, dealers in intangibles, financial institutions and insurance companies are excluded from the CAT. A particularly

unique feature of the Ohio tax is the taxation of imports but exclusion of gross receipts associated with exports.

Texas margin tax
In 2006 Texas modified its franchise tax, the Texas margin tax. The modifications apply to tax years 2007 and forward. Under the modifications the tax applies to all corporations, S-corps, limited liability companies, limited partnerships and limited liability partnerships. The tax does not apply to businesses organized as sole proprietorships or general partnerships that have only natural persons as partners. In addition, entities with gross receipts of $300,000 or less, tax-exempt entities, insurance companies, REITs (Real Estate Investment Trust), REMICs (Real Estate Mortgage Investment Conduit), and some passive entities are among the list of firms that are not subject to the tax. The tax is computed as the lower of three possible bases. The first is total revenue minus the cost of goods sold. The second is total revenue minus employee compensation and benefits but not subtracting payroll taxes. The third possible base is computed as 70 percent of total revenue. The final tax base is apportioned using a receipts-only apportionment formula. The applicable tax rate is 0.5 percent for firms engaged primarily in retail or wholesale trade and in general 1 percent for all other entities.

Delaware gross receipts tax
The Delaware tax is a more standard gross receipts tax based on the sum of a firm's gross revenue from sales, rent, services and commissions with no deductions allowed for the cost of goods sold, compensation or interest expenses. The tax applies to most business entities. There is an exclusion of, in general, $80,000 per month, though this increases to $1 million per month for manufacturers. The rate varies from 0.096 percent to 1.92 percent depending on the business of the firm. For example, retailers face a tax rate of 0.576 percent while manufacturers face a tax rate of 0.144 percent. While not specifically apportioned, the tax is levied only on revenues associated with sales and services rendered in Delaware.

Other state experiences
Several other states have somewhat similar taxes. For example, New Mexico has a very broad-based sales tax that has often been referred to as a gross receipts tax. Hawaii, as well, has a broad-based sales tax. In 2005, Kentucky implemented an alternative minimum gross receipts tax that operates in conjunction with the corporate income tax.

The GRT Argument

Arguments for and against a GRT have been made since the GRT first arrived on the scene. On the pro-side, the GRT is a tax that encompasses a broad base, which allows for a much lower rate. Mikesell (2007) argues that the base may in fact be too broad, as gross receipts for Washington in 2005 were 177 percent of gross state product. This is not a recent phenomenon either, for back in 1962 Indiana's ratio was 135 percent.

Another argument is how the wide base of a GRT provides greater stability as a revenue source. Testa and Mattoon (2007) report that, although the GRT is more stable than the corporate income tax, there is little difference in stability between the GRT and a retail sales tax. As a result, the GRT is unable to reduce the volatility of a state's overall tax portfolio.

A third argument is how a GRT avoids penalizing a business for being profitable, since it is not a tax on net income or profits. On the other hand, a GRT may create a positive tax liability for firms not making a profit, because a firm's tax liability under a GRT is not reduced for the cost of business inputs, labor or capital investments. This will be particularly burdensome for small start-up firms with low sales and high business costs (Wheeler and Sennoga, 2007; Testa and Mattoon, 2007). More importantly, because a GRT taxes capital investment, it not only discourages such investment (McClure, 2005), but it also creates an incentive for firms to substitute away from capital into other inputs (Mikesell, 2007).

Some advocates of a GRT promote the simplicity of the GRT as its major advantage. Simplicity is often not a function of the underlying base. Rather, complexity stems from using the tax code to redistribute income or encourage certain activities (Wheeler and Sennoga, 2007). As discussed in the previous section, both Washington and Ohio make exceptions to the base, increasing the complexity of the tax.

While a GRT may not be passed on to consumers directly, it can be passed on indirectly via price increases. Thus, a major concern against a GRT is the notion of tax pyramiding or cascading, in which taxes are imposed upon earlier taxes. This effect increases as the number of taxable transactions in the production process increases. This creates the potential for the effective tax rate from a GRT to be significantly higher than the statutory rate (Mikesell, 2007). However, Pogue (2007) found for the cases of Washington and New Mexico that the variation in pyramiding tax rates 'is not large'.

Besides creating different rates for different firms, tax pyramiding also has the ability to impact firm structure by creating an artificial incentive for vertical integration (McClure, 2005). The tax burden under a GRT can be lower for these types of firms, as there is no resale of inputs from one firm to the other. Firms with fewer steps in the production process also benefit under a GRT.

Finally, there are equity concerns in dealing with a GRT. On the one hand, the GRT is imposed on nearly all business entities, which creates an equal treatment of firms regardless of business structure. On the other hand, two firms with similar profits but different production processes can have different tax liabilities, violating notions of horizontal equity.

To conclude, there are numerous arguments for and against the GRT. These arguments have yet to be settled because the data needed to quantify these arguments have been hard to come by. As we describe in the next section, our unique Georgia corporate tax return data provide information on gross receipts that allows us to shed some light on both the equity and stability arguments associated with a gross receipts tax.

GEORGIA'S CORPORATE INCOME TAX

Because our goal is to compare a GRT to the corporate income tax in Georgia, a discussion of Georgia's current tax system is in order. The Georgia corporate income tax is similar to most other state corporate income taxes. The statutory rate is 6 percent on a base of adjusted federal taxable income.[7] Firm income is apportioned to Georgia using the standard three-factor formula of 25 percent weight on compensation and property and a 50 percent weight on receipts. Beginning in 2006, Georgia transitioned from a three-factor apportionment formula to a receipts-only apportionment factor. This transition was fully in place for the 2008 tax year. All corporations must file, though most do not owe any tax and corporations with anticipated tax liabilities in excess of $25,000 must make quarterly tax payments.[8]

DATA

This analysis makes use of the corporate return data file prepared by the Georgia Department of Revenue. This file consists of the population of Georgia Form 600 corporate filers from 1998 to 2005 and contains 90,000 observations, annually.[9] Table 6A.1 of the Appendix provides a general overview of this corporate data file.

Approximately one-third of all firms each year apportion their multistate corporate income. Apportioning firms report the values of property, receipts and compensation paid nationally and within the state of Georgia. These data fields are captured on the DOR Corporate file. Unfortunately, these data are only reported for firms that apportion their corporate income and are not available for the remaining two-thirds of firms which do not have corporate income from other states. Therefore, the results presented here are based only on the analysis of apportioning corporate entities which was approximately 30,000 returns per year. While the degree of required data cleaning was fairly minimal, several outliers existed each year. Twenty firms were found to have an extremely large share of annual corporate tax payments over the eight years of data. Since their inclusion in the analysis strongly skewed our results, these 20 were dropped from the analysis.[10] These 20 observations represent only eight unique firms over the eight-year period as several firms are excluded in multiple years.

The descriptive statistics for the apportioning firms are shown in Table 6A.2 in the Appendix. The descriptive statistics for the remaining data, referred to in this work as the non-apportioned data, and the pooled set of omitted observations, are shown in Table 6A.3 and Table 6A.4 of the Appendix, respectively.[11] The descriptive statistics of the dataset used in the analysis (apportioning firms excluding the 20 outliers) are shown in Table 6A.5 of the Appendix. In general, the dataset is comprised of firms with slightly higher than average federal and Georgia taxable income than compared to the non-apportioning firms.

HERFINDAHL–HIRSCHMANN INDEX

One purpose of this research is to determine the degree of concentration of tax payments among corporate entities under the different tax scenarios. We compare the concentration of tax payments under the standard three-factor corporate apportionment, the single-factor corporate apportionment and a gross receipts tax. To measure the degree of concentration of tax payments among firms under these three scenarios we construct a Herfindahl–Hirschman index for each type of tax. A Herfindahl–Hirschman index (HHI) is used to measure concentrations of market share across industries. The HHI is constructed by summing the squared market share across all firms. It ranges from approximately zero (an infinite number of firms of equal size) to 10,000 (one firm with 100 percent market share). In our case, market share is going to be the percentage of overall corporate taxes in a given year paid by an individual firm in that year.

Our main goal is to consider the effect of moving from a three-factor corporate apportionment system to a gross receipts system. But in making that transition we recognize that two effects are occurring simultaneously. First, a gross receipts tax is not only a tax of a different base but also a single apportionment tax since only gross receipts are involved in the tax calculation. Thus, the switch from a three-factor apportioned corporate tax to a gross receipts tax involves first a change in the tax base and a change in apportionment. To isolate the marginal effect of each, we consider them separately.

Moving from a three-factor apportioned corporate income tax to a single-factor system is expected to result in a higher degree of concentration of tax payments and a higher HHI value. This is because it is anticipated that a number of firms paying tax under the three-factor system will have lower tax liabilities under a single-factor system. On the other hand, moving from a single-factor corporate tax to a gross receipts tax is expected to decrease the degree of concentration of tax shares.

In calculating our tax shares, we took three steps. First, for any firm that had a negative tax liability under the corporate income tax, we made their tax bill equal to zero for the purposes of the HHI. Second, we aggregated these new tax bills across all firms in our sample to generate the total amount of corporate income tax paid. For each firm, we then divided their new tax bill by the total corporate taxes paid, multiplied by 100, and used this value as market share.

In calculating tax liability under a GRT, we wanted the tax to be revenue-neutral, so that the same amount of revenue generated under the three-factor apportionment system would be generated by our GRT. Thus, we divided the aggregated corporate income tax bills (with negative tax bills once again brought to zero) by aggregate gross receipts to generate a revenue-neutral gross receipts tax rate. We then applied this rate to each firm's gross receipts to calculate their tax liability under the GRT. Doing so yielded very reasonable tax rates that ranged from a high of 0.0026 in 1998 to a low of 0.0016 in 2005. By comparison, the rate used by Ohio is 0.0026. We then calculated tax shares in a similar manner as outlined above.

To calculate the single-apportionment tax liability, we again constructed an equal revenue tax rate on the base of single-apportioned corporate income. Under this alternative, we summed the simulated tax base of single-apportionment corporate income and divided this by the annual aggregate tax payment of the three-factor apportioned corporate income. These rates ranged from 0.072 in 1998 to 0.048 in 2005. It is expected that the single-apportionment rate would be higher for an equal yield tax as the base is lower under single apportionment. Thus, the rate of 0.048 in 2005 is lower than anticipated and requires further investigation. Based on the derived annual tax rates, we computed the tax shares in the usual manner.

Figure 6.1 shows the HHI calculations for all three tax regimes. There are two broad trends to notice. As expected, the concentration under the GRT is relatively stable, and the broad base of the GRT is illustrated by the very low HHI value. More interestingly, however, is how both

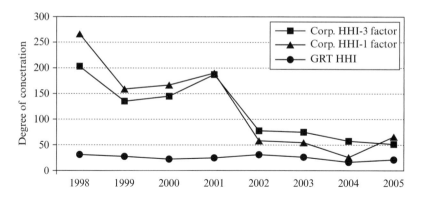

Figure 6.1   HHI by tax type

the three-factor and single-factor corporate apportionment systems are trending downward, indicating that the degree of concentration has been widening and approaching that of a GRT. There is very little difference in concentration between the three-factor and single-factor regimes.

For all three tax regimes, the value of the HHI is very low, indicating a high degree of concentration among corporate taxpayers. While the HHI values for the GRT are consistently under 50, the highest corporate income tax HHI is only slightly above 250. Thus, it is hard to argue from these calculations that a three-factor or single-factor apportionment system is any less broad than a GRT.

One final caveat concerning the HHI is that the HHI only calculates market share for those firms with a tax liability, as a zero liability results in zero share. In our sample, between 34 percent (in 2001) and 47 percent (in 1998) of firms actually have a positive corporate income tax liability. By comparison, under our hypothetical GRT, between 68 percent (in 1998) and 78 percent (in 1999) have a positive GRT liability. So while firms that face a tax liability under the various regimes appear to have similar tax shares, the number of firms that face that a liability differs dramatically under the regimes.

PROBIT EQUATIONS

To capture the effect of a change in tax payments between tax regimes, we run a simple probit of the form:

$$INCREASE_t = \alpha + \beta INCOME_t = \gamma APPORTIONMENT_t$$
$$= \delta CREDITS_t + \mu PAYMENTS_t \qquad (1)$$

where *INCREASE* is a 1/0 dummy variable indicating if a firm's tax bill increased as a result of a switch between two tax regimes. Included in *INCOME* are the firm's federal taxable income, along with any Georgia additions and subtractions to that amount. The more additions (subtractions) a firm has, the higher (lower) its corporate tax bill will be. We also include a firm's net worth and any amount of loss carry-forward that the firm had. The net worth is a crude measure to capture the size of a firm. The carry-forward allows a firm to reduce its tax liability, thus we would expect a firm's bill to increase should it lose this reduction.

In *APPORTIONMENT*, we include how much a firm has listed for Georgia property and compensation separately. Because property includes capital investment, we would expect the tax bill to increase when switching to a GRT, whereas compensation is a sign that the firm is using more labor. Thus, the bill is likely to decrease, given the GRT's supposed bias against capital.

We include two variables for *CREDITS*. The first is the amount a firm receives in the Georgia job credit, and the second is an aggregation of all other credits available. Tax credits have an impact of lowering corporate tax liability, so both credits will likely have a negative impact in our probit. We treat the job credit separately because it is one of the larger credits available and we wish to see if there is a different effect for this credit versus the others.

Finally, we include estimated payments and tax penalties under *PAYMENTS*. A higher estimated payment might indicate that a firm had higher profits and thus would pay more with a corporate income tax. Firms with high penalty payments may have incurred higher-than-expected profits or have tight cash flows, both of which would lead to a negative effect.

The model also includes year fixed effects, to account for any changes in Georgia law that may affect all firms in a different year. Tax payments are calculated as described previously. Because approximately 25 percent of firms have no change in their tax liability between regimes, we also re-estimate the probit model using a 1/0 dummy variable indicating a firm had a decrease in its tax liability. As a final note, we consider our probit estimates to be descriptive in nature, as we make no attempt to address econometric issues of mulitcolinearity, simultaneity, selection and other issues.

Changing from Triple Apportionment to Hypothetical GRT

Table 6.1 reports the marginal effects from our probit estimation for whether or not a firm faces an increasing tax bill. Column 1 deals with the

Table 6.1   Marginal effects from probits for increasing tax bill

Independent variable	Marginal effect for increase tax bill from GA corp. tax to gross receipts tax	Marginal effect for increase tax bill from GA single apportionment to gross receipts tax	Marginal effect for increase tax bill from GA corporate tax to GA single apportionment
Federal taxable income	−4.71E-07	−7.73E-07	7.11E-07
	(−34.46)	(−48.75)	(50.08)
GA additions to federal income	−3.35E-08	−2.63E-07	2.24E-07
	(−1.52)	(−12.27)	(14.39)
GA subtractions to federal income	6.87E-07	9.30E-07	−4.35E-07
	(20.98)	(27.79)	(−15.74)
Net worth amount	6.42E-09	3.25E-09	−1.80E-08
	(8.00)	(4.01)	(−15.70)
GA carry-forward amount	0.00072	0.0004333	0.00002
	(22.88)	(14.21)	(1.22)
GA property amount	7.72E-10	6.60E-07	−1.13E-07
	(8.54)	(7.67)	(−1.92)
GA compensation amount	−7.66E-10	−6.54E-07	1.14E-07
	(−8.47)	(−7.60)	(1.94)
GA job credit amount	−0.04240	−34.91887	25.31022
	(−10.66)	(−8.82)	(8.00)
Other GA credit amount	−0.00250	−6.15E-05	−0.00008
	(−6.33)	(−2.08)	(−7.90)
GA estimated payments	−0.00057	−0.000354	0.00001
	(−39.68)	(−27.85)	(1.28)
GA penalty amount	−8.87E-06	−2.08E-03	−1.13E-04
	(−15.54)	(−8.23)	(−1.96)
Observed probability	0.546	0.522	0.272
Predicted probability (at x-bar)	0.544	0.522	0.267

Notes:
Z-values in brackets.
Year fixed effects included, but not reported.

switch from triple apportionment in Georgia to a revenue-neutral GRT. We find that while subtractions to federal income will increase the probability that a firm's tax bill will increase, additions have an insignificant impact. The higher a firm's carry-forward amount, the more likely it is to pay more under a GRT. Higher net worth is also associated with a higher

Table 6.2   Marginal effects from probits for decreasing tax bill

Independent variable	Marginal effect for decrease tax bill from GA corp. tax to gross receipts tax	Marginal effect for decrease tax bill from GA single apportionment to gross receipts tax	Marginal effect for decrease tax bill from GA corporate tax to GA single apportionment
Federal taxable	5.74E-07	7.44E-07	1.09E-07
income	(41.90)	(51.88)	(17.27)
GA additions to	−1.05E-08	1.21E-07	2.94E-08
federal income	(−0.40)	(8.42)	(2.69)
GA subtractions to	−5.89E-07	−6.95E-07	−7.46E-08
federal income	(−19.36)	(−24.95)	(−4.04)
Net worth amount	−4.06E-08	−2.90E-08	−6.57E-09
	(−29.04)	(−22.92)	(−7.54)
GA carry-forward	−0.00097	−6.72E-04	0.000038
amount	(−55.42)	(−41.36)	(4.85)
GA property	−1.08E-10	−4.44E-08	−9.46E-08
amount	(−1.61)	(−0.73)	(−1.95)
GA compensation	1.06E-10	4.34E-08	−1.95E-08
amount	(1.58)	(0.71)	(−0.40)
GA job credit	0.05792	39.34052	23.50941
amount	(19.45)	(13.98)	(10.67)
Other GA credit	0.00026	4.70E-05	0.0000191
amount	(8.72)	(2.37)	(3.15)
GA estimated	0.00106	7.82E-04	0.0000457
payments	(92.19)	(81.90)	(15.34)
GA penalty amount	1.48E-05	4.99E-03	0.0004862
	(31.00)	(24.68)	(8.86)
Observed probability	0.229	0.221	0.144
Predicted probability	0.227	0.216	0.137
(at x-bar)			

Notes:
Z-values in brackets.
Year fixed effects included, but not reported.

tax bill under a GRT. Property and compensation have equal and opposite effects, with property making it more likely that the GRT bill will be higher. Somewhat surprisingly, both credit measures decrease the likelihood that a firm will pay more under a GRT.

Column 1 from Table 6.2 reports marginal effects from our probit estimation for whether or not a firm faces a decreased tax bill with a GRT. Most variables switch signs, so that if the variables increased the probability of having an increased tax bill, they decreased the probability of having a lower tax bill. The two exceptions are the property and compensation variables. While the coefficients remained equal and opposite and they also changed signs as we would expect, they are now no longer statistically significant.

Changing from Three-Factor Apportionment to Hypothetical Single-Factor Apportionment

Column 3 from Table 6.1 reports marginal effects from our probit estimation for whether or not a firm faces an increased tax bill when we switch from a three-factor to single-factor apportionment. Now, additions are more likely to increase a firm's tax bill, whereas subtractions decrease. The higher a firm's net worth, the more likely it is that it would pay less under a single-factor apportionment rule. Property and compensation still work equally and opposite, with more property decreasing the tax bill and more compensation increasing it. Having a high job tax credit will increase taxes paid, which makes sense as it should follow the effect of compensation. Other credits, however, decrease taxes paid. Finally, note that the carry-forward amount, while positive, is insignificant.

When we repeat the exercise for a decrease, shown in column 3 of Table 6.2, we see a similar pattern, albeit with smaller coefficients across the board. A notable exception is the carry-forward amount, which is now significant and positive, indicating that carry-forwards increase the likelihood that the tax bill will decrease. Compensation is no longer statistically significant, although property still is. Other credits, estimated payments and penalties all increase the likelihood that a firm will face a lower tax bill.

Changing from Hypothetical Single-Factor Apportionment to Hypothetical GRT

The second column of Table 6.1 shows results from switching from our hypothetical single-factor apportionment system to a hypothetical GRT. We see similar patterns across the board as we did when considering the switch from three-factor to single-factor apportionment. This is to be expected as for most firms, the estimated change in taxes from three-factor apportionment to single-factor apportionment was either an increase or a slight decrease. Tax bills change most dramatically for a GRT, which is why the results are very similar when we switch from either a three- or a single-factor apportionment rule to a GRT.

We do see some differences for the likelihood of facing a decreased tax bill, as reported in column 2 of Table 6.2. Additions to federal income increase the likelihood of facing a lower bill. Property and compensation amounts remain statistically insignificant, whereas the carry-forward amount decreases the likelihood that a firm would face a lower bill. With the exception of our penalty, job credit and federal income variables, most of our estimated marginal effects are lower when we start from a single-factor than a three-factor apportionment rule.

To conclude, in moving from a three-factor apportionment corporate income tax to a GRT, the larger the carry-forward amount, the more net worth a firm has and the more property it owns, will lead to higher GRT taxes than corporate income taxes. Large credits, compensation and federal taxable income will lead to lower GRT taxes. When we divide this overall movement into steps (change apportionment, change base), we find that the results of changing apportionment rules by themselves yield contradictory results, as most variables increase the likelihood of increased and decreased tax payments. This may be due to the small overall change in tax bills for most firms. When we switch from either apportionment factor to the GRT, however, we get a much more consistent story.

CONCLUSION

In general the data yielded the expected results in terms of the degree of concentration among taxpayers. The analysis revealed as expected that the degree of concentration of tax shares widens as we move from a three-factor corporate apportionment formula to a single-factor formula, and narrows as we move from a single-factor formula to a gross receipts tax. The unexpected finding was that the degree of concentration associated with each of the three taxes considered here was fairly small, indicating no significant change associated with one choice over the other. The true difference between the tax regimes is masked by the treatment of firms with negative income tax liabilities. While firms that face a tax liability under the various regimes may appear to have similar tax shares, the number of firms that actually face such a liability differs dramatically under the regimes. For instance, in our sample, between 34 percent (in 2001) and 47 percent (in 1998) of firms actually have a positive corporate income tax liability. By comparison, under our hypothetical GRT, between 68 percent (in 1998) and 78 percent (in 1999) have a positive GRT liability.

NOTES

1. The State of Washington does not impose either a corporate income tax or a personal income tax.
2. This represents 0.79 percent of gross state product for Washington State. By contrast, Georgia total tax collections represent about 4.4 percent of gross state product in 2000 (Georgia Department of Revenue, 2002).
3. Since the state of Washington does not levy an individual income tax, the lack of an exemption of the labor costs from the B&O tax base does not lead to the double taxation on wages.
4. Some non-profit organizations such as public and non-profit hospitals are subject to the B&O tax.
5. Banks and other financial institutions, insurance companies, public utilities and dealers in intangibles such as securities are subject to special taxes and are excluded from the CAT. Further, most affiliates of financial institutions and insurance companies are also excluded from the CAT.
6. Businesses with gross receipts of less than $150,000 are not required to register as CAT taxpayers.
7. The additions to federal taxable income vary from year to year but include such items as taxes paid to other governments, the value of the federal deduction for the domestic production activities deduction and the value of the bonus depreciation deduction.
8. For example, in 2005, only 34 percent of all corporate filers had a positive tax liability. (Rork and Wheeler, 2008)
9. All corporate entities are required to file a Form 600. S corporations file a Form 600S.
10. In addition, a limited number of observations, less than 20 each year, were deleted because they gave nonsensical responses to the data fields, such as negative values for receipts.
11. In actuality, a few of the observations included in the analysis are firms which do not apportion their income but did report the value of their receipts, compensation and property.

REFERENCES

Georgia Department of Revenue (2002). Annual Statistical Report for FY2002. Atlanta, GA: 2003.

Georgia Department of Revenue (1998–2005). Corporate return data file, not publically available.

McClure, C. (2005). Why Ohio should not introduce a gross receipts tax: testimony on the proposed commercial activity tax. *State Tax Notes* 36: 213–15.

Mikesell, J. (2007). Gross receipts taxes in state government finance: a review of their history and performance. Tax Foundation Background Paper 53.

Pogue, T. (2007). The gross receipts tax: a new approach to business taxation? *National Tax Journal* 60 (4): 799–819.

Rork, J.C. and Wheeler, L. (2008). Distribution of the Georgia corporate and net worth tax liabilities, 1998 and 2005. Fiscal Research Center Brief 185, Georgia State University.

Testa, W. and Mattoon, R. (2007). Is there a role for gross receipts taxation? *National Tax Journal* 60 (4): 821–40.

Wheeler, L. and Sennoga, E. (2007). Alternative state business tax systems: a comparison of state income and gross receipts taxes. Fiscal Research Report 154, Georgia State University.

APPENDIX

Table 6A.1   General data description, 2005 ($ values in 000 $)

Variable	Number of observations	Mean	Median	Standard deviation	Minimum	Maximum
Federal taxable income base	82 614	1 094	0	185 944	−38 545 912	9 698 604
Georgia taxable income base	82 614	-301	0	18 436	−2 608 459	2 532 504
Value of Georgia net worth	82 614	5 933	6	420 141	−12 663 041	100 980 450
Georgia tax liability	82 164	7	0	128	0	25 518
Georgia tax liability among payers	27 525	22	1	220	0	25 518
Value of Georgia receipts	29 929	32 488	372	3 421 318	0	589 700 000
Average apportionment ratio	82 164	0.69	1	0.44	0	1

Table 6A.2 Descriptive statistics, apportioned observations ($ values in 000)

Variable	Mean	Median	Standard deviation	Minimum	Maximum
YEAR 1998 (N = 31651)					
Federal taxable income	1023	13	107342	−7413019	6727715
Net federal taxable income	1085	14	108243	−8045904	6727715
National net worth	72439	700	784098	−14563029	49047045
Georgia taxable income	−219	0	10227	−452876	1274535
Georgia corporate tax liability	19	0	493	0	76472
Georgia apportionment ratio	0.13	0.02	0.25	0	1
Carry-forward amounts	6	0	138	0	17184
Total value of credits	2	0	88	0	13091
Estimated payment indicator	0.55	1		0	1
Penalty indicator	0.12	0		0	1
Value of national property	137746	2921	1375450	0	110935399
Value of Georgia property	13483	10	1237033	0	219144008
Value of national compensation	30281	1650	253223	0	20583206
Value of Georgia compensation	13003	11	1236981	0	219144008
Value of national receipts	260653	6919	5403791	0	532074865
Value of Georgia receipts (FRC)	7338	225	71515	0	5723331

147

Table 6A.2 (continued)

Variable	Mean	Median	Standard deviation	Minimum	Maximum
YEAR 2002 (N = 31 228)					
Federal taxable income	−5466	0	222028	−18 963 554	9 512 138
Net federal taxable income	−1604	0.91	184 282	−17 194 274	14 344 738
National net worth	114 165	983	1 294 986	−17 722 930	63 430 713
Georgia taxable income	−854	0	17 937	−1 790 697	336 274
Georgia corporate tax liability	15	0	226	0	20 176
Georgia apportionment ratio	0.16	0.02	0.28	0	1
Carry-forward amounts	5	0	76	0	7564
Total value of credits	3	0	125	0	13 220
Estimated payment indicator	0.7	1	0.46	0	1
Penalty indicator	0.09	0	0.29	0	1
Value of national property	193 716	5668	1 753 267.51	0	123 762 491
Value of Georgia property	8168	25	106 432.12	0	12 299 269
Value of national compensation	43 231	3042	391 453.92	0	41 583 613
Value of Georgia compensation	7239	30	105 049.24	0	12 299 269
Value of national receipts	3 224 757	11 649	411 764 120	0	70 399 633 224
Value of Georgia receipts (FRC)	332 600	318	56 879 967	0	10 069 058 347

YEAR 2005 (N = 29929)

Federal taxable income	3 090	2	306 434	−38 545 912	9 698 604
Net federal taxable income	5 151	52	146 918	−7 284 683	6 571 275
National net worth	181 509	1 410	2 464 152	−25 703 694	159 454 367
Georgia taxable income	−476	0	13 456	−1 035 797	628 612
Georgia corporate tax liability	17	0	206	0	25 518
Georgia apportionment ratio	0.16	0.02	0.29	0	1
Carry-forward amounts	6.7	0	63	0	3 513
Total value of credits	1.6	0	54	0	4 759
Estimated payment indicator	0.73	1	0.44	0	1
Penalty indicator	0.09	0	0.29	0	1
Value of national property	198 221	5 891	1 662 076	0	140 598 075
Value of Georgia property	8 599	17	147 830	0	19 623 733
Value of national compensation	43 976	3 706	266 438	0	14 750 176
Value of Georgia compensation	7 410	29	146 318	0	19 623 733
Value of national receipts	1 710 350	14 807	152 506 972	0	20 600 462 881
Value of Georgia receipts (FRC)	32 494	373	3 421 318	0	589 732 777

Table 6A.3   Descriptive statistics, non-apportioned observations ($ values in 000)

Variable	Mean	Median	Standard Deviation	Minimum	Maximum
YEAR 1998 (N = 63 582)					
Federal taxable income	-222	0	40176	-7649967	4245950
Net federal taxable income	-218	0	40139	-7649967	4245950
National net worth	5679	7	240953	-5592890	40996822
Georgia taxable income	-439	0	32516	-7650034	146321
Georgia corporate tax liability	2.27	0	55538	0	8779280
Georgia apportionment ratio	1	1	0.06	0	1
Carry-forward amounts	0.39	0	12	0	2276
Total value of credits	0.16	0	12	0	2090
Estimated payment indicator	0.29	0	0.45	0	1
Penalty indicator	0.14	0	0.35	0	1
YEAR 2002 (N = 59 522)					
Federal taxable income	-320	0	46111	-6037768	6753948
Net federal taxable income	-230	0	43682	-5650721	7060349
National net worth	5405	4000	248095	-9848043	44829777
Georgia taxable income	-325	0	18707	-2934963	726457
Georgia corporate tax liability	3	0	188	-1	43587
Georgia apportionment ratio	1	1	0.05	0	1
Carry-forward amounts	0.63	0	27	0	3352
Total value of credits	0.91	0	144	0	34014
Estimated payment indicator	0.3	0	0.46	0	1
Penalty indicator	0.13	0	0.33	0	1

YEAR 2005 (N = 52 235)

Federal taxable income	−49	0	24 094	−3 452 912	2 464 682
Net federal taxable income	−56	0	22 426	−3 369 364	2 532 504
National net worth	8 706	1 755	621 093	−9 599 185	100 980 450
Georgia taxable income	−201	0	20 758	−2 608 459	2 532 504
Georgia corporate tax liability	2	0	36	0	3 794
Georgia apportionment ratio	1	1	0.05	0	1
Carry-forward amounts	0.71	0	19	0	3 382
Total value of credits	0.18	0	11	0	1 903
Estimated payment indicator	0.32	0	0.47	0	1
Penalty indicator	0.12	0	0.33	0	1

Table 6A.4   Descriptive statistics, outlier observations ($ values in 000)

Variable	Mean	Median	Standard deviation	Minimum	Maximum
ALL YEARS (N = 20)					
Federal taxable income	291970	140766	914509	−1192354	3175901
Net federal taxable income	237272	178489	744501	−1240380	1896983
National net worth	5644741	3536553	11124312	0	50919506
Georgia taxable income	559	2317	54042	−177822	92437
Georgia corporate tax liability	936	0.07	1439	0	5546
Georgia apportionment ratio	0.08	0.03	0.09	0	0.32
Carry-forward amounts	224	0.05	547	0	2088
Total value of credits	277	0	1240	0	5546
Estimated payment indicator	0.8	1	0.41	0	1
Penalty indicator	0.2	0	0.41	0	1
Value of national property	8719493	4453646	15333822	3322	60295763
Value of Georgia property	356864	79614	760441	7.21	3320726
Value of national compensation	4292612	5708835	4528567	45767	17062063
Value of Georgia compensation	356864	79614	760441	0	3320726
Value of national receipts	17719902897	1879780596	27339903767	179666061	74927101988
Value of Georgia receipts (FRC)	1633266043	38024142	3803479447	246592	10820111188

Table 6A.5 Descriptive statistics, apportioned observations/no. outliers ($ values in 000)

Variable	Mean	Median	Standard deviation	Minimum	Maximum
YEAR 1998 (N = 31651)					
Federal taxable income	1023	13	107342	−7413019	6727715
Net federal taxable income	1085	14	108243	−8045904	6727715
National net worth	72439	700	784098	−14563029	49047045
Georgia taxable income	−219	0	10227	−452876	1274535
Georgia corporate tax liability	19	0	493	0	76472
Georgia apportionment ratio	0.13	0.02	0.25	0	1
Carry-forward amounts	6	0	138	0	17184
Total value of credits	2	0	88	0	13091
Estimated payment indicator	0.55	1		0	1
Penalty indicator	0.12	0		0	1
Value of national property	137746	2921	1375450	0	110935399
Value of Georgia property	13483	10	1237033	0	219144008
Value of national compensation	30281	1650	253223	0	20583206
Value of Georgia compensation	13003	11	1236981	0	219144008
Value of national receipts	260653	6919	5403791	0	532074865
Value of Georgia receipts (FRC)	7338	225	71515	0	5723331

Table 6A.5 (continued)

Variable	Mean	Median	Standard deviation	Minimum	Maximum
YEAR 2002 (N = 31 225)					
Federal taxable income	−5461	0	222027	−18963554	9512138
Net federal taxable income	−1600	0.92	184281	−17194274	14344738
National net worth	113768	982	1294076	−17722930	63430713
Georgia taxable income	−855	0	17937	−1790697	336274
Georgia corporate tax liability	15	0	226	0	20176
Georgia apportionment ratio	0.16	0.02	0.28	0	1
Carry-forward amounts	5.13	0	75.42	0	7564
Total value of credits	3.44	0	125	0	13220
Estimated payment indicator	0.7	1	0.46	0	1
Penalty indicator	0.09	0	0.29	0	1
Value of national property	193252	5666	1752589	0	123762491
Value of Georgia property	8153	25	106418	0	12299269
Value of national compensation	42783	3041	387778	0	41583613
Value of Georgia compensation	7224	30	105035	0	12299269
Value of national receipts	382978	11645	13748825	0	2294768952
Value of Georgia reciepts (FRC)	9125	318	90907	0	8667204

YEAR 2005 (N = 29929)

Federal taxable income	3070	2	306350	-38545912	9698604
Net federal taxable income	5123	52	146663	-7284683	6571275
National net worth	181059	1409	2463568	-25703694	159454367
Georgia taxable income	-471	0	13417	0	628612
Georgia corporate tax liability	17	0	206	-1035797	25518
Georgia apportionment ratio	0.16	0.02	0.29	0	1
Carry-forward amounts	6.72	0	62.84	0	3513
Total value of credits	1.57	0	53.97	0	4759
Estimated payment indicator	0.73	1	0.44	0	1
Penalty indicator	0.09	0	0.29	0	1
Value of national property	197847	5885	1661501	0	140598075
Value of Georgia property	8595	17	147836	0	19623733
Value of national compensation	43481	3705	260153	0	14750176
Value of Georgia compensation	7406	29	146325	0	19623733
Value of national receipts	973163	14806	93257815	0	15979821660
Value of Georgia reciepts (FRC)	10538	372	83817	0	5887733

7. Can Georgia move from income tax to consumption tax?

Sally Wallace

INTRODUCTION

Since 1985, there have been numerous calls for flat taxes in the US and abroad. These calls have led to substantial rethinking of income taxes for the first time in many years. Flat tax reforms often call for an income tax system that limits deductions, exemptions and credits, and imposes one statutory tax rate. In some countries, flat tax reforms have integrated the corporate and individual income taxes. Flat tax reforms have simplified the structure of the income tax in countries such as Jamaica, Estonia, Russia and Lithuania.

While the flat rate income tax reforms of Jamaica, Estonia, Russia and other countries have their merits, they are aimed at simplifying the tax system through elimination of various exemptions and deductions, and by simplifying the tax rate structure. They do not fundamentally change the base of taxation. There is, however, another type of income tax reform (which, unluckily, is also referred to as flat tax reform) that stems from a long-standing debate over the merits of a general consumption tax versus a broad-based income tax. This kind of reform fundamentally changes the base of taxation from realized income (wages, realized capital gains, interest income and the like) to consumption. It may be accomplished using a reporting mechanism that is similar to an income tax, but one which exempts savings from taxation.

In the United States, there have been numerous consumption tax proposals at the federal government level. Hall and Rabushka (1983, 1995) proposed a direct consumption tax for the US, where income from savings is exempt from tax and a single tax rate is imposed on businesses and individuals. Zodrow and McLure (1988) and McLure and Zodrow (2006) have presented the case of consumption taxes in developing countries and demonstrate the potential for a progressive tax that serves to exempt savings (and therefore effectively taxes consumption via the income tax system) as a replacement for a more traditional income tax that taxes wages and savings. The focus of the consumption tax literature since 1985 has been taxation at the federal government level (in the United States, for example) and the general appeal of consumption taxes (in various countries). There has been scant work that presents a conversion from income to consumption tax in the United States at a subnational level.[1] The focus of this chapter is the conversion of a state income tax to a state consumption tax using the case of a US state – the state of Georgia.

The arguments for a consumption tax are widely known, but are summarized in the next section. The third section provides a brief overview of the state tax system in Georgia, and compares it to that of other states. In the fourth section, we decompose the current income tax system and 'rebuild' it as a consumption tax, with an eye toward revenue neutrality. We do not take on local taxes such as the property tax. This is an important caveat and is discussed later in this chapter. The final section concludes with a summary of lessons that might be gleaned from the Georgia example for use in other states.

Which Flat Tax?

The flat rate income taxes that have become widespread in Eastern Europe and in Russia typically feature a single tax rate and a limited number of deductions and exemptions (Martinez-Vazquez et al., 2006; Hadler et al., 2006; Keen et al., 2006). In the United States, at the state government level, flat rate income taxes are used in seven states: Colorado, Illinois, Indiana, Massachusetts, Michigan, Pennsylvania and Utah. These rates range from 3 to 5.3 percent and are applied to different definitions of state taxable income. The flat rate income tax structures have typically emphasized a base broadening that has moved them closer to being a tax on comprehensive income. But they are not by and large consumption taxes. The 'flat tax' that is of concern in this chapter is an individual income tax that is levied at a single rate on what is consumed and not saved, and is fully integrated with the corporate income tax. The composition of the tax base, rather than a single flat rate, is the distinguishing feature of the flat tax that we discuss in this chapter. Hall and Rabushka's (HR) flat tax proposal (1983, 1995) is taken as a convenient starting point for our discussion.[2]

The HR proposal is an integrated tax on individuals and businesses that is levied through a 'postcard tax return'. The HR proposal was for a national consumption-based tax – not necessarily a state-level tax. This postcard tax return requires the taxpayer to report wage income plus pension and retirement benefits, and provides a deduction for family status and for dependents. Under the HR proposal, businesses would report gross revenues and deduct allowable costs (wages and salaries, pension contributions, purchase of goods, services and materials, and purchases of capital equipment, but not fringe benefit payments). Presumably, if this calculation were done by multistate corporations, there would be a need for an allocation rule to attribute the correct net revenue to the correct state. This is similar to what is currently done in many states to calculate state corporate income tax liability. Under the proposal, interest income is exempt and deductions of interest expense are not allowed. All income is therefore subject to consistent treatment and is taxed at one rate (above the standard deduction or personal exemption level). The tax on withdrawals from savings accounts (that might eventually be used for consumption) is treated as 'prepaid' in that savings and non-retirement investments are made from after-tax income.[3] The HR tax is essentially a two-part tax that taxes compensation of individuals and separately taxes businesses through a value added approach.[4]

In general, the treatment of savings and investment is the critical feature of a consumption-based tax (with the HR proposal a specific example of a consumption-based tax proposal) relative to a more typical US federal or state income tax. Under the consumption base, individuals are taxed only on that part of their income and asset accumulation that is consumed. There are two ways to do this. The tax can be prepaid by making contributions to qualified accounts from after-tax income and exempting the withdrawal from taxation. Or, the tax can be post-paid (by making deductible contributions and subjecting withdrawals to tax). In either case, businesses fully deduct the purchase prices of assets including equipment, buildings, land and the like; however, they must include revenue from the sale of assets as taxable income. Interest and dividend payments are not business deductions, so effectively, the returns to capital are taxed once at the business level – a form of integration of individual and corporate taxes.[5]

THE ADVANTAGES OF A FLAT TAX ON CONSUMPTION

Why might a consumption tax, levied at a flat rate, have appeal in a country or a state? Simplification of the tax system and the resulting reduction in the cost of tax administration and compliance is usually cited as a major benefit of a move to a consumption-based flat tax. The prepaid version of the consumption tax eliminates the need to audit deductions for interest payments and pension contributions, and depreciation schedules would be eliminated in favor of expensing capital asset purchases. On the individual income tax side, since only wage income would be taxed, this could lead to a reduction in the number of returns filed. More generally, if all income is taxed only once, we would expect that the tax administration could do a better job than it could through monitoring and enforcing double taxation of the same income sources. If individual and company rates are equalized, the flat rate structure reduces the incentives for arbitrage and in that way simplifies the job of tax administration. Expensing and ignoring financial transactions also would be major steps in the direction of simplification. All of this could free up tax administration resources to concentrate on other areas of enforcement (for example, taxpayer identification, collections) or could lead simply to a reduction in administration costs that could be passed back to the general public.

Simplification is an advantage that we can attribute to a consumption tax, but a consumption tax may not deal with the compliance problems of the self-employed or small businesses and the informal sector in general.[6] Also, while a national consumption tax would offer potentially significant benefits to capital, there is a question of how much a state consumption tax could offer in the way of reduced welfare costs on capital.

Another important benefit of a consumption tax is the elimination of the distorting effects of inflation. Since activity is taxed on a cash flow basis, inflation does not play a role at a national level (McLure and Zodrow, 2006). The benefit from a flat rate consumption tax that most interests economists is that it eliminates the current penalty for future consumption and thus probably increases savings. While, theoretically, the switch to a state-level flat tax (for all states) could result in increased domestic investment due to an increase in the relative after-tax return to investment, if one or two states imposed the tax, the benefits to capital may be difficult to realize by any one state. Nationally, the economic growth effects might be quite significant. Auerbach (1997) reports potential increases in output of 2 to 4 percent over the first nine years of pure flat tax and 4 to 6 percent over the long run at the national level.

There are many possible disadvantages inherent in shifting to a consumption tax. Whether the shift will draw additional investment to a state depends on several factors, and the net impact for a state could be quite different than what would be expected at the national level. Certainly there are conditions in the open economy case under which a revenue-neutral consumption tax might actually repel certain types of investment. First, even if the shift is revenue-neutral, there could be an increase in the effective tax rate that might dampen the after-tax return to investors. Second, if there is a shift in the tax burden to labor, production costs in labor-intensive industries could be driven up, and the after-tax return to investment could be reduced, reducing competitiveness in any one state. Third, even if increased domestic savings did lead to a reduction in the average cost of capital, it might not lead to a reduction for all investors.[7]

The specific tax treatment within a state tends to pick 'winners and losers'. For example, in the case of the state of Georgia, the present income tax regime features exemptions for elderly (who are substantial capital owners), tax credits for various economic development incentives and other exemptions. These specific features could make the cost of capital lower for some investments than would be the case under a flat rate consumption tax – so a switch to a revenue-neutral flat rate consumption tax need not reduce the after-tax return to capital. At the national level, the technical issue of whether a consumption-based direct tax is eligible for foreign tax credits in capital-exporting countries is still an open one (McLure and Zodrow, 2006, p. 14). Finally, there are transition costs to be reckoned with. The switch to expensing to replace deductions would result in unused write-offs and declines in asset prices. These impacts may be less important at the state level (relative to the national level), but they are still important, especially in times of tough competition for economic development. Net operating losses (NOLs) present a special transition difficulty. To achieve neutrality, NOLs (for example, deductions greater than income) should be carried forward with interest reflecting inflation as well (McLure and Zodrow, 2006) or should be refunded in the year realized.

All of these considerations help to make the case, we believe, that the impacts of a consumption tax are best evaluated in the context of a specific case.

GEORGIA'S TAX SYSTEM

The state of Georgia relies heavily on the individual income tax, corporate income tax and general sales tax. The composition of total state revenues is summarized in Figure 7.1. The personal income tax (PIT) is the largest state tax revenue source, comprising 50 percent of all state tax revenues ($8 billion in FY06), while the sales tax is second (35 percent or $5.7 billion in FY06). The corporate income tax – an important tax in this analysis – is about 5 percent of state tax revenue in 2006 ($811 million in FY06).

The individual income tax has a progressive rate structure, but with a relatively low taxable income threshold. As a result, most taxpayers face the top 6 percent tax rate (Table 7.1). The Georgia individual income tax is imposed on the taxable net income of all residents and non-residents of Georgia. Taxpayers can file returns based on one of the following categories: single, married filing separately, head of household or married filing jointly.

Two sets of adjustments are made to FAGI (Federal Adjusted Gross Income) to arrive at Georgia Adjusted Gross Income (GAGI). First, the

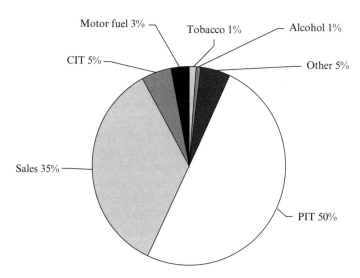

Source: Georgia Department of Revenue (2007).

Figure 7.1   Distribution of state tax revenues, Georgia FY2006

Table 7.1   Georgia's personal income tax structure

	Single	Married filing separate		Joint, head of household	
Rate	Taxable income	Rate (%)	Taxable income	Rate (%)	Taxable income
1%	< $750	1	< $500	1	< $1000
2%	750–2250	2	500–1500	2	1000–3000
3%	2250–3750	3	1500–2500	3	3000–5000
4%	3750–5250	4	2500–3500	4	5000–7000
5%	5250–7000	5	3500–5000	5	7000–10 000
6%	> 7000	6	> 5000	6	> 10 000

following items are subtracted from FAGI: (1) retirement income for tax-payers aged 62 and older or for totally disabled persons up to but not to exceed $35,000 ($70,000 if married and filing jointly when both individuals earn sufficient income to qualify separately for the $35,000 exclusion); (2) social security benefits and tier 1 railroad retirement benefits to the extent included in FAGI; (3) interest or dividends on federal obligations to the extent included in FAGI if these amounts are exempt from state taxation by federal law; and a few others. In the second set of adjustments, the following items are added to FAGI: (1) dividend or interest income on obligations of any state or political subdivision except Georgia and its political subdivisions, to the extent excluded from FAGI; (2) interest or dividends on federal obligations if exempt from federal income tax but not state income tax; (3) lump-sum distributions from an annuity, pension plan or similar source that were removed from FAGI because of special federal tax treatment; (4) loss carry-overs from years when the taxpayer was not subject to Georgia income tax; and some more minor other additions.

Georgia taxable income is then derived by subtracting the following amounts from GAGI: (1) either itemized non-business deductions used in computing the federal taxable income, or a standard deduction of $2300 for single and head of household, $3000 for married joint and $1500 for married separate filers, with additional $1300 deductions allowed when the taxpayer and/or spouse (for joint returns) is blind or aged 65 or older; and (2) Georgia's personal exemptions of $2700 for each taxpayer (and an additional $2700 for spouse in the case of joint filers), with $3000 allowed for each dependent.

A graduated rate structure ranging from 1 to 6 percent is applied to the Georgia taxable income to arrive at the before-credit tax liability. A number of credits are allowed, including: taxes paid to other states, a low-income credit and credits for physicians who establish a practice in a rural county after 1 July 1995.

Over the past thirty years, there have been limited changes to the individual income tax in Georgia. The tax brackets and rate structure have in fact been unchanged for decades. Notable changes are the increase in income exemptions for the elderly, addition of various credits (low income, jobs creation, rural physicians, and so on), and an increase in the dependent exemption.

The corporate income tax in Georgia is closely aligned with the federal income tax. Georgia taxable income is derived from federal taxable income, and is taxed at a flat 6 percent rate. Georgia also levies a net worth tax on a sliding scale from $10 for net worth of $10,000 or less to $5000 on net worth over $22 million. The apportionment of Georgia taxable income is now based on sales only (1 January 2008).

Georgia's income tax allows for a number of specific credits including: employer's jobs tax credit, manufacturer's investment credit, low-income housing credit, optional investment tax credit, bank tax credit and the like. There are other taxes that one would consider in this analysis including the tax on financial institutions, insurance premiums tax (possibly), property tax and the intangible taxes (real estate transfer and recording). For purposes of the current analysis, we focus only on state-level taxes, so we ignore property taxes and intangibles taxes, which are mainly local taxes.

MOVING TO A CONSUMPTION TAX

Georgia's basic tax system has not been substantially reformed in more than 40 years. Revenue growth has typically been quite strong for the individual income tax and sales tax, although the buoyancy of these taxes has declined since the early 1990s. While corporate income tax revenue growth was stagnant in the 1980s–1990s, beginning in 2002, the growth in corporate income tax receipts has been higher than it was in the period of the 1980s–1990s.

Georgia has not seriously considered a major income tax reform in modern history. None of the tinkering in the past thirty years amounted to a dramatic shift in tax burden or elasticity of the entire tax system. To our knowledge, no state has completely replaced an income-based tax system with a consumption-based system. Some states have added consumption-type taxes to their tax mix while continuing to impose an income tax (Michigan and New Hampshire). So taking a state through the transition of an income tax to a consumption tax would be quite novel.

A number of changes are necessary to take Georgia's income tax structure to a direct consumption tax. Some of these policy changes have to do with integration of the individual and corporate income tax, and others are more directly focused on limiting the tax base to consumption. Overall, movement to a consumption tax means that the state would have to decouple from the federal income tax, and impose a new definition of taxable income. In the remainder of this section, we track through these necessary changes and estimate their revenue impacts.[8]

Wage and Salary Income

All income that is available for consumption expenditure should be taxed as personal income under a consumption tax. None should be taxed twice. In the current income tax structure of most states (and the federal government), fringe benefits are allowed as an expense (deduction) by corporations and are not included by individuals as income. To 'fix' this under a consumption tax requires some important adjustments to the present income tax structure. It will be necessary to bring non-taxed fringe benefits into the individual income tax structure by disallowing the corporate deduction for benefits or including the value of those benefits in individuals' taxable income. By requiring that contributions to pension and other savings programs be made from after-tax income at the state level (employers and employees), the tax on future consumption would be prepaid and all withdrawals from these accounts would be exempt.

We estimate the revenue impact of bringing fringe benefits into the tax base by using the federal data on tax expenditures for health and other insurance and retirement savings, apportioned to Georgia as explained below. Note that federal reported tax expenditure does not include all fringe benefits, but it does reflect the most important non-taxed fringe benefits in terms of revenue impact. In 2007, the federal government estimates the foregone revenue is $210 billion off of a base of $954 billion in non-taxed fringe benefit expenditures (assuming an average effective federal tax rate of 22 percent; Joint Committee on Taxation, 2007). We assume that Georgia's share is proportional to Georgia's share of personal income in the total personal income of the US, which is 2.7 percent (based on data from the Bureau of Economic Analysis, 2008). In Georgia, the estimated level of non-taxed fringe benefits is $25.8 billion in 2007. Assuming a state corporate income tax rate of 4 percent on average and an average individual income tax rate of 3.2, taxing these fringe benefits amounts to an increase in corporate revenues of $1 billion (if all fringes were currently able to be deducted) or, if taxed on the individual side, an increase in individual income tax revenues of $0.83 billion.

It is unlikely that corporations will be fully liable for that increased liability due to the usual level of loss carry-forwards. If we make a conservative assumption that 25 percent of the liability will actually be paid in a given year, the value of taxing currently non-taxed fringe benefits is $250 million, which represents a 30 percent increase in Georgia state corporate income tax revenues in 2006, or a 1.5 percent increase in all state tax revenue. It is probably easier to tax fringe benefits via the corporate side versus the individual side due to the mechanisms currently in place for accounting for fringe benefits paid by companies.

As noted earlier, the move to a consumption tax from the current income tax will break the close tie that Georgia's income taxes have with the federal income taxes. Companies filing tax in Georgia would have to add back fringe benefits to their taxable income. A question arises as to whether the companies should do this only for payments made to employees in Georgia. Our thought is that to reduce complexity, all Georgia return filers should add back the cost of fringe benefits. This does, admittedly, spread Georgia's flat tax policy beyond its borders, and would reduce the accounting and compliance burden facing the corporation.

Private Pension Income

Companies and individuals can currently deduct some of the expense associated with private pension funding, and some pensions received by individuals are untaxed in the present system at the state level (Social Security benefits and some older state pensions). Pension income would be taxed at the ordinary personal income tax rate under a consumption tax since it represents income available for consumption. As noted above, the tax could be prepaid by allowing contributions to be made from after-tax income (that is, by disallowing deductions for contributions at the corporate and individual levels). An alternative for businesses and individuals is to allow a deduction for contributions to savings and pension funds, but to include withdrawals in taxable income. McLure and Zodrow (2006) note that on the business side the prepaid option could lead to various types of arbitrage.

We use IRS data on corporate deductions for 'pensions, profit-sharing, stock bonus and annuity plans' to gauge the size of this adjustment on the corporate side. The IRS reports total deductions for this category of $137 billion in 2003. Using the same 2.7 percent 'Georgia' ratio as earlier, this suggests a potential increase in corporate taxable income of $3.7 billion (disallowing the deduction). If 25 percent of that lost deduction made it into taxable income, we expect an increase in corporate taxable income of $975 million, and an increase in state corporate tax liability of $39 million which translates to direct revenue for the state. Assuming a growth in the value of the deduction of 5 percent per year, the elimination of this deduction would yield about $45 million in 2006 for Georgia – or 0.3 percent of all state tax revenue.

On the individual side, we should exclude deductions for contributions to retirement plans but also exclude pension payments from corporations (as those are picked up on the corporate side) or pension payments made out of after-tax dollars. There are some big transition issues to deal with in this case of pensions at the individual level. Individuals who have contributed to retirement via Individual Retirement Accounts (IRAs) or other tax-preferred pension plans may begin receiving their retirement savings distributions under the new, consumption tax regime. Under our scenario, the distributions would not be taxable. If the state were not able to track when the contributions were made, there would be some leakages in the system and distributions received from retirement accounts that were funded by after-tax dollars may escape taxation inadvertently.

The IRS reports taxable IRA distributions, pensions and annuities, and self-employed retirement plan distributions by state. For Georgia, these amounted to $13 billion (2004). No longer including these in Georgia taxable income would reduce the personal income tax by about $340 million in 2004, or about $375 million in income tax revenues in 2006. This is about 2.4 percent of all tax revenues. There would be some pick-up, however, since there are currently deductions from AGI

(Adjusted Gross Income) for pension contributions that would be disallowed. Using data from the IRS, this offset of disallowing deductions would amount to 0.8 percent of all tax revenues so that the net impact at the individual level would be a decrease in state tax revenues of 1.6 percent.

Interest Income and Dividend Taxation

In Georgia, interest income paid to individuals (or corporations) is taxed, while interest payments are allowable deductions under the corporate income tax. The corporate and individual income taxes are not integrated, hence there is potentially preferential treatment for corporate debt (for example, the statutory corporate tax rate at which the deduction occurs is 6 percent while the individual income tax rate ranges from zero to 6 percent). This may lead to arbitrage in the system, and provides an incentive to adopt certain business structures, albeit on a very limited scale at the state level (versus the national level). However, this is a case where full integration of the income tax system at one tax rate may increase the user cost of capital in the short run due to lack of deductibility of interest expense. Under a consumption-based tax, interest income received by individuals would not be taxed, interest expenses would not be deductible at the company level, and the corporate and individual income tax rates would be equal.

Dividends are taxed at the individual level but are not deductible by corporations in Georgia (or under the federal tax system). There would be no revenue impact of the consumption tax preferred treatment of dividends as it is the same as under current law.

The revenue impact of a change in the taxation of interest is again estimated using the IRS reported 'deductions for interest paid' on corporate tax returns. In 2003, the national total was $818 billion. Applying 2.7 percent as Georgia's share we arrive at $22 billion, and using our now familiar convention of assuming that 25 percent of that ends up in the tax base, we would expect an increase in state corporate tax revenues of $255 million at 2006 levels (1.5 percent of total state tax revenues). The offset on the individual side must be worked into these numbers. If dividends and interest are paid in after-tax dollars by the corporations, then individuals should not include those items in their taxable income. Using data from the IRS on interest and dividends reported in federal adjusted gross income, we estimate that excluding those items from the individual income tax in Georgia under the consumption base would cost the state $185 million (about 2.3 percent of income tax revenue and 1.15 percent of all state tax revenue).

Elimination of Corporate Incentives

Georgia has an abundance of corporate tax incentives, just as many states do. Various deductions, credits and incentives create an uneven playing field for companies in the state. Unfortunately there is no annual tax expenditure budget for Georgia, which would allow us to report easily the value of incentives. A study by the Fiscal Research Center (Edmiston et al., 2002) estimated the cost of corporate tax incentives to be about $120 million in 2001. There have been changes since 2001, but due to data constraints, we use this figure in this analysis. The $120 million accounts for about 14.7 percent of corporate tax revenues or 0.7 percent of total state tax revenues.

Asset Purchases, Asset Sales and Capital Gains

Under a consumption tax, asset sales would be taxed at the income tax rate, and capital gains would not be brought into tax under a separate levy. Capital investments would be expensed rather than depreciated. We know that the expensing of capital asset purchases (versus depreciation) would lead to a government revenue loss in the short run, but some revenue increases would come from the taxation of the sale of assets. For the revenue cost of expensing, we make an estimate based on data from the IRS on corporate tax depreciation. The IRS reports total depreciation of about $700 billion in 2003 – or $19 billion for Georgia (using the same conventions used above). If we assume that the effective rate of depreciation is 20 percent and that 20 percent of capital is new each year, then full expensing could completely wipe out the corporate income tax as it currently stands – reducing revenues by $880 million (5.3 percent of total tax revenues) at 2006 levels.

To the extent that asset sales are currently included in the tax base, there need not be an adjustment for those assets. Individuals would not include capital gains in their taxable income. The IRS reports capital gains in Georgia of about $10 billion (2004). The revenue loss to the state of excluding those gains is about $330 million, or 1.9 percent of total state tax revenue at 2006 levels.[9]

Excluding Itemized Deductions and other Special Treatment

Itemized deductions do not have a place in the consumption tax structure. Elimination of these deductions will increase individual income tax revenue by approximately $900 million (5.6 percent of state tax revenues).

Major exemptions under the individual income tax would also be removed. While there are many, we focus here on the exemption for the retirees. The current level of exemption is $35,000 per taxpayer. The tax expenditure estimate for this exemption is $170 million. Eliminating this exemption would increase income tax revenues commensurately, to the tune of 1.1 percent of total revenue.

Rate Harmonization

At present, there is little difference in the corporate and individual statutory marginal rates. The individual rates range from 1 to 6 percent while the corporate is a flat 6 percent. There is likely to be little incentive related to the impact of these differences on the incentive to incorporate, and also the corporations are likely to be more affected by the federal rate structure. However, to be consistent with the exercise here, we estimate the impact of a flat 6 percent rate (keeping the current personal exemptions and standard deduction amounts). Income tax revenues could grow by $300 million (or more – this is an early estimate): 1.9 percent of total tax revenue.

Total Impact

The net impact of all changes except the rate harmonization is a revenue loss of 0.45 percent of tax revenue (Table 7.2, line 10). The revenue losses due to the elimination of taxation of pension income and interest and dividends on the individual side and expensing of capital assets on the corporate side is more than the revenue recapture associated with disallowing pension expenses, fringe benefits and itemized deductions. This estimate suggests that, roughly, the change from an income tax to a consumption tax as presented in this chapter would be revenue-neutral. A cushion (in the form of harmonized rates) might be added to any legislation for this type of tax policy change. If a harmonized flat 6 percent rate for the individual income tax were instituted, income tax revenue would increase by about 1.9 percent. This amounts to $600 million in additional revenue in 2006.

Though the net impact of this structural reform is close to revenue-neutral, the individual changes that are required may be substantial. Elimination of the individual income tax on dividend and interest income and pensions reduces the tax on individuals. However, the disallowance of itemized deductions and taxation of fringe benefits (via corporations) increases the overall burden on individuals. Corporations see a larger percentage increase in tax burden under this proposal, largely through the disallowance of deductions under the corporate tax. This implies, also,

Table 7.2   Revenue effects of a shift to a direct consumption tax: the case of Georgia (% total tax revenues)

Required change	PIT	CIT	Net	Comments
1. Tax fringe benefits	NA	+1.5	+1.5	Taxing fringes via the corporate income tax
2. Bring income from private pensions fully into the tax system	−1.6	+0.3	−1.3	
3. Disallow corporate deductions for interest costs				Tax once at the corporate level
4. Eliminate individual income tax on interest and dividends	−1.15		−1.15	Tax once at the corporate level
5. Eliminate company tax incentives		+0.7	+0.7	Eliminate all incentives
6. Expensing of capital assets		−5.0	−5.0	
7. Exclude capital gains	−1.9		−1.9	Gains are effectively taxed only at business level
8. Exclude itemized deductions	+5.6		+5.6	
9. Eliminate personal income tax exemptions	+1.1		+1.1	Elderly exemption
10. Impact of (1) – (9)	+2.05	−2.5	−0.45	
11. Harmonize individual and company income tax rates at 6%	+1.9		+1.9	Flat rate for personal income tax

Source: Estimates by the authors.

a major shift in collections to the company level. This may (or may not) make it an easier tax to collect. The windfall revenue could be used to reduce the corporate and individual income tax rates.

CONCLUSIONS: A CONSUMPTION TAX IN A US STATE?

Is a state-level consumption tax levied through the income tax system in a US state feasible? Is it worthwhile? Would it be 'undone' by actions of the federal governments and other states? These are all important questions;

perhaps the last one being the most important. The benefits of a consumption tax hinge on it increasing the economic neutrality regarding the tax treatment of savings, labor and consumption. Regarding wage income, the change in tax treatment may serve to retain the positive impacts associated with consumption taxes, but in the case of capital, the net impact is less clear given the exercise that we have performed here. This is seen by the relative increase in taxes from the corporate sector – although a number of those could be passed on to wage earners.

The potential for economic benefits under a state consumption tax are probably relatively small unless a number of states made similar moves. The change in the net rate of return to capital in Georgia from a move to a consumption tax is debatable. However, in general, a consumption tax is a tax that, at least theoretically, reduces the relative burden of taxation on capital – signaling a friendly investor climate. In the world of hot competition for investment and business expansion, even a small move to reduce taxes on capital by a single state could be enough to encourage economic development.

NOTES

1. Bahl and Wallace (2007) provide such an analysis for the developing country of Jamaica.
2. HR was by no means the first proposal to replace the income tax with a consumption tax. Among those to whom flat tax ideas are attributed are: Milton Friedman (1962), David Bradford (1986), Nicholas Kaldor (1955), William Andrews (1974) and the Meade Commission (Institute for Fiscal Studies, 1973).
3. Several other versions of the consumption tax have been discussed. See Meiszkowski (1977) for a discussion of a specific cash flow expenditure tax: http://www.treasury. gov/offices/tax-policy/library/ota26.pdf. The 'X-tax' proposal is attributed to David Bradford (1986). A helpful summary of the flat tax and X-tax proposals is available from the President's Advisory Panel on Tax Reform, at http://www.taxreformpanel.gov.
4. McLure and Zodrow (2006, p. 4) point out that combining this treatment of expenditures on real assets with the tax prepaid treatment of financial transactions yields what the Meade Commission called the real business cash flow tax base, or 'R-base', and combining it with the tax postpaid approach yields the 'real plus financial' business case flow tax base, or 'R+F base'.
5. The FairTax proposal is also a consumption tax – but is set up using a retail sales tax.
6. For a discussion of the size of the underground economy, and some estimates for individual countries, see Alm et al. (2004).
7. It is unlikely that the tax policy of one state would have enough impact on the overall capital markets to affect the rate of return in the market. However, if multiple states committed to a consumption tax, changes in tax rates nationwide could result in a change in the overall supply of capital.
8. The revenue analysis includes behavioral impacts of tax changes but does not use a dynamic model in that there are no second-round effects associated with changes in investments, pensions, personal savings and the like.

9. Under the plan evaluated here, the existing property tax and intangible taxes would continue as supplementary wealth taxes. In fact, the intangible taxes are taxes on sales rather than on the value of holdings, but they are mostly (75 percent) levied against real estate.

REFERENCES

Alm, J., Martinez-Vazquez, J. and Schneider, F. (2004). 'Sizing' the problem of the hard-to-tax. In J. Alm, J. Martinez-Vazquez and S. Wallace (eds), *Taxing the Hard-to-Tax: Lessons from Theory and Practice.* Amsterdam: Elsevier.

Andrews, W. (1974). A consumption-type or cash flow personal income tax. *Harvard Law Review* 87: 1113.

Auerbach, A. (1997). Quantifying the current US fiscal imbalance. National Bureau of Economic Research Working Paper 6248, October.

Bahl, R. and Wallace, S. (2007). From income tax to consumption tax? The case of Jamaica. *FinanzArchiv: Public Finance Analysis* (Mohr Siebeck, Tübingen) 63 (3): 396–414.

Bradford, D. (1986). *Untangling the Income Tax.* Cambridge, MA: Harvard University Press.

Edmiston, K., Essig, A., Freeman, C., Sjoquist, D. and Wallace, S. (2002). Revenue implications for Georgia of tax changes since 1987. FRP report 68.

Friedman, M. (1962). *Capitalism and Freedom.* Chicago, IL: University of Chicago Press.

Georgia Department of Revenue (2007). *Annual Report.* Atlanta, GA: Georgia Department of Revenue.

Hadler, S., Moloi, C. and Wallace, S. (2006). Flat or flattened? A review of international trends in tax simplification and reform. *USAID Fiscal Reform in Support of Trade Liberalization Report.* http://www.fiscalreform.net/research/pdfs/Flat%20or%20Flattened%20USAID%20final%2007-11-06.pdf.

Hall, R.E. and Rabushka, A. (1983). *Low Tax, Simple Tax, Flat Tax.* New York: McGraw-Hill Book Company.

Hall, R.E. and Rabushka, A. (1995). The flat tax: a simple, progressive consumption tax. In M. Boskin (ed.), *Frontiers of Tax Reform.* Stanford, CA: Hoover Institution Press.

Institute for Fiscal Studies (1973). *The Structure and Reform of Direct Taxation: Report of a Committee Chaired by Professor James E. Meade.* London: George Allen & Unwin.

Joint Committee on Taxation (2007). *Estimates of Federal Tax Expenditures for Fiscal Years 2007–2011.* Washington, DC: US Government Printing Office.

Kaldor, N. (1955). *An Expenditure Tax.* London: George Allen & Unwin.

Keen, M., Kim, Y. and Varsano, R. (2006). The 'flat tax(es)': principles and evidence. International Monetary Fund Working Paper 6/218, Washington, DC: International Monetary Fund.

Martinez-Vazquez, J., Rider, M., Qibbayth, R. and Wallace, S. (2006). Russia's flat rate income tax reform and revenue growth. *Proceedings of the Ninety-Eighth Annual Conference*, Boston, MA: National Tax Association.

McLure, C. and Zodrow, G. (2006). 'Consumption-based direct taxes: A guided tour of the amusement park'. Presented at the conference *Alternative Methods of*

Taxing Individuals. Stone Mountain, GA, 8–9 June, suspended by the International Studies Program, Andrew Young School, Georgia State University.

Mieszkowski, P. (1977). A cash flow version of an expenditure tax. Washington, DC: US Department of Treasury, Office of Tax Analysis Working Paper 26.

Zodrow, G. and McLure, C. (1988). Implementing direct consumption taxes in developing countries. World Bank Working Paper WPS 131, Washington, DC: World Bank.

Comments on 'Can Georgia move from income tax to consumption tax?'

William J. Smith

This chapter describes the theoretical justification and a practical route for repurposing a personal and corporate income tax into a single flat consumption tax. The author uses Georgia as a case study for the potential for such a tax reform. In 2006, Georgia's personal and corporate income tax revenues comprised 54.1 percent of total state revenues, or about $8.8 billion, thus Georgia appears to be a reasonable candidate for such a transition. Particular attention is focused on describing a revenue-neutral shift from the current combination of corporate and individual income taxes to a substantially integrated single-rate consumption-based tax.

Although the chapter focuses on Georgia, the author suggests that a consumption tax could be effectively administered within the corporate and personal income tax structures that currently exist in many states. The move to a flat consumption-based tax would have several key benefits for a state. Not only would the move simplify the rate structure, limit deductions, exemptions and credits, but it would also fundamentally change the tax base from realized income to consumption. According to the author, the basic administrative aspects of the tax would remain substantially unchanged from the current income tax; however, savings would be exempted from taxation. Currently, state and federal income taxes include savings (interest) income in the tax base, thus penalizing individuals who forgo current for future consumption by taxing income generated from saved post-tax earnings.

Under the proposed system, individuals would only be taxed on the part of their income and asset accumulation that is consumed. The author suggests a couple of ways in which this can be accomplished. First, after-tax income that is saved could be deposited into qualified accounts that can be later withdrawn tax-free. Second, saved income that was not taxed going into a savings account could be taxed as it was later withdrawn and consumed.

On the corporate side, businesses would be allowed fully to deduct inputs such as plant and equipment, but must include any subsequent sales in taxable revenues. Furthermore, rather than depreciating capital expenditures over time, firms would be allowed to expense the full cost of capital purchases.

Interest and dividend payments would not be deductible, thus returns to capital are taxed only once at the corporate level, effectively eliminating a source of double taxation (corporate income and individual investment income) and, thus, substantially integrating aspects of Georgia's individual and corporate income taxes. As a result, the author suggests that the integration and simplification could increase the efficiency for the taxing authority and increased compliance, both of which could subsequently generate tax savings that may be returned to the taxpayer.

Although some effort is made to assess the effectiveness of implementing the tax at the state level, there are also important questions that remain unanswered, not the least of which is how the shift affects a state's competitiveness at attracting new businesses. Currently, Georgia and other states have an array of tax incentives aimed at attracting new businesses into the state.

Another potentially important issue revolves around single-state adoption of the consumption tax, capital assets and the shift from depreciation to expensing. Under a consumption tax, the elimination of depreciation in favor of expensing is expected to reduce state revenues by about $880 million. However, the author suggests some of that lost revenue would be recaptured as assets are sold. Since Georgia firms would be taxed on the sale of used equipment and other states' firms may not, there may be an opportunity for arbitrage between states. For example, a Georgia firm could sell its used equipment to an Alabama subsidiary at below-market prices. From there, assuming Alabama does not adopt a similar tax, the assets could be resold without tax.

Currently, Georgia's sales tax does not tax the majority of services. One issue that is not mentioned by the author is that by implementing a consumption tax, both goods and services purchased within the state would be part of the consumption tax base. Furthermore, Georgia's sales tax code contains almost 100 specific sales tax exemptions targeted at specific industries or groups. For example, food purchased for home consumption is currently exempt from the state sales tax and accounted for $880 million in revenue loss in 2004. In addition to broadening the base to cover services, some of the sales tax base lost from statutory exemptions could be partially recaptured by a state consumption-based tax.

Individual retirement plans present a important problem. Because distributions from these plans would not be taxable under the author's consumption tax, there would be substantial tax leakages. Retirement accounts that accumulated from pre-tax dollars would not be taxed upon withdrawal. This could make Georgia an even more attractive retirement location than it currently is.

When taken by itself, the consumption tax is viewed as a tax that is easy to understand and it comes with a simple administration. However, the author points out that Georgia's current income tax is coupled to the federal income tax, and that moving to a consumption tax would require decoupling. It is not clear if decoupling would substantially decrease the complexity of Georgia's current income tax for individual taxpayers.

Because Georgia's income tax comprises such a large and important component of the state's tax base, any proposed changes should be carefully examined. This chapter does a good job of outlining the various potential benefits and likely pitfalls associated with a transition. The estimates of revenue losses and gains presented in the chapter are fiscally conservative, but considerable difficulties remain in estimating the effects of implementing a consumption tax in a single state.

PART IV

Evaluating state and local government
finances and budgeting

8. Reaching and maintaining structural balance: leaders in the states

Katherine Willoughby

INTRODUCTION

This chapter examines state governments in the USA indicating strong 'structural balance' as defined and examined by the Government Performance Project (GPP), a research effort supported by the Pew Charitable Trusts. The initial and primary goals of the GPP are to gather data that supports 'governments' understanding of their management functions, including where to make improvements and how their systems compare to the management systems of other governments. In addition, the public is made more aware of how their government is performing and so is better able to hold leadership accountable' (Crawford, 2002, p. 15). Structural balance is defined here as the ability of government to support ongoing expenditures with ongoing revenues – this concept is measured by examining tax structures, the existence of countercyclical devices, financial management strategies and various fiscal ratios.

This research uses information generated by the most recent iteration of the GPP survey of the 50 US state governments, conducted in 2007 with results published in 2008 (see Barrett and Greene, 2008). The chapter begins with an overview of the recent fiscal condition of state governments and relays the concerns of current governors regarding reaching and maintaining structural balance. Then, an accounting of the GPP grading methodology and criteria used to measure state budget and financial management is provided. The next section assesses the results of the 2008 GPP, concentrating on state management in those governments indicating positive structural balance. This exploratory effort seeks to characterize the budget and financial management strategies of state governments for which structural balance is rated as strong by the GPP. Results identify nine state governments as leading states in reaching and maintaining structural balance.

THE FISCAL PICTURE

Although the state fiscal picture in recent years has been stable, steady recovery from the 2002 recession has ended. The National Bureau of Economic Research (NBER) (2008) indicates that recovery from the 2002 recession peaked in December 2007 and that: 'the subsequent decline in economic activity was large enough to qualify as a recession'. The national economic decline has been driven by the housing crisis, credit crunch and rising oil prices. Specific regions of the country have suffered additionally due to local circumstances such as droughts in the Southeast, storms in the Midwest, fires in California and other such disasters. States are also beginning to be held more accountable to various long-term obligations regarding both aging populations (retiree benefits and other post-employment benefits) and infrastructure. Elizabeth McNichol and Iris Lav (2008, p. 1) claim that states face:

> a great fiscal crisis. At least 41 states faced or are facing shortfalls in their budgets for this and/or next year. Over half the states had already cut spending, used reserves, or raised revenues in order to adopt a balanced budget for the current fiscal year – which started 1 July in most states. Now, their budgets have fallen out of balance again.

Revenue growth was slow in fiscal 2008, with 'collections from all sources higher than projections in 20 states, on target in 16 states and below projections in 12 states' (NASBO, 2007, p. 10). In 2007 and 2008, in particular, state revenue changes declined substantially. Table 8.1 illustrates enacted revenue actions by type in the states from 1998 to 2008. From 1998 through 2001, when revenues were fairly plentiful, states cut taxes involving state governments' most predominant sources – sales and income taxes. States realized a net decrease in revenues in millions of dollars in every one of these years. From 2002 through 2006, tax bases and rates were changed in order to realize increases from all sources, except personal income taxes in 2006. Still, net increases in revenues were realized in every one of these years. The use of 'sin taxes' to bring in revenues was a staple in these years. States realized approximately $6.6 billion (nominal) in new revenues from cigarette and tobacco taxes from 1997 to 2006. By 2007, state confidence in a growing economy was exhibited by the substantial cuts to personal and corporate income, motor fuel and other taxes, cuts yielding a net decline in tax revenues of approximately $2.1 billion. By 2008, net tax yields had declined by just $115.5 million, indicative of the slowing economy.

According to the National Association of State Budget Officers (NASBO) (2007, p. viii and 2008, p. vii) state spending growth going forward reflects the effects of such economic decline; general fund spending grew by 5.3

Table 8.1 *Enacted revenue actions by type/net increase or decrease (in millions), 1998–2008*

Fiscal year enacted	Revenue source								Net
	Sales	Personal income	Corporate income	Cigarette/ tobacco	Motor fuel	Alcohol	Other taxes	Fees	
2008	(104.6)	(1033.1)	610.1	761.8	22.5	0.0	(581.3)	208.1	(115.5)
2007	622.4	(2321.9)	(239.7)	487.9	(115.2)	5.4	(772.75)	279.2	(2054.7)
2006	994.5	(739.2)	119.6	1249.1	81.1	36.4	141.7	685.6	2568.8
2005	710.6	428.5	272.0	888.4	1.2	25.0	707.7	508.7	3542.1
2004	2569.7	2461.4	601.0	751.1	132.9	46.5	1178.2	1809.5	9550.3
2003	1436.5	1073.2	999.4	2965.7	34.9	12.6	677.1	819.0	8018.4
2002	186.1	(671.2)	381.6	98.7	–	–	126.4	182.2	303.8
2001	(926.7)	(2594.4)	(708.9)	41.6	(104.1)	(41.3)	(1426.9)	(56.1)	(5816.8)
2000	(366.8)	(2200.8)	(821.1)	218.8	212.5	42.9	(2808.5)	524.7	(5198.3)
1999	(582.2)	(4442.6)	(395.6)	223.1	22.1	–	(1267.3)	(584.3)	(7026.8)
1998	(671.4)	(3454.1)	(280.5)	118.7	462.0	(4.7)	(982.8)	231.4	(4581.4)

Source: NASBO 1998–2008, Table 7.

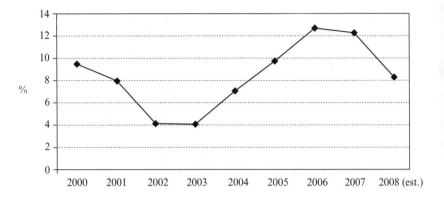

Note: *Alaska's year-end balances as a percent of general fund expenditures have been consistently and substantially larger than the rest of the states, even those that are also dependent on severance taxes. In 2003, for example, Alaska's average balances to expenditures ratio from 2000 to 2008 stood at 83.8 percent compared with the next highest average ratio, 24.6 percent, in Wyoming, another state heavily dependent upon severance taxes.

Figure 8.1   Mean end of year balances as a percentage of general fund expenditures, 2000–2008 (est.) (all states except Alaska*)

percent in fiscal 2008, well below the 30-year average of 6.4 percent and a little more than half of spending growth experienced by states in fiscal 2007 (9.3 percent). Declining total balances as a percentage of expenditures from the 2006 fiscal year to the 2008 fiscal year also suggest the necessity for belt-tightening by states. Balances as a percent of expenditures were 11.5 percent in 2006, 9.6 percent in 2007 and an estimated 6.7 percent in 2008 (NASBO, 2007, p. viii). Figure 8.1 illustrates mean end-of-year balances as a percentage of general fund expenditures of states from 2000 to 2008 (estimated). The trend indicates that states rebounded from the depths of the recession in 2002 and 2003 – the two worst budget years in five decades for most states. But since 2006, state balances as a percentage of expenditures have declined.

STATE CHIEF EXECUTIVES HAVE BALANCE ON THE BRAIN

Willoughby (2008, pp. 162–3) examined the 2008 State of the State addresses by governors in which they report to their legislatures and to citizens about the fiscal condition of their state.[1] Through these oral reports, governors are able to highlight their budget and policy agendas. Chief executives can educate citizens on the necessity for fiscal discipline and warn of the impending pain related to either tax increases, expenditure cuts or both. Content analysis of the 2008 addresses indicates that a majority (55 percent) of governors were concerned enough about structural balance to bring it up. For example, New Jersey's Governor laid out his state's problems:

> Our fiscal practices, balance sheet, and most vitally, our culture must be restructured. We are in a hole, and if we want to get out, we have to stop digging . . . we have to put an end to the financial culture that allowed the proliferation of spending, borrowing and mismanagement to take hold of our state finances. We must recognize we are at the end of the line on the ways of the past. I will introduce a budget in February that freezes spending at this year's current level; for future budgets, spending will not be allowed to exceed recurring revenue growth . . .

Rhode Island's Governor also noted to the citizens of that state that: 'our government has been spending beyond its means, and has been depleting its savings to pay the bills'. The Governor of Ohio exclaimed that: 'the weak economy is a burden to all Ohioans and a burden to our state government. And, like most states, we now confront a budget gap'. Kentucky's Governor explained that: 'the revenue outlook is grim. Because of the economic slowdown . . . and a gap between what we spend and what we earn, we are facing an unprecedented budgetary shortfall'. Maryland's Governor recognized: 'no wonder many of us are frustrated when – in the midst of this national economic downturn – we were also forced to confront a long neglected and huge structural deficit'. Mississippi's Governor urged a duty 'to live within our means . . . to pass an honest balanced budget'. In California, the Governor clarified that: '[our] problem is that while revenues are flat, automatic formulas are increasing spending by 7.3 percent. Now, even a booming economy can't meet that kind of increase. So the system itself is the problem'. In Hawaii, the Governor was blunt: 'Government will never be able to solve all of society's problems'.

South Carolina's Governor discussed a plan to reduce spending and to equate ongoing revenues better with ongoing expenditures that involved a number of components, including prohibiting one-time money to start or fund recurring programs. The Governor in South Dakota agreed that: 'we cannot commit to expensive new programs or huge increases in existing programs, because we don't have the money to do so. We must live within our means. If you decide you want to spend more, please make sure we have the money available to do so or be willing to identify ongoing sources of revenue or new revenues'.

Even states with a strong revenue base and flush resources called for fiscal discipline. For example Wyoming, like other mineral- and oil-rich states, has been able to reap the bounty of high oil prices of the recent past. Wyoming's Governor recommended:

> [a] need to have the discipline to recognize that even with this abundance we cannot and should not fund every request that comes before us. We have to have the discipline to reduce the increases in the standard budget. When you go to add things to the budget, please do it on the basis that it is not a continuing appropriation.

THE GPP METHODOLOGY AND STATE MONEY MANAGEMENT GRADES

Using a criteria-based approach, the GPP has graded the management capacity of the 50 states four times since 1996 in specific areas that include budget and finance, human resources, information and infrastructure. The survey component of the GPP was conducted using a mailed questionnaire to states in 1998 and 2000 and electronically to states in 2004 and 2007. Resulting grades are published in *Governing* magazine in the spring of the year following the survey as well as other data collection efforts.

The GPP engages academics and journalists to collect and analyze quantitative and qualitative data about the states in the selected management areas, using these data and analyses to assign grades to the states. Data sources that underpin the grades include: (1) interviews conducted by the journalists; (2) research provided by university faculty and graduate students; and (3) the survey of state officials, administrators, and staff and managers. The criteria applied in each management area are determined through an identification of best practices, with input from professional organizations and upon reaching consensus among team members as to how to measure such practices.[2]

Once the data are collected from the three sources, the academic and journalist teams work independently of one another to analyze the available information and to determine criteria scores (strong, mid-level or weak) that are used to calculate the management area grade; then management area grades are used to calculate an overall management grade (A, A-, B+ and so on) for each state. The two teams then meet to review and agree on scores and grades for each state. These grades are meant to reflect a government's capacity in each management area rather than its performance alone. According to the GPP:

> the grades assess the capacity of state governments as a whole to produce results – including the cumulative skills and leadership of elected and appointed

officials, career civil servants, and not-for-profit and private-sector partners. The grades do not represent a judgment of any individual, branch, or department within state government.

GPP Budget and Financial Management Criteria

The five criteria used to arrive at the 2008 GPP grades for budget and financial management capacity (money management area) of states were based on best practices related to budget planning, budget process, structural balance, internal controls and reporting. The components that measure each criterion are explained below.

Criterion 1: Government should have a multiyear budgeting perspective
A high grade for this criterion requires that a state engages revenue and expenditure forecasting processes that are thorough, accurate and transparent, and include a multiyear perspective. The accuracy of revenue forecasting is of prime importance given that states are revenue-driven entities with 49 having some type of budget balancing requirement.[3] Other measures of this criterion examine state consideration of the long-term impact of tax and expenditure decisions, for example by virtue of the production and use of a tax expenditure budget. The state's long-term liabilities, including pensions and other post-employment benefits, consider realistic and timely valuations and are managed with an emphasis on long-term benefits and consequences. Finally, the state should maintain low credit risk status by managing a reasonable level of debt.

Criterion 2: Government should have a budget process that is transparent, inclusive and easy to follow
To obtain a high grade in this criterion from the GPP, a state must indicate a budget format and process that is results-oriented and consistently passes its budget prior to the start of the fiscal year. Also, the state provides citizens with opportunities for public input about the budget and supports citizen access to clear and understandable budget information.

Criterion 3: Government financial management activities should support structural balance between ongoing revenues and expenditures
To obtain a high grade on this criterion, states must indicate the maintenance of structural balance at current levels of revenues and expenditures. The state's revenue structure should indicate the ability to support annual expenditures in fluctuating economic climates. The state should have countercyclical and/or contingency planning devices available to address economic downturns and should keep such funds stocked. States receiving

a high grade in structural balance are not overly dependent on windfalls or 'one-time' revenues, added debt or accounting changes to finance current expenditures.

Criterion 4: Government procurement activities should be conducted efficiently and supported with effective internal controls
To obtain a high grade on this criterion requires that a state minimize waste, fraud and abuse related to purchasing goods and services. Executive agencies should have the necessary flexibility to buy goods and contract for services while the state maintains the ability to monitor and account for such spending effectively. State leaders on this criterion should indicate a strong electronic procurement facility that advances the efficient control of, as well as equitable access to, purchasing and contracting.

Criterion 5: Government should systematically assess the effectiveness of its financial operations and management
State leaders in financial and performance reporting should consistently generate clean audits in accordance with generally accepted accounting principles. Strong assessment of financial operations and management requires the state to report periodically on linkages between financial costs and operational performance.

2008 GPP Grades for Budgeting and Financial Management

In 2008, based on the five criteria above, five states earned an A or A-grade in budgeting and financial management from the GPP, 15 earned a B+ or B, 10 scored a B-, 13 received a C+ or C, and 7 earned a C- or D+ (see Table 8.2).

States averaged a score of 2.7 on a grade scale of 4 for budgeting and financial management. Table 8.3 illustrates a ranking of all GPP criteria used to measure every management area in 2005 and 2008. This table shows advancement, backsliding or status quo of states on the individual criteria (five criteria for each of four management areas); for example, states received the highest average score for intergovernmental coordination, a criterion used to measure infrastructure management, in both years. Regarding structural balance, states advanced from an average score that ranked 18th in 2005, to one that ranked 11th in 2008. In 2008, the GPP ranked structural balance as a strength in nine states, as mid-level in 29 states and as a weakness in 12 states; in 2005, the GPP determined structural balance to be a strength in eight states, as mid-level in 26 states, and as a weakness in 16. Table 8.4 lists states (in no particular order) in which structural balance is ranked as a strength in each of these years.

Table 8.2   2008 GPP grades for state money management

Region/state	Grade	State	Grade	State	Grade	State	Grade
Utah	A	Louisiana	B	Oklahoma	B-	New York	C+
Delaware	A-	North		South		Oregon	C+
Nebraska	A-	Dakota	B	Carolina	B-	Wisconsin	C+
Virginia	A-	Ohio	B	Tennessee	B-	Maine	C
Washington	A-	Pennsylvania	B	Vermont	B-	Alabama	C-
Georgia	B+	Texas	B	Arizona	C+	Alaska	C-
Idaho	B+	West Virginia	B	Colorado	C+	Illinois	C-
Indiana	B+	Wyoming	B	Hawaii	C+	New	
Iowa	B+	Arkansas	B-	Kentucky	C+	Hamp-	
Maryland	B+	Connecticut	B-	Massachusetts	C+	shire	C-
Minnesota	B+	Florida	B-	Michigan	C+	New Jersey	C-
Missouri	B+	Kansas	B-	Mississippi	C+	California	D+
South	B+	New Mexico	B-	Montana	C+	Rhode	
Dakota		North	B-	Nevada	C+	Island	D+
		Carolina					

Source: 2008 Government Performance Project, http://www.pewcenteronthestates.org/uploadedFiles/Money%20Performance.pdf.

STATE LEADERS IN STRUCTURAL BALANCE

One data point used by the GPP to measure structural balance is year-end unreserved budget balance (general fund balance plus rainy-day fund balance) as a percentage of general fund expenditures. This is a commonly used ratio measuring state fiscal condition; unreserved balances provide states with some support should revenues fall short or expenditures rise unexpectedly. The GPP examined this ratio for states from 2005 to 2007, specifically looking for ratios of 5 or over as a sign of strength, using the generally accepted 'rule-of-thumb' that balances as a percentage of expenditures below 5 are a sign of fiscal stress.[4] Table 8.5 provides average ratios in fiscal 2005, 2006, 2007 and 2008 by 2008 GPP ranking of structural balance of states.

For every year noted, states with structural balance ranked as a strength indicate larger ratios than other states, and much larger ratios when compared to states with structural balance ranked as a weakness. An analysis of variance of means by rank indicates significant differences in the mean ratios in the years 2006, 2007 and 2008.

The tax structures and burdens of state leaders in structural balance vary a bit from those of other states, although there are no significant differences (see Table 8.6). State leaders in structural balance, on average, have

Table 8.3   GPP management average ranking of criteria, 2005 and 2008

	2005 GPP ranking	GPP management criterion	2008 GPP ranking	Advance (↑) Backslide (↓) No change (↔)
Strong ↑	1	Intergovernmental coordination	1	↔
	4	Financial controls/ reporting	2	↑
	6	Online services and information	3	↑
	10	Budget process	4	↑
	2	Internal coordination	5	↓
	5	Long-term outlook	6	↓
	8	Project monitoring	7	↑
	14	Performance evaluation	8	↑
	15	Retaining employees	9	↑
	3	Contracting/purchasing	10	↓
	18	Structural balance	11	↑
	12	Capital planning	12	↔
	17	Managing employee performance	13	↑
	7	Hiring	14	↓
	13	Managing for performance	15	↓
	9	Strategic direction	16	↓
	16	Budgeting for performance	17	↓
	11	Training and development	18	↓
	20	Maintenance	19	↑
Weak	19	Strategic workforce planning	20	↓

balanced tax structures. That is, most depend upon a mix of taxes made up predominantly of individual income and sales taxes, rather than on one sole tax source. The average proportions of taxes of states ranked mid-level in structural balance look about the same, except that these states have a stronger reliance on property taxes (making up, on average, 4.67 percent of total taxes) than state leaders (making up, on average, 0.17 percent of total taxes). There is also a bit of disparity in dependence on sales and corporate income taxes between the top two ranked groups (structural balance ranked as strength or mid-level) and the group ranked weakest

Table 8.4   GPP State leaders in structural balance, 2005 and 2008

2005	2008
Delaware	Delaware
Pennsylvania	Pennsylvania
South Dakota	South Dakota
Utah	Utah
Kansas	Georgia
Minnesota	Idaho
Vermont	Indiana
Virginia	Nebraska
	North Dakota

Table 8.5   2008 GPP rankings of structural balance and average end-of-year balances as a percentage of general fund expenditures*

Ranking in structural balance		EOY balances/GF expenditures			
		Fiscal 2005	Fiscal 2006	Fiscal 2007	Fiscal 2008
Strength	Mean	12.20	15.54	17.68	13.19
	N	9	9	9	9
	Std. Deviation	7.92	9.93	14.67	9.91
Mid-level	Mean	10.49	14.03	13.12	8.17
	N	28	28	28	28
	Std. Deviation	7.02	7.93	6.86	4.11
Weakness	Mean	6.35	7.96	6.46	4.72
	N	12	12	12	12
	Std. Deviation	4.40	6.60	4.69	2.72
Total	Mean	9.79	12.82	12.33	8.25
	N	49	49	49	49
	Std. Deviation	6.85	8.36	9.04	5.94

Note: *Excluding Alaska for reasons noted in Figure 8.1.

in structural balance. States weakest in structural balance indicate that a smaller proportion of total taxes are comprised of sales taxes and a greater proportion of total taxes are comprised of corporate income taxes than indicated in the other states. Still, these differences are not significant.

Eight of nine state leaders depend upon both sales and individual income

Table 8.6 *2008 GPP rankings of structural balance and average 2006 tax collections, proportions of total*

Ranking in structural balance		State government tax source (proportion of total tax sources)					
		Property	Sales	Selective sales	Individual income	Corporate income	Other taxes
Strength	Mean	0.17	34.39	15.23	37.28	6.74	13.42
	N	6	9	10	9	10	10
	Std. Deviation	0.12	10.54	4.34	10.26	1.58	11.80
Mid-level	Mean	4.67	35.79	16.20	35.25	6.97	14.85
	N	20	25	28	22	24	28
	Std. Deviation	7.80	13.14	5.27	13.59	5.95	13.01
Weakness	Mean	3.49	29.08	16.65	36.03	9.21	8.23
	N	11	11	12	12	12	12
	Std. Deviation	5.68	6.47	7.51	13.93	5.54	3.60
Total	Mean	3.59	33.87	16.11	35.89	7.50	12.98
	N	37	45	50	43	46	50
	Std. Deviation	6.61	11.48	5.63	12.80	5.21	11.37

Sources: US Bureau of Census, 2006 Tax Collections by Source, percentage of total. Selective sales taxes are state excise taxes including motor fuel, alcoholic beverages, etc. GPP rankings of structural balance by state are tabulated from Barrett and Greene, 2008.

taxes predominantly to generate revenue. In only one state scored as strong in structural balance does just one tax source make up more than 50 percent of tax collections. South Dakota depends almost entirely on sales taxes for revenue; general sales taxes comprise 58 percent and selective sales taxes make up 24 percent of total tax collections in 2006. This state does not impose an individual income or state property tax. North Dakota also depends predominantly on sales and other taxes, including severance taxes (together, these sources make up over 75 percent of tax collections in 2006). This state does have an individual income tax, however. Delaware does not impose general sales or state property taxes, depending predominantly on other taxes (39 percent of total 2006 tax collections) that include licenses and documentary and stock transfer taxes.

According to the GPP, other factors support fiscal restraint and economic diversification in these states, however. For example, the political culture in Delaware supports slow to no growth of government; the long-range budgeting perspective of the state highlighted by the GPP has created a culture of budget restraint. In Georgia, officials responding to the GPP credited a diversified economy that is growing and not confined to one sector. Indiana cited efforts to diversify the state's economy as well. North Dakota officials confirmed an economy tied largely to natural resources, but highlighted that the state's economy has become more diversified in recent years with the addition of technology companies and other industries. This has helped to smooth out boom–bust cycles.

In the rest of the 41 states there are six that do not implement an individual income tax, four that do not impose general sales taxes, and four that do not have corporate income taxes. Still, in five of the states that impose an individual income tax, revenues from this tax make up from 50 to slightly more than 70 percent of total state tax collections in 2006. In six states that impose the general sales tax, revenues from this tax make up from 50 to 61 percent of total state tax collections in 2006. And in two states, severance taxes make up more than 50 percent of total tax collections in 2006. Severance taxes are those levied by a state on the extraction and use of natural resources of the state such as coal, petroleum and/or minerals. In other words, over 30 percent of the remaining 41 states have tax structures indicating overwhelming dependence upon one tax source. Regardless of policy decisions and fiscal management strategies of these states, tax collections in these states are particularly sensitive to a variety of exogenous variables.

The Federation of Tax Administrators provides an annual accounting of tax burden by state; the 2007 state tax collection data indicate an average burden of 7.4 (calculated average of individual state burdens, measured as state taxes as a percentage of personal income).[5] Mean burden for

Table 8.7　Balanced budget requirements and/or tax and expenditure limits (TELs) in the states, leaders in structural balance and the rest of the states (% of states)

Balanced budget requirement or TEL	State leaders (N = 9) (%)	Rest of states (N = 41) (%)
Governor must submit a balanced budget	55.6	82.9
Legislature must pass a balanced budget	66.7	70.7
Anti-deficit rule that deficit cannot carry over to next fiscal year	44.4	61.0
Supermajority rule for tax increases	22.2	19.5
Revenue limitation	0	14.6
Expenditure limitation	33.3	46.3

states scored strong in structural balance is 7.19; for those scored as mid-level, 7.69; and for the weakest states, 6.87. States with structural balance ranked as a weakness indicate the lowest tax burdens, on average, than other states. Of the states scored strong in structural balance, Delaware's tax burden is highest at 8.7; North Dakota and Idaho also have burdens above 8 (8.5 and 8.1, respectively). Still, of the states leading in structural balance, five have burdens that rank in the bottom 30 or below. Indiana, Pennsylvania, Nebraska, Georgia and South Dakota have burdens of 6.9 or less, South Dakota's tax burden is ranked 47th at 5.

Table 8.7 presents the existence of balanced budget requirements and/or tax and expenditure limitations in states leading in structural balance compared to the rest of the states. These requirements and limitations place constraints on states in their ability to reach and maintain structural balance. Except for the supermajority rule regarding tax increases, states indicating strong structural balance by the GPP are less likely to have any of the requirements noted.

Table 8.8 compares budget-balancing strategies of states in which structural balance is scored as a strength and the rest of the states that responded to the online survey component of the GPP. Scanning the various strategies for enhancing revenues across states, it seems that the two groups of states engage many of the same strategies, but to a lesser or greater extent, depending upon the group. For example, states leading in structural balance indicate a greater likelihood of applying carry-forward balances to the general fund in the years under study. These states are more likely to lease state assets and/or to borrow more to balance the budget. On the other hand, these states do not seem to resort to transferring normally earmarked funds into the general fund, increasing

*Table 8.8　Budget-balancing actions in the states, fiscal years 2005–06 (%
of states taking action)*

	State leaders		Rest of states	
	FY2005 (%)	FY2006 (%)	FY2005 (%)	FY2006 (%)
Revenue-enhancing actions	*N = 8*		*N = 33*	
Apply carry-forward balances to the general fund	62.5	62.5	51.5	48.5
Increase tax collection enforcement	25.0	37.5	33.3	45.5
Make non-routine transfers from other funds to the general fund	50.0	37.5	51.5	42.4
Increase and/or add fees and/or charges	25.0	25.0	36.4	33.3
Change tax structure to generate revenue increase	25.0	12.5	24.2	30.3
Transfer normally earmarked funds to the general fund	0	0	18.2	27.3
Refinance debt	25.0	25.0	18.2	15.2
Conduct the sale of state asset(s)	12.5	25.0	12.1	15.2
Increase short-term borrowing	0	0	6.1	12.1
Initiate tax amnesty program	25.0	12.5	18.2	6.1
Draw down budget stabilization or other contingency fund	0	0	18.2	9.1
Lease state asset(s)	0	12.5	6.1	6.1
Accelerate tax payments	0	0	9.1	3.0
Increase debt financing	12.5	12.5	6.1	0
	FY2005 (%)	FY2006 (%)	FY2005 (%)	FY2006 (%)
Expenditure-reducing actions	*N = 7*		*N = 33*	
Make targeted spending cuts	42.9	28.6	60.6	45.5
Lapse unspent agency appropriations to the general fund	42.9	28.6	39.4	36.4
Initiate program reorganizations	28.6	28.6	33.3	30.3
Increase employee contributions to health benefits	42.9	42.9	15.2	21.2
Conduct across the board spending cuts	14.3	14.3	15.2	15.2

Table 8.8   (continued)

	State leaders		Rest of states	
	FY2005 (%)	FY2006 (%)	FY2005 (%)	FY2006 (%)
Implement privatization initiatives	14.3	28.6	9.1	9.1
Cut local aid	14.3	0	12.1	9.1
Reduce contribution(s) to pension fund(s)	14.3	0	9.1	6.1
Increase retiree contributions for health benefits	14.3	14.3	0.0	3.0
Initiate lay-offs	0	0	3.0	6.1
Freeze hiring	0	0	15.2	15.2
Freeze employee salary increases	0	0	15.2	6.1
Freeze program increases	0	0	21.2	18.2
Initiate early retirement program	0	0	3.0	3.0
Suspend annual employee cost-of-living adjustment	0	0	12.1	3.0
Suspend transfers from the general fund	0	0	9.1	3.0
Delay payments for purchases	0	0	6.1	6.1
Delay payments to local schools	0	0	6.1	3.0
Terminate and/or amend state contracts	0	0	9.1	9.1
Implement monthly agency spending targets	0	0	9.1	9.1

Source: 2008 GPP, Survey of the States, MONEY section, Questions 12–13.

short-term borrowing, drawing down budget stabilization or contingency funds, or accelerating tax payments. The rest of the states indicate conducting these strategies in fiscal 2005 and/or 2006.

The engagement of various expenditure reduction strategies across groups is more distinctive. Similar proportions of both groups of states conducted across-the-board spending cuts in 2005 and 2006, although states leading in structural balance were less likely than other states to make targeted cuts in either year. States strong in structural balance were much more likely than the rest of the states to require employees to contribute more toward health benefits and to implement privatization initiatives. Yet, there are numerous strategies that no state scoring well in structural balance needed to engage in – for example, freezing hiring and program increases are two strategies that other states needed to conduct in order to reach balance in the fiscal year noted.

Indiana provides an example of a state scoring well in structural balance that indicated a number of revenue-generating strategies in fiscal years 2005 and 2006 to balance, including advanced tax collection enforcement and conduct of an amnesty program, non-routine transfers into the general fund, the sale and lease of assets, and refinancing of debt. But importantly, most of the actions taken by Indiana were not used to balance the budget, but were made as one-time expenses such as paying down debt or investing in the state's infrastructure. For instance, only $65 million of the nearly $250 million generated from the Tax Amnesty Program was used to balance the budget (as it was included in the budget bill). The remainder of these proceeds was used to pay back payment delays incurred by the previous administration. Likewise, the leasing of the Indiana Toll Road was not initiated to balance the state's budget, but to make new investments in the state's transportation infrastructure. The lone, notable exception was the non-routine transfer of funds to the general fund in fiscal 2005. The previous administration used pension stabilization funds to balance the budget. This action was sharply criticized by Governor Mitch Daniels, who publicly committed to not raiding pension funds or using other funding gimmicks to balance the budget.

Given the fiscal climate evidenced during the conduct of the most recent GPP, states were asked about revenue-reducing and expenditure-enhancing actions conducted in the years 2005 and 2006. Table 8.9 shows some distinction in chosen strategies by states, depending upon strength in structural balance. States scoring well in reaching and maintaining structural balance were more likely than other states to create new programs in both years. These states were much more likely to increase funding for existing programs beyond inflationary amounts in 2005, and about as likely as other states to increase such funding in 2006. None of the states leading in structural balance indicated increasing employee benefits or issuing a tax refund to citizens in either year, as some other states indicate. This squares with Table 8.7 that indicated no states that scored well in structural balance are being held to any sort of revenue limitation that might require issuing a tax refund to citizens.

Examination of countercyclical devices in the states indicates that those scored as strong in structural balance have various devices and funding requirements that support budget-balancing. Delaware's Constitution mandates that unencumbered budgetary general fund resources, as much as 5 percent of general fund revenue in any fiscal year, be transferred to the Budget Reserve Account, which was fully funded at the time of the

Table 8.9 *Revenue-reducing or expenditure-enhancing actions in the states, fiscal years 2005–06 (% of states taking action)*

	State leaders		Rest of states	
	FY2005 (%)	FY2006 (%)	FY2005 (%)	FY2006 (%)
Revenue-reducing or expenditure-enhancing actions	*N = 8*		*N = 33*	
Increase funding for existing programs beyond inflationary amounts	87.5	75.0	54.5	78.8
Create new programs	75.0	75.0	57.6	63.6
Make transfers into budget stabilization or other like fund	62.5	62.5	54.5	63.6
Conduct debt refinancing	25.0	37.5	42.4	36.4
Increase local aid	37.5	37.5	36.4	57.6
Increase contribution(s) to pension fund(s)	37.5	37.5	36.4	51.5
Cut taxes	12.5	50.0	33.3	45.5
Pay down debt or pay off bonds	12.5	25.0	30.3	30.3
Increase employee benefits	0	0	21.2	21.2
Increase retiree benefits	12.5	12.5	9.1	12.1
Tax refund to citizens	0	0	12.1	9.1
Set aside funding for other retiree health and non-pension post-employment benefits	12.5	0	3.0	3.0

Source: 2008 GPP, Survey of the States, MONEY section, Question 14.

2008 GPP. This funding may only be accessed by a three-fifths vote of the members of each house. Georgia has a Revenue Shortfall Reserve that cannot exceed 10 percent of the previous fiscal year net budgetary revenue for any given fiscal year; up to 1 percent of the preceding fiscal year's budgetary net revenue collections may be appropriated from the reserve to fund increased K-12 educational needs. This state's Governor also has an emergency fund; the Governor has discretion in using the fund, but it cannot be used for activities that have defined funding by the legislature. Idaho has a budget stabilization and economic recovery reserve fund. These reserve monies are set aside specifically to plug general fund revenue shortfalls, to meet expenses incurred as a result of a major disaster, or to provide tax relief to the citizens of Idaho.

Other states leading in structural balance include Indiana that maintains a counter-cyclical revenue and economic stabilization fund to assist in stabilizing revenue of the state's general fund in times of recession. Nebraska maintains a cash reserve fund that can only be accessed when the cash balance of the general fund is insufficient to meet obligations and for legislatively mandated transfers to other funds. Any money transferred must be repaid as soon as there is sufficient cash in the general fund to do so. Further, by law, the extent to which state tax receipts exceed appropriations at the end of the fiscal year is transferred to a cash reserve fund. North Dakota has a budget stabilization fund; any amount over $70 million at the end of the biennium goes into the fund – $100 million was in this fund in 2005 and $200 million estimated in 2007 and recommended in 2008. Actual revenues must be 2.5 percent below forecasted before the Governor can access the funds. North Dakota also has a contingency fund; this fund can be spent on natural disasters, deficiencies and to cover unexpected expenditures and is managed by an Emergency Commission.

In Pennsylvania, for the fiscal year beginning 1 July 2002 and in any fiscal year thereafter in which the Secretary of the Budget certifies that there is a surplus in the general fund, 25 percent of the surplus is to be deposited by the end of the next succeeding quarter into the state's Budget Stabilization Fund. South Dakota ended fiscal year 2006 by transferring $317,535 to its Budget Reserve Fund, as required by law. The State's Budget Reserve Fund then held a balance of $43 million, and the Property Tax Reduction Fund ended the fiscal year with a balance of $94.2 million. The maximum level of funds in this state's budget reserve is set at 10 percent of general fund appropriations. The use of money from this fund requires an Act passed by the South Dakota Legislature. Finally, Utah has a budget reserve account into which 25 percent of general fund year-end surplus is transferred; the account's balance cannot exceed 8 percent of the general fund appropriation in any fiscal year. This reserve has had a positive balance for 2006, 2007 and 2008. Expenditures from the account are limited to retroactive tax refunds and operating deficits and must be made by legislative appropriation. Utah also has a Medicaid transition account that does not have a cap. The Governor of Utah also has an emergency fund; unexpended funds may be carried over year to year and the Governor has discretion in using these funds, but cannot use funds for activities that have defined funding by the legislature.

CONCLUSIONS ABOUT STATES WITH STRONG STRUCTURAL BALANCE

This research provides a first look at states scoring well in structural balance, as measured by the GPP in 2007 with results published in *Governing* in March 2008 (see Barrett and Greene, 2008). Structural balance is defined as the ability to support ongoing expenditures with ongoing revenues – an issue of concern to more than half of governors in 2008 as indicated in their State of the State addresses for that year. States responding to the GPP survey indicated financial strategies taken during fiscal years 2005 and 2006, a brief period of recovery directly following the two worst budget years experienced by states in five decades (2002 and 2003) and just before the onset of recent fiscal decline (2007 and 2008). Overall, states improved their ranking in structural balance from the previous iteration of the GPP in 2005, when this criterion ranked 18th compared to all other management criteria graded. Structural balance moved up in rank to 11th in the 2008 GPP, undoubtedly the result of a more positive economy, but also attributable to advancements in budgeting and fiscal capacity in the states across these years.

States scoring well in structural balance do exhibit significantly larger end-of-year balances as a percentage of general fund expenditures. Also, these states have relatively balanced tax structures, with just one state predominantly dependent on one tax source for revenues, compared to over 30 percent of the rest of states similarly dependent. Five of the nine states that scored the highest in structural balance (55 percent) have tax burdens below the state average. Examination of the budget-balancing strategies engaged in by these leading states and other states in fiscal 2005 and 2006 indicates a reduced likelihood that states with strong structural balance have to engage an assortment of revenue-raising and expenditure-reducing strategies to balance, when compared to the rest of the states. Specifically, states scoring well in structural balance did not transfer normally earmarked funds into the general fund, increase short-term borrowing, draw down budget stabilization or contingency funds, or accelerate tax payments in the years under study. On the expenditure side, these same states did not resort to hiring or program increase freezes, but were more likely than other states to require employees to contribute additionally toward health benefits and to implement privatization initiatives in 2005 and/or 2006. Also, none of these states indicated increasing employee benefits or issuing a tax refund to citizens in either year. While states with strong structural balance are less likely than the rest of the states to have constraints like budget-balancing requirements, or tax or expenditure limitations that can constrain the ability to balance, these states do have rainy-day, budget stabilization and other funds, often with specified funding requirements, that can be used when revenues decline or expenditures soar unexpectedly. And generally, these states consistently fulfill funding requirements in order to have some flexibility on the inevitable rainy day.

One might ask whether reaching and maintaining structural balance allows for thinking 'outside the box'. That is, the states with strong structural balance examined here reveal traditional 'best practices' in budgeting and financial management – by maintaining balanced tax structures, relying less on traditionally volatile corporate taxes and keeping tax burdens low, by shoring up resources for the proverbial 'rainy day', through minimal use of short-term debt and by keeping debt levels well under state limits in order to be able to tap such resources in downtimes. These states were less likely to resort to increasing taxes and cutting expenditures to manage through fiscal stress. On the other hand, these states demonstrate some less customary, even unpopular approaches to managing in tough times that certainly can be considered 'outside the box'. Refinancing debt, selling and leasing state assets, instituting tax amnesty programs and, especially, increasing employee and retiree contributions for health benefits and implementing privatization initiatives were more likely to be conducted by states with strong structural balance than other states. Such unconventional strategies helped these states to manage in difficult fiscal times.

Thus, the nine states pegged here as leading ones in reaching and maintaining structural balance demonstrate adherence to traditional best practices in financial management as well as the engagement of a variety of less traditional strategies. The policy-makers in these states appear to have a good understanding of the future effects of current taxing and spending as well as management decisions, hence the disciplined yet strategic approaches to budgeting and finance that are illustrated. Future research will examine tax administration and auditing compliance strategies engaged in by states, to distinguish states with strength in this area of management from the rest in their efforts to advance the flow of funds into their governments. Also, there are a number of other variables – political, economic and organizational – that influence the ability of these states to manage and that need to be considered in future research. Finally, a fuller comparison of results here with those from the previous iteration of the GPP in 2005 (directly on the tail of the last recession) provides fertile ground for further inquiry.

NOTES

1. This section takes advantage of Willoughby's (2008) examination of State of the State addresses that were accessed from January through 18 March 2008 at www.stateline.org, www.nga.org, or at the state government homepage. All quotes presented in this section are from the addresses accessed on these websites, unless otherwise noted.
2. See http://www.pewcenteronthestates.org/template_page.aspx?id=35362 for the summary of the 2008 GPP project methodology and criteria development. The views expressed here are those of the author and do not necessarily reflect the views of the GPP or The Pew Charitable Trusts.
3. In 2008, all states except Vermont have a constitutional and/or statutory requirement that the state budget must balance. These requirements vary. In 43 states the Governor must submit a balanced budget to the legislature; in 39 states, the legislature must pass a balanced budget; and in 37 states, the budget must be balanced at year-end (the state cannot carry over a deficit into the next fiscal year). Thirty states are held to all three of these requirements (Snell, 2004).
4. See recent work by Rubin and Willoughby (2009) that discusses the '5 percent rule' and examines thresholds of 8 and 16 percent in the states in fiscal years 2002 and 2003.
5. See http://www.taxadmin.org/fta/rate/07taxbur.html for the 2007 tax burden by state.

REFERENCES

2008 GPP. Online survey of the states, MONEY section of questionnaire.
Barrett, K. and Greene, R. (2008). Grading the states: the mandate to measure. *Governing* (March): 24–34.
Crawford, J. (2002). Overview. In *Paths to Performance in State and Local Governments: A Final Assessment from the Maxwell School of Citizenship and Public Affairs.* http://sites.maxwell.syr.edu/gpp3/2002full.html. Accessed 2 December 2008.
McNichol, E. and Lav, I. (2008). State budget troubles worsen. http://www.cbpp.org/9-8-08sfp.pdf. Accessed 2 December 2008.
National Association of State Budget Officers (NASBO) (2007). *The Fiscal Survey of the States.* Washington, DC: NASBO.
National Association of State Budget Officers (NASBO) (2008). *The Fiscal Survey of the States.* Washington, DC: NASBO.
National Bureau of Economic Research (NBER) (2008). Determination of the December 2007 peak in economic activity. http://wwwdev.nber.org/dec2008.html. Accessed 2 December 2008.
Rubin, M.M. and Willoughby, K. (2009). Financial management grades for the states: a prospective use. *Public Budgeting and Finance* 28 (1): 1–19.
Snell, R.K. (2004). State balanced budget requirements: provisions and practice. http://www.ncsl.org/programs/fiscal/balbuda.htm. Accessed 20 December 2007.
Willoughby, K. (2008). The state of the states: governors keep agendas short. In K.S. Chi (ed.), *The Book of the States*, Vol. 40. Lexington, KY: Council of State Governments.

9. Fiscal limitations on local choice: the imposition and effects of local government tax and expenditure limitations

Daniel R. Mullins

INTRODUCTION

Of the 89,528 units of government in the United States, all but one are subnational and 89,476 are local (see Table 9.1). These governments are the first line of representation and service delivery for all citizens of the nation. They deliver autonomous basic services and coordinate joint services and policy across all levels of government. These jurisdictions provide the critical foundations for economic activity, education, and cultural and social development. They respond to and reflect the subsets of desires of populations with differing tastes, capacities and needs for public services. Essential to the successful completion of their functions is discretion over service levels and packages, and the authority to raise revenue in a manner which effectively exploits their fiscal capacity consistently with the desires of their local populations. This discretion must obviously be limited to assure proper coordination with the policy objectives of overlying governments; however, beyond this there is little justification for policies which constrain the ability of these jurisdictions to respond to the demands of their populations. The ability of local (and state) jurisdictions to serve the wants and needs of their populations in the United States has come under increasing strain over the past few decades for reasons that appear to defy rational explanation and which have contributed to distortions in their fiscal, service delivery and governance structures.

The subtlety of these changes belie their importance in shaping the ability of the sector to respond to and meet the varied needs of local populations. They may also reflect the most significant erosion of local autonomy since the establishment of home rule beginning in the nineteenth century. Some of these changes may have been driven by external economic forces and perceptions of heightened spatial competition, resulting in a perceived

Table 9.1   Subnational governments, by type

Type	1972	1982	1992	1997	2002	2007	Change 1972– 2007 (%)
County	3 044	3 041	3 043	3 043	3 034	3 033	−0.4%
Municipal	18 517	19 076	19 279	19 372	19 372	19 492	5.3%
Town or township	16 991	16 734	16 656	16 629	16 506	16 519	−2.8%
Special district	23 885	28 078	31 555	34 683	35 356	37 381	56.5%
School district	15 781	14 851	14 422	13 726	13 522	13 051	−17.3%
Total	78 218	81 780	84 955	87 453	87 790	89 476	14.4%

Source: US Bureau of the Census (2002, 2008).

need to respond to a new level of mobility of both residents and business investment. Constraints on revenues and expenditures have, however, been imposed via both local political processes and through statewide initiatives and referenda and state legislative enactments. Constraints imposed by the initiative and referenda process have attempted to restrain the ability of state and local governments. State legislative bodies have also been active in limiting the revenue access of substate jurisdictions. For local jurisdictions, constraints have been largely imposed externally, in statewide processes. This chapter focuses on these constraints, imposed through political and institutional mechanisms (rather than economic processes), and their effects on reshaping state and local fiscal structures.

GENERAL CHARACTER AND EFFECTS OF STATE AND LOCAL GOVERNMENT REVENUE AND EXPENDITURE LIMITATIONS[1]

Local revenue limitations are traceable to the nineteenth century and earlier. The more recent decades (beginning in the early 1970s) have often reinforced previously existing limitations (see Mullins and Cox, 1995). However, this period has also brought new, more stringent constraints. In the most recent period (since the 1990s), much of the attention has focused on state governments. Thirty-three states function under measures to limit state taxes and/or expenditures (NCSL, 2007).[2] Sixteen states limit increases in some or all taxes, and 26 limit appropriations, although in four of those states these are anti-deficiency requirements. Ten limit both revenue and spending. These state limitations often tie the growth in state revenues and appropriations to a rate less than or equal to the growth in state personal income, with a variety of override provisions. While initially perceived to be relatively non-constraining, the severity of state limitations more recently imposed has increased. These state-level constraints also have implications for local resource availability and expenditure responsibility, as state-level constraints may limit the availability of state transfers to localities and encourage a devolution of spending responsibility.

At the local level, the bulk of the limitations initiatives have been directed at the property tax; however, their scope has broadened since 1990. Local revenue or expenditure limitations exist in 47 states, but vary widely in the actual constraint they impose. Over the years, these limitations have substantially altered the structure of local finance, and have created shifts in the distribution of service responsibilities between units of government. Limitations on local property taxes and general expenditures have stimulated shifts toward non-tax sources of revenues (fees and charges, state transfers and debt) and have encouraged vertical shifts of revenue and expenditure authority and responsibility to the state. They also inspire horizontal shifts of local functional responsibility (through increased roles of special service and finance districts; see Figure 9.1). Service affects attributed to them have included reduced educational inputs, lower teacher qualifications, poorer educational performance and generally lower-quality municipal services. Increased borrowing at the state and local levels has also been attributed to tax limitations (see Mullins and Joyce, 1996; Joyce and Mullins, 1991; Mullins, 2001, 2004; Danziger, 1980; Downs and Figlio, 1999; Downes et al., 1998; Doyle, 1994; Bowler and Donovan, 2004; Carr, 2006). Limitations have also had differential effects across governments within states. As would be expected, they are likely to have the most serious implications for central cities and less prosperous communities. The overall outcome may be impaired responsiveness, as relationships between local governments and local populations are substantially altered, and local government's capacity to provide for public needs and wants declines. The effects vary by type of government and service subgroups, and by the demographics of resident populations (Mullins, 2001, 2004).

The effects of tax and expenditure limitations (TELS) increase over time. Colorado's Taxpayer Bill of Rights (TABOR), the nation's most comprehensive and stringent package of state and local tax and expenditure limitations, was enacted in 1992. State-level provisions were suspended in 2005 in a wave of concern for TABOR's detrimental effect on both state and local services (see Box 9.1). Still, tax and spending limitations of all varieties continue to be placed on state ballots and considered by state legislatures, often with the assistance of national anti-tax associations

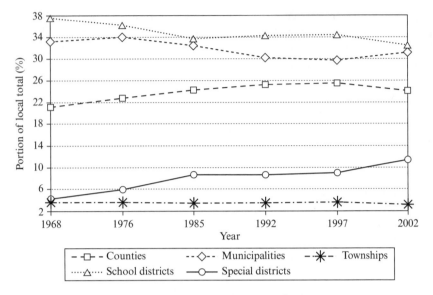

Figure 9.1   Total local general revenue by type of government

(see below). Limitations complicate budgeting at the state or local level, sometimes mandating expenditure increases or privileged status to certain program areas while elsewhere limiting the ability of government to finance them. The large number of states facing court-ordered reform of their systems of financing K–12 (Kindergarten to grade 12) education must work within their frameworks.

Expenditure and revenue authority and responsibility has shifted away from local governments in general (and local general-purpose governments in particular), altering access and voice within a framework of constraint. The result may entail serious implications for local autonomy and the ability of communities to match their service–tax packages to the preferences of their residents, seriously reducing the efficiency of resource allocation within the sector.

PERVERSION OF THE PROPERTY TAX

Statewide Responses Engender Local Costs

The property tax has often been a motivator for supporting local tax and expenditure limitations. Particularly in the present environment (one of ballooning market prices followed by a contraction and mortgage crisis),

---

BOX 9.1 TABOR-ATTRIBUTED EFFECTS IN COLORADO

Colorado's Taxpayer Bill of Rights fostered a substantial decline in the availability and quality of nearly all public services.

- Colorado K–12 education funding. Declined from 35th in the nation to 49th as a portion of personal income. Average per pupil funding fell by more than $400 relative to the nation and teacher salaries declined from 30th to 50th.
- Cuts in higher education funding. Funding per resident student declined 31 percent in real terms. Higher education's share of personal income declined from 35th to 48th. Real tuition increased 21 percent in four years.
- Cuts in funding for public health. Colorado declined from 23rd to 48th in the percentage of pregnant women receiving adequate prenatal care and fell from 24th to 50th in the share of children receiving full vaccinations.
- Medical insurance for children and adults. The portion of low-income children lacking health insurance doubled and Colorado ranks last among the 50 states in coverage. Colorado fell from 20th to 48th low-income non-elderly adults covered under health insurance and ranked 49th in low-income non-elderly adults and low-income children covered by Medicaid.

Source: Lay and Lyons (2006). Original source, Bradley and Lyons (2005).

---

one of the primary challenges facing local government is fending off attacks on its basic revenue source from state actors desiring to take credit for providing 'relief'. State actions vary to the degree that they place the burden for 'tax relief' on state or local resources. For example, in 2006, Pennsylvania enacted $800 million in property tax relief during a special legislative session for 2008–09. Revenues from gaming are to be used to reduce school district taxes by 10 percent and an option was provided for further tax relief through the adoption of local income taxes. In New York, in 2007 the Governor proposed a $6 billion school property tax relief program for fiscal years 2008–2010 (FY2008–10) for middle-income homeowners using state funds, but also proposed a cap on school property tax levies. New Jersey allocated $1.7 billion from the state budget for residential property tax 'rebates' for 2005–07. New Jersey also, however, enacted limits on property tax levy increases for all local governments from 2007 to 2012.

Other states have sought to enact property tax relief in manners that more significantly infringe on local discretion. In 2007, Florida required all local jurisdictions (including school districts) to freeze FY2008 tax levies at FY2007 levels and then imposed additional reductions of 3 percent for school districts, and in amounts based on previous growth history for cities and counties. Further growth was restricted to the rate of growth of population and income. In January 2008, a referenda incorporated relief into the Florida Constitution, doubling the homestead exemption, allowing portability of valuation reductions due to the existing 3 percent cap on annual assessment growth, retaining a 3 percent residential assessed value cap and instituting a 10 percent cap on non-homestead property.[3] In March of 2008 the Indiana Legislature provided $870 million in property tax relief and at the same time enacted statutory property tax rate limits on all local governments expected to produce a 30 percent reduction in local government revenue. Beginning in 2010, homestead property taxes are limited to 1 percent of assessed value, apartments and agricultural property taxes are limited to 2 percent, and businesses 3 percent. Local spending limits were also enacted. A referenda scheduled for 2010 would place these limitation into the state's Constitution. In Georgia, a constitutional amendment has been proposed that would freeze residential real property values and another has been proposed ('The GREAT Plan') that would eliminate property taxes for education, establish a property tax revenue cap and acquisition value assessment (see Box 9.2).

Relief provided by many of these proposals and initiatives come at the direct expense of local government revenue. They are often shortsighted at best, scrambling to provide relief in the form of a statewide policy response (in an environment of a short-term economic cycle) to a local taxation issue. State responses usurp local choice, as mechanisms of local political responsiveness and representation are circumvented. Instead of relying on a response by a local governing body to moderate tax rates in the face of cyclical base changes, uniform statewide responses are enacted which likely produce intermediate- and long-term revenue difficulties for local governments faced with future market readjustments and potentially declining property values. The ramifications of these constraints are already at hand, given the deflation of housing values brought on by the subprime mortgage and liquidity crisis and the general economic contraction. In the current environment, states and localities have gone from revenue-rich to increasing austerity in the span of a single year. The largest revenue shortfalls since 2001 emerged in planning for FY2009 budgets in at least 29 states. These states faced a combined revenue shortfall of more

BOX 9.2 ILLUSTRATIVE EXAMPLES OF STATE PROPERTY TAX RELIEF INITIATIVES

State	Initiative
Pennsylvania	Enacted in June of 2006 (Special Session Act 1) provides $800 million in statewide property tax relief for 2008–09. Gaming revenue to reduce school district property taxes by 10 percent. An option exists for school districts to place a referenda on the November 2009 ballot to institute a local income tax to provide property tax reduction via homestead and farmstead exclusions (or, under certain circumstances, millage reductions).
New Jersey	Homestead (owner and tenant) rebates for 2005, 2006 and 2007 property tax payments. For 2008, $1.7 billion was allocated from the state budget for property tax relief to 1.3 million New Jersey households. Rebates are for 20 percent of the first $10,000 in tax payment for households with income less than $100,000 and 10 percent for households with income between $101,000 and $150,000. Different provisions exist for seniors and disabled taxpayers.
New York	January 2007, New York's Governor proposed a three-year, $6 billion expansion in property tax relief programs directed toward middle-income homeowners. The Budget proposal for FY 2007-08 increased the school tax relief program by $1.5 billion, with increases of $2 billion and $2.5 billion for FY2008–09 and 2009–10. Relief is based on a new sliding income scale with 100 percent increases in benefits to as much as $2300 for families with incomes of $80,000 or less. In June of 2008, New York's Governor also proposed a cap on school property tax levies and the New York State Commission on Property Tax Relief proposed additional restructuring.

State	Initiative
Indiana	19 March 2008 legislation provided $870 million in property tax relief, cutting average homeowner property taxes by more than 30 percent. Beginning in 2010, homestead property taxes are limited to 1 percent of assessed value, apartment and agricultural taxes are limited to 2 percent of assessed value, and businesses are limited to 3 percent. Additional reductions accrue through increased sales tax revenues. Also included are limits on local government spending. An amendment will be voted on in November of 2010 to permanently enter these caps into the state Constitution. Significant education costs (including operating costs) are shifted to the state. Referenda will be required on school and local governments' capital projects and local government discretion in 'levy appeals' will be eliminated. Eliminates most township assessors and places most assessing responsibility in the hands of counties.
Florida	June 2007, Florida introduced statutory property tax relief. Local jurisdiction and school districts were required to roll-back 2007–08 property tax levies to 2006–07 levels (except for new construction). Cities and counties were required to additionally reduce levies based upon a factor which directly related required reductions to previous year's level of levy growth. School districts were required to reduce levies by 3 percent. Revenue growth is restricted to the rate of growth in population and income. Overrides require supermajority legislative votes, with some requiring public referenda. 29 January 2008, a referenda was held on including expanded relief in the state's Constitution. It provides for expanded (and doubled) $50,000 homestead exemptions (except for school district levies); allows valuation reductions of up to $500,000 due to the 3 percent limit on residential assessment increases on homes of existing homeowners to

State	Initiative
	be transferred to homes purchased in 2007 or later; retains the 3 percent homestead assessment cap, while capping non-homestead property at 10 percent; and establishes a $25,000 exemption for business personal property.
Georgia	12 February 2008, a proposed constitutional amendment to freeze residential real property values at 2008 levels and adopt acquisition value assessment (limiting assessment increases to an inflation factor) passed the state senate. A second proposal has also been advanced to eliminate property taxes for education, cap property tax revenue for other local jurisdictions (limiting levy growth to the change in a price index) and adopt acquisition value assessment. Known as 'The GREAT Plan' (Georgia's Repeal of Every Ad Valorem Tax) lost local revenue will be partially replaced by increases in sales taxes.

than $48 billion. Mid-year, 21 states had seen a shortfall in revenue execution necessitating more than $8.9 billion in additional revenue reductions (McNichol and Lav, 2008).

Local jurisdictions, whether cities, school districts, transportation districts or villages, find themselves in similar circumstances. Two-thirds of city financial officers indicate a decline in their ability to cover fiscal needs in 2008 and four-fifths expected the situation to worsen in 2009. Aggregate average real revenue reductions of more than 4 percent are expected for 2008 with property tax revenue declines of more than 3.5 percent. This is occurring in the face of significant cost escalation driven by increases in the cost of energy and fuel, public safety, infrastructure, pensions and health insurance. The result is real (and in some cases significant nominal) declines in public services. However, outcomes are buoyed by the existence of historically high reserves (Pagano and Hoene, 2008). Many jurisdictions across the United States are finding that significant retrenchment is required to close revenue shortfalls that have developed in current year budgets and even more drastic measures are needed to deal with projected shortfalls in the following year (see Box 9.3). This is occurring at a time when state governments such as California, Maryland, Virginia and Massachusetts (and many others) are considering sharp reductions in

---

BOX 9.3   EXAMPLES OF MAGNITUDES
OF LOCAL FISCAL STRESS AND
BUDGETARY ADJUSTMENTS

Local government	Revenue shortfall and remedy
Los Angeles	Current year revenue shortfall of $400 million with expected employment and service cuts. Fiscal year 2010 budget instructions call for submission of two proposals by department heads (freezing spending and a 9 percent across the board budget reduction). Reductions in state aid are also likely due to the state of California's own budget difficulties. (Wilson, P. [2008]. LA expects big budget shortfall. *Los Angeles Times*, 4 October, part B, p. 3)
Long Island Towns	Current year shortfall in nearly all of Long Island's 13 towns due to slumping 'mortgage tax revenue'. Hiring freezes and bond issues are being considered. Shortfalls are as follows. Brookhaven, at least $19.3 million. Previous budget cuts of 5 percent were enacted along with current additional cuts in 'discretionary spending' and a hiring freeze. Islip, at least $10 million. Budgets were previously trimmed by 5 percent in the spring of 2008, additional operating cost reductions are planned, as is a 5 percent reduction in personnel cost for FY 2009. Similar issues face East Hampton, Huntington, Smithtown, Hempstead, North Hempstead and Oyster Bay. (Whittle, P. et al. [2008]. Economy zaps LI towns. *Newsday*, 29 September, A16.)
Philadelphia	Projected five-year, $850 million, revenue shortfall, five months after approval of the current year budget and $400 million greater than one month earlier. Bonuses for 4500 employees have been frozen,

Local government	Revenue shortfall and remedy
	10 percent across-the-board budget cuts. All options are being considered. (Shields, J. and Gelbart, M. [2008]. Five year gap in Phila: Spending could hit $850 million. *Philadelphia Inquirer,* 9 October, B1.)
Prince George's County, MD	Current year shortfall, $57 million. Proposed forced two-week furlough of all county employees (except school district), $14 million reduction in education budget and across-the-board operating cuts. (Helderman, R. [2008]. Johnson proposes two-week furloughs. *Washington Post,* 16 September, B5.)
Hoboken, NJ	Current year $10 million shortfall. State oversight to close the gap. New Jersey's Local Finance Board is now required to approve all city expenditures and contracts, all city employees' deployment and departments will be audited. (*The Bond Buyer.* [2008]. Hoboken needs approval for all borrowing. 11 September, p. 24.)
Camden, NJ	Current year, $24 million shortfall in a city of 80,000 residents. Layoff of 40–60 (non-public safety) employees. Governor appointed chief operating officer. (Katz, M. [2008]. Camden workers protest proposed lay-offs. *Philadelphia Inquirer,* 19 September, B1.)
Fairfax County, VA	Expected 2009 revenue shortfall of $430 million. Delayed capital projects, budget reviews. (Chandler, M. [2008]. Supervisors turn away Fairfax schools proposal. *The Washington Post,* 23 September, B1.)
Duluth, MN	Current year, $6 million revenue shortfall. Occurred after laying-off 160 employees and retrenching recreation programs in the adopted budget. (Saulny, S. [2008]. Financial crisis takes a toll on already-squeezed cities. *New York Times,* 7 October, A16.)

Local government	Revenue shortfall and remedy
Phoenix	Budget reduction of $89 million adopted for current fiscal year. Based on a 12.5 percent spending reduction. Lagging revenue has required new proposals for an additional 30 percent reduction. (Saulny [2008]; Uchitelle, L. [2008]. Lawmakers weight plans for stimulus. *New York Times*, 10 October, B1.)

local government transfers. Local jurisdictions in states allowing broader and more diversified revenue options and without constraining tax and expenditure limitations are better able to cope with current economic conditions and to continue to meet the public service needs of their populations (Hoene and Pagano, 2008).

A Love–Hate Relationship

For good or ill, much of the focus of the local portion of the 'tax revolt' has been the property tax, either in general or for education purposes.[4] Indicators suggest that we may be on the cusp of a third wave. What explains this outcome? On all economic counts, this tax has positive attributes as a local revenue generator. Public opinion polls, however, consistently rate the property tax as among the 'worst' or 'least fair' taxes, and limitations and 'reforms' have not altered the general view of the public. A 2007 survey of the Tax Foundation reported the local property tax as the least fair of broad-based state and local taxes, with fully half of all respondents rating it as somewhat unfair or not at all fair (Chamberlain, 2007). At the same time the public consistently shows equal or more trust and confidence in local government compared to national and state governments, and favors local governments in value received for their dollar in taxes. More surprising is that the Western states, those imposing the most serious limitations, are among the least likely to view the property tax as the worst tax, equally as likely to have trust and confidence in local government, and feel as though they are receiving value for their tax dollars (Cole and Kincaid, 2000). How is it that the primary revenue source for the level of government for which the public has most confidence, and perceives the greatest value, is held in such disrepute? An argument can be made that 'reforms' enacted to limit local government's access to property tax revenue have seriously impaired equity and efficiency, resulting in desire for a new series of 'reforms'.

Favoring the Resident Homestead/Differential Burdens as Political Nullifiers?

There have certainly been legitimate concerns raised regarding the property tax over time (see Fisher, 1996), but these do not supersede its basic appeal as a local revenue source. The marginal adjustments in the general implementation of the property tax over the last several decades, to the degree to which they have created departures from the theoretical property tax in its administration, tend to have benefited the resident citizen voter (Gold, 1979) and more specifically those with the longest tenure.

Classification

A review of property tax classification structure across the states shows that through varying assessment ratios or directly applying differential property tax rates, 22 states (and the District of Columbia) apply lower effective tax rates to the taxable value of residential property than do commercial and industrial property. For 14 states, the resulting differential produces a tax rate on commercial and industrial property that is at minimum twice that of residential property (see Table 9.2). This application to taxable value also seriously underestimates this residential differential because of reductions in the base value of residential property and tax liability through homestead exemptions, deferrals and circuit-breaker programs (not to mention differences in assessing practices and methods).

Homestead exemptions

Homestead exemptions in the form of a reduction of assessed value or credit against tax payments are provided in every state except Missouri. Twenty-eight states provide a general homestead exemption to all homeowners, with two providing similar relief to renters, while the remainder provide it to other classes of homeowners, such as the elderly, veterans, blind, disabled or low-income homeowners. Twenty-five states provide special relief to elderly homeowners (with five also providing relief to elderly renters). Forty-four states offer additional targeted relief to the blind, disabled or disabled veterans (nine offer this exemption without providing relief to general homeowners or elderly homeowners). Eleven states provide additional relief to low-income homeowners and elderly homeowners, or require an income test for eligibility. The value of the exemptions range from a maximum total exemption of assessed value (generally for disabled veterans) in 18 states, to exemptions for all homeowners of $100,000 for school taxes in South Carolina, an $89,000 exemption in Idaho and an $80,000 exemption in Hawaii. Mississippi exempts 34 percent of assessed value and North Dakota 10 percent. New York

Table 9.2 *Property tax classification and homeowner relief*

State	2008 classification/rate favoring owner-occupied housing (OO% of C/I)[1]	Homestead exemption (2006/08)		Circuit-breaker (2006/08)			State deferral program
		Eligibility	Amount range	Year of adoption	Eligibility	Highest amount	
Alabama	50.00	AH,AE,EH,B,D	$6000–Total	–	–	–	–
Alaska	–	AH, EHR,DV,S	$20k–150k(AV)	–	–	–	–
Arizona	41.67	AH,S,D,V	$540(c)–$3k(av)	1973	EH,AR	$502	EH
Arkansas	–	AH,DV,S,M	$350(c)–Total	1973	EH,S	$118	–
California	–	AH, DV,S	7000–161,420	1967	EHR,D	$473	EH,D
Colorado	27.45	EH,DV	50% to 100k	1971	EHR,D	$600	EH
Connecticut	–	D,V,DV	Local option	1974	AH,EHR,D	$1250	–
Delaware	–	EH,LID	50% – 500(c)/LO	–	–	–	–
District of Columbia	45.95	AH,EH,D	60,000(AV)/50%(c)	1974	AHR	$750	AH,EH
Florida	–	AH,D,S,DV	$25,000(AV)–Total	–	–	–	AH.EH
Georgia	–	AH,EH,DV	$2,000–50,000(AV)	–	–	–	EH
Hawaii	29.99[2]	AH,E,B,D,DV	$80k – Total	1977	EH,AH,AR	Amount > 3% income	EH
Idaho	40.00[3]	AH	$89,000/50%	1974	EH,S,D,V	$1320	EH,S,D,V
Illinois	40.00[3]	AH,EH	5500–75,000(DR)	1972	EHR,D	$700	EH
Indiana	33.33[4]	AHR,E,B,D,V	20%(t)+45k(AV) + 25k	–	–	–	–
Iowa	–	AH,DV	$4850(AV)–Total	1973	EHR,D	$1000	SSI
Kansas	46.00	AH	2300(AV)/20K(MV)	1970	EHR,D,B	$700	–
Kentucky	–	EH,D	$29,400(AV)	–	–	–	–
Louisiana	66.67	AH	$7500(AV, NM)	–	–	–	–

214

State							
Maine	—	AH,EV,D,B,S	13k – 50k(AV)	1971	AHR,EHR,DS	$400–2000	EH,D
Maryland	—	B,DV	$6000–Total	1973	AH,ER	$750 – Taxes paid	—
Massachusetts	43/37[5]	EH,V,S,B,DV,LO	2k – Total(AV)	2001	EH R	$930	EH
Michigan	—	DV	Total	1973	AHR	$1200	EH R, DV
Minnesota	50.00[6]	AH	State credit (to 304)	1967	AHR	$1700	EH
Mississippi	66.67	AH,D,EH	$300(c)/$7500(AV)+	—	EH R	$750	—
Missouri	59.38	—	—	1973	EH R,LI	$1000	—
Montana	77.65[7]	AH, DV	34%(AV)–Total	1981	—	—	—
Nebraska	—	EH,D,V,DV (LI)	40k–50k(AV)	—	EH R	$500	—
Nevada	—	W,O,V,DV	$1100–$22,000	1973	AH	Edu. Tax	—
New Hampshire	—	EH&D(LI),B,DV	$5k–15k–Total	n/a	AHR	$2000	EH,D
New Jersey	—	EH,D,S,V,DV,R	$250(tax)–Total	1990	EH R	$250	—
New Mexico	—	AH,V	2000–4000(AV)	1977	AHR	$375	—
New York	20.46[8]	AH,(EH,V,DV(LO))	30k–56.8k(AV)	1978	—	—	—
North Carolina	—	EH, D,V	$20k–38k(AV)	—	EH R,D	$240	—
North Dakota	90.00	AH,EH,D,V,ER	10–100%	1969	—	—	EH
Ohio	—	AH,EH,D	12.5%(T)/25k(AV)	—	EH,D	$200	—
Oklahoma	—	AH,LIHH,DV	$1,000(AV)+Total	1974	ER	$2100	—
Oregon	—	DV,W	$15,450–18,540(AV)	1971	EH R,D,S	$650	EH,D
Pennsylvania	37.00[9]	AH(LO),B,D,DV	50%(AV)–Total	1971	EH R,D	$300	AH(LO)
Rhode Island	38.10	B,V,DV,POW	$1000–15,000(AV)	1977	—	—	LO
South Carolina	—	AH,EH,B,D,DV	$100,000–Total	—	EH,D	35–55%	—
South Dakota	—	D(LI),DV	8k–Total(AV)	1976	—	—	EH
Tennessee	62.50	EH(LI),D,DV	6250–43,750(AV)	—	—	—	EH,D
Texas	—	AH,E,D,DV	$15k–25k(AV edu.)	—	—	$816	EH,D
Utah	55.00	DV,B,LI	$816(C)–219,164(AV)	1977	EHR,W		EH,D

Table 9.2 (continued)

State	2008 classification/ rate favoring owner-occupied housing (OO% of C/I)[1]	Homestead exemption (2006/08)		Circuit-breaker (2006/08)			State deferral program
		Eligibility	Amount range	Year of adoption	Eligibility	Highest amount	
Vermont	Local[10]	DV	$10,000–40,000(LO)	1969	AHR	% of over threshold taxes	–
Virginia	–	(EH,D)LI	Local	–	–	–	EH,D(LO)
Washington	–	(EH,D)LI	All voted levies	n/a	EH,D	50k(AV)	AH
West Virginia	40 to 55[11]	EH,D/EHLI	$20k(AV)/+20k(c)	1972	AHR	$1000	–
Wisconsin	–	AHR,DV,SS	300(c)–Total(c)	1964	AHR	$1160	EH,D
Wyoming	82.61[12]	AH(LI),V,DV	$250(C)–50%(tax)	1975	EHR,D	$900	EH,D (LO*)

Notes:
[1] The assessment ratio (or rate) for owner-occupied housing is divided by that for commercial/industrial property and then multiplied by 100 to produce this column. The District of Columbia, Hawaii, Indiana, Massachusetts, Minnesota, New York, Rhode Island and West Virginia apply differential rates to classes rather than differential assessment ratios.
[2] Hawaii allows for local rate variation. This ratio is that existing in Honolulu, where residential rates are 3.59/1000 and commercial/industrial are 11.97/1000.
[3] Classification applies only in Cook County.
[4] In 2008, Indiana adopted a reform (to take effect in 2010) restricting tax rates to 1 percent of a home's assessed value, 2 percent of the assessed value of apartments and agricultural land, and 3 percent for commercial and industrial property.

216

5   Massachusetts relies on a split tax rate. Maximum differentials for the commercial/industrial property to residential rate is 2.31–2.69, depending upon previous year's residential levy.

6   Minnesota residential rates are 1 percent for property under $500,000, 1.2 percent above. Commercial/industrial rates are 1.5 percent under $150,000 and 2 percent above.

7   Montana applies a uniform rate to residential and commercial property of 3.01 percent for 2008 to property values derived through differential exemptions for base values of 34 percent for residential and 15 percent for commercial/industrial property ((3.01*.66)/(3.01*.15) = 77.65).

8   New York City and Nassau County vary both assessments ratio and rates applied by class of property. For 2008, residential property in NYC is assessed at 6 percent of value and taxed at a 15.434 rate, while commercial and industrial property is assessed at 45 percent of value and taxed at 10.059 ((0.06*0.15434)/(0.45*0.10059) = 0.2046). Nassau County assessment ratio is 0.25 percent and 0.96 percent.

9   Rhode Island allows local governments to vary rates across categories of property. The locality with the greatest disparity taxes commercial and industrial property at a rate 2.67 times residential.

10   Local jurisdiction vary rates. Different rates are applied to residential and commercial/industrial property for education levies.

11   Commercial and industrial property is taxed at a different rate depending on whether it is inside (2.21 percent) or outside (2.99) a municipality. The residential tax rate is 1.21 percent.

12   The differential is only for industrial property. Residential and commercial are assessed at a uniform portion of value (9.5 percent), while industrial property is assessed at a high proportion (11.5 percent).

A – all; C – tax credit; HH – head of household; M – minor; R- renter; AV – assessed value; D – disabled; H – homeowner; P – periodically; S – surviving spouse; B – blind; E – elderly; LI – low income; POW – prisoner of war; W – widow; LO – Local Option; DR – disaster reconstruction; SSI – supplemental security income recipients; MV – market value; NM – not municipal taxes, except New Orleans; LO* – LO, before 1988; V – veterans

Sources: ACIR (1990, 1992, 1994); Baer (2008); Lyons et al. (2007); NCSL (2002); updated and confirmed via various state websites, Fall 2008.

exempts $30,000 in property value and Florida and Alaska exempt $25,000 and $20,000 respectively. The values of some of these exemptions are adjusted upwards periodically as home values increase. The fixed nature of these exemptions in most states results in greater relative base relief for lower-valued properties, reducing effective tax rates the most for owners of lower-valued homesteads. In aggregate, these exemptions reduce the relative value of the residential component of the property tax base (compared to commercial and industrial components) and shift a greater portion of property tax burdens to commercial and industrial classes. This burden shift is magnified by assessment processes and differential classifications.

Commercial and industrial burdens
The result is that for 2000 in the largest urban areas in each state, typical effective tax rates on commercial property averaged more than double that of typical residential housing, while the rate on industrial property was 1.75 times higher (see Table 9.3, last four columns).[5] This differential had declined somewhat in 2004, with effective commercial and industrial property tax rates at a level 1.92 and 1.49 times the residential rates across the states. This, of course, assumes that valuations are accurately calculated. For 2004, the highs for relative tax burdens for commercial property were 16.4 times that of residential property in Massachusetts (with a commercial effective tax rate of 3.01 percent), 6.39 times in New York (at 3.92 percent) and 3.58 times in Colorado (at 1.83 percent). For 2000, in no jurisdictions were commercial effective tax rates less than residential rates; for 2004 they were in five states (Delaware, New Hampshire, New Jersey, North Dakota and Pennsylvania). Industrial property was taxed at a level 9.04 times the residential rate in Massachusetts (at 1.65 percent), 3.84 times in New York (at 2.35 percent), 2.89 times in the District of Columbia (at 1.94 percent), and at 2.86 times in Colorado (at 1.46 percent). While in only five states was industrial property taxed at a rate less than the residential rate in 2000, this was so in 19 states for 2004, reflecting a shift toward lessened industrial tax burdens.

Circuit-breakers and deferrals: more targeted relief
Circuit-breakers, however, are also used in 33 states and the District of Columbia for targeted residential property tax relief (Table 9.2). Relief is generally calculated as a portion of property tax liabilities that exceed a certain percentage of income and is provided as a refundable income tax credit. Relief is available for all homeowners in 13 states, for all renters in 11, and for both renters and homeowners in 10. Renter circuit-breakers are often provided to compensate for the absence of homestead exemptions for commercial rental property, with property taxes calculated as an

Table 9.3 Property tax burdens across classes of property

State	Average PT on OOH as % of household income		Variation across income deciles in burden of PT on OOH		Residential homestead ETR, higher-valued property, largest urban area		Ratio, high-valued homestead ETR to lower-valued homestead ETR	Commercial ETR, largest urban area		Industrial ETR, largest urban area		Ratio, commercial ETR to residential		Ratio, industrial ETR to residential	
	1999	2006	1999	2006	2000	2004	2004	2000	2004	2000	2004	2000	2004	2000	2004
Alabama	1.1	1.5	110.0	115.4	0.44	0.66	1.09	1.30	1.39	1.06	1.11	2.92	2.11	2.38	1.69
Alaska	3.5	4.7	107.1	165.3	1.27	1.54	1.00	1.61	1.55	1.35	1.58	1.27	1.01	1.07	1.03
Arizona	2.6	3.2	98.8	106.4	0.87	0.96	1.00	3.56	2.92	3.08	2.66	4.09	3.04	3.54	2.77
Arkansas	2.0	1.8	96.3	104.6	0.87	1.24	1.33	1.17	1.39	1.21	1.38	1.34	1.12	1.38	1.12
California	3.9	5.4	105.9	104.9	0.89	1.19	1.09	1.25	1.25	1.00	1.00	1.40	1.05	1.12	0.84
Colorado	2.9	3.1	92.7	109.5	0.49	0.51	1.00	1.89	1.83	1.53	1.46	3.87	3.58	3.12	2.86
Connecticut	6.9	7.8	106.7	111.9	1.50	2.28	1.00	3.78	2.73	3.03	2.18	2.53	1.20	2.02	0.96
Delaware	2.1	2.2	91.9	114.4	0.85	1.09	1.00	1.45	0.91	0.87	0.55	1.71	0.84	1.03	0.50
District of Columbia	3.3	4.2	129.5	156.9	0.50	0.67	2.02	2.19	1.97	2.00	1.94	4.36	2.93	3.97	2.89
Florida	4.2	5.2	96.0	102.8	1.64	2.05	1.44	2.69	2.48	2.12	1.99	1.64	1.21	1.29	0.97
Georgia	2.6	3.1	99.5	104.9	0.67	1.18	1.95	1.19	1.61	1.24	1.65	1.78	1.37	1.85	1.40
Hawaii	1.8	2.8	114.2	92.9	0.19	0.27	1.58	0.76	0.89	0.45	0.53	3.90	3.26	2.38	1.96
Idaho	3.4	3.8	97.2	79.7	0.99	1.16	1.66	1.76	1.70	1.44	1.38	1.78	1.47	1.45	1.19
Illinois	5.2	6.4	87.1	83.4	2.41	1.41	1.27	6.92	3.24	3.94	2.00	2.88	2.30	1.64	1.42
Indiana	2.8	3.2	88.5	94.0	1.26	1.53	1.84	2.38	2.52	2.86	2.32	1.89	1.64	2.27	1.51
Iowa	3.3	3.8	82.2	83.4	1.52	1.85	1.14	3.18	3.55	2.26	2.14	2.09	1.91	1.48	1.16
Kansas	3.0	3.6	86.7	90.2	0.77	1.22	1.04	2.16	2.79	2.36	2.88	2.83	2.28	3.09	2.36

Table 9.3 (continued)

State	Average PT on OOH as % of household income		Variation across income deciles in burden of PT on OOH		Residential homestead ETR, higher-valued property, largest urban area		Ratio, high-valued homestead ETR to lower-valued homestead ETR	Commercial ETR, largest urban area		Industrial ETR, largest urban area		Ratio, commercial ETR to residential		Ratio, industrial ETR to residential	
	1999	2006	1999	2006	2000	2004	2004	2000	2004	2000	2004	2000	2004	2000	2004
Kentucky	2.1	2.3	94.1	75.4	1.10	1.09	1.00	1.44	1.23	1.46	0.81	1.31	1.12	1.33	0.74
Louisiana	1.1	1.6	119.6	98.0	0.62	0.89	12.44	2.28	2.43	2.33	2.49	3.65	2.72	3.74	2.79
Maine	4.3	5.2	93.2	94.6	1.72	2.12	1.09	2.40	2.28	1.92	1.90	1.40	1.07	1.12	0.90
Maryland	4.1	4.3	102.3	104.0	1.57	2.24	1.00	2.89	2.77	1.44	1.37	1.84	1.24	0.92	0.61
Massachusetts	5.7	6.5	112.6	119.5	0.74	0.18	6.02	2.85	3.01	1.71	1.65	3.87	16.42	2.32	9.04
Michigan	4.3	5.4	98.3	99.9	2.23	3.20	1.00	3.87	4.02	3.10	3.28	1.74	1.26	1.39	1.02
Minnesota	3.9	3.9	90.0	92.0	1.06	1.25	1.29	3.64	2.69	2.29	2.05	3.45	2.16	2.17	1.65
Mississippi	1.7	2.1	114.1	112.4	0.93	1.34	1.22	2.16	2.54	1.78	2.03	2.32	1.90	1.92	1.52
Missouri	2.5	3.2	86.2	94.1	1.03	1.43	1.00	2.73	2.80	2.13	2.20	2.66	1.95	2.07	1.53
Montana	3.9	4.3	103.5	101.4	0.69	1.37	0.99	1.27	1.73	1.01	1.39	1.83	1.27	1.46	1.02
Nebraska	4.7	5.2	86.0	76.2	1.34	2.03	1.00	1.79	2.07	1.47	1.69	1.33	1.02	1.09	0.83
Nevada	3.2	3.8	101.8	112.1	0.80	1.12	1.00	1.08	1.13	0.87	0.91	1.36	1.01	1.09	0.81
New Hampshire	7.5	8.1	92.6	98.4	2.06	1.72	1.00	2.62	1.43	1.37	0.86	1.27	0.83	0.67	0.50
New Jersey	8.8	10.5	108.1	114.2	2.02	2.00	1.47	3.38	1.94	2.03	1.17	1.67	0.97	1.00	0.58
New Mexico	2.3	2.6	110.5	116.4	0.07	1.06	1.09	1.21	1.34	1.00	1.11	1.73	1.26	1.43	1.05
New York	7.0	7.9	97.0	101.4	0.62	0.61	2.42	3.42	3.92	2.05	2.35	5.50	6.39	3.30	3.84
North Carolina	2.5	3.1	101.1	104.0	0.85	1.13	1.00	1.14	1.14	0.92	0.91	1.35	1.00	1.09	0.81

220

State															
North Dakota	3.5	4.2	98.7	94.6	1.46	2.02	1.00	1.83	1.88	1.10	1.13	1.25	0.93	0.75	0.56
Ohio	3.8	4.6	89.6	96.5	1.03	1.19	1.00	1.80	1.48	1.78	1.90	1.76	1.24	1.73	1.60
Oklahoma	1.9	2.2	98.0	90.3	0.79	1.15	1.11	1.18	1.28	1.30	1.39	1.49	1.11	1.65	1.21
Oregon	4.6	4.9	95.6	96.7	1.53	2.23	1.00	2.03	2.23	1.63	1.78	1.33	1.00	1.07	0.80
Pennsylvania	4.7	5.5	96.3	101.1	1.96	2.19	1.00	3.40	1.83	2.04	1.10	1.73	0.83	1.04	0.50
Rhode Island	6.2	7.3	100.6	121.0	1.79	2.08	1.00	4.40	3.51	2.43	2.67	2.46	1.69	1.35	1.28
South Carolina	2.1	2.5	106.5	115.1	0.57	1.48	1.24	1.51	2.97	2.08	3.73	2.65	2.01	3.66	2.52
South Dakota	4.1	4.1	94.3	89.8	1.34	1.50	1.00	2.17	1.73	1.30	1.04	1.62	1.16	0.97	0.69
Tennessee	2.6	2.8	101.6	94.9	1.19	1.73	1.00	2.48	2.67	1.90	2.04	2.08	1.54	1.60	1.18
Texas	3.9	5.5	91.0	95.5	2.04	2.24	1.13	2.77	2.74	2.84	2.96	1.36	1.23	1.39	1.33
Utah	2.4	2.8	88.8	95.6	0.72	0.86	1.00	1.42	1.57	1.14	1.26	1.98	1.83	1.58	1.47
Vermont	6.8	7.9	99.2	102.5	1.60	1.90	1.00	2.56	2.28	2.04	1.94	1.60	1.20	1.27	1.02
Virginia	2.8	3.8	86.9	86.5	0.99	1.24	1.00	1.77	1.49	1.11	1.28	1.79	1.20	1.12	1.04
Washington	4.3	5.0	97.3	94.2	0.82	0.98	1.00	1.11	0.98	0.91	0.79	1.36	1.01	1.11	0.81
West Virginia	1.4	1.8	105.5	96.3	0.51	0.82	1.00	1.82	1.73	1.80	1.77	3.57	2.11	3.54	2.16
Wisconsin	5.7	6.8	88.0	96.3	1.91	2.48	1.04	2.68	2.51	1.47	2.02	1.41	1.01	0.77	0.82
Wyoming	2.3	2.0	105.7	109.2	0.53	0.67	1.00	0.71	0.67	0.69	0.64	1.33	1.00	1.29	0.97
Average	3.67	4.3	98.92	102.17	1.14	1.42	1.49	2.26	2.09	1.73	1.69	2.18	1.92	1.75	1.49
Coef. Of Variation	47.0	46.1	9.6	15.6	46.6	43.0	49.0	38.5	41.1	41.6	45.4	117.4	49.7	86.9	

Notes: Abbreviations: OOC, owner-occupied housing; PT, property tax; ETR, effective tax rate.

Sources: Calculations for 2000 and 2004, Minnesota Taxpayers Association (2001, 2005); calculations for 1999 and 2006, *Census of Population and Housing* and *Annual Community Survey.*

assumed percentage of gross rent. In 21 states, circuit-breakers only apply to elderly homeowners and renters. For three states, special additional relief is available for elderly renters or homeowners above that provided to all renters and homeowners. Overall, special provisions exist that are applicable to only elderly homeowners in 22 states and elderly renters in 18 states, with 17 states having special provisions for both. The magnitude of relief includes a credit of up to the full property tax liability in Maryland, and of any amount over 3 percent of income in Hawaii. Nearly all other states cap absolute maximum credit amounts, but 11 cap this at $1000 or more. The maximum equals or exceeds $2000 for Maine, New Jersey and Oregon, with New Jersey's program available to all homeowners and renters and Oregon's available to elderly renters.

Deferral programs also exist in 22 states plus the District of Columbia which allow portions of property tax payments to be deferred until sale of the property or for a specified period of time (Table 9.2). These programs are less universal, with only three applying deferrals to all homeowners and 22 limiting eligibility to the elderly or disabled (and one only to the disabled). In addition to state programs, numerous localities also offer deferrals in cases of hardship to relieve excess property tax burdens.

Property Tax Reliance

Still, public attitudes are reflected in patterns of reliance on the tax (see Figure 9.2). Use of the property tax for local government finance has been in decline for the past 40 years. The period of greatest decline (from 1961 to 1981) was the era of California's Proposition 13 and the flurry of property tax constraints.

However, the relative shift away from the property tax does not provide the full picture. Over that same period, the property tax burden, adjusted for inflation, has been increasing at a near unrelenting pace (Figure 9.3). Total real property tax collections grew from $84,602.8 million to $290,828.9 million, measured in constant 2000 dollars, a compound annual rate of 2.9 percent. The growth rate was only slightly interrupted in the late 1970s to early 1980s. Since 1982, after a subsidence of the initial wave of 'property tax revolts', the compound annual growth rate has been 3.7 percent. Property tax collections have been increasing more rapidly than inflation, by a considerable amount. However, as a share of income, property taxes declined until 2000, then increased with escalating residential property values. Still, as a portion of income, 2007 property taxes are 22 percent lower than in 1961 (0.0327 in 2007 versus 0.0420 in 1961, see Figure 9.4).

The average burden (local property tax collections in a state divided by

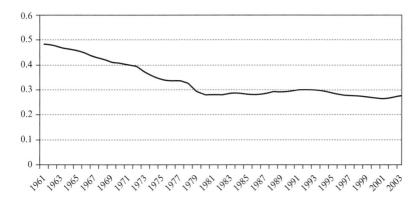

Figure 9.2   Local property tax as share of local general revenue, 1961–2004

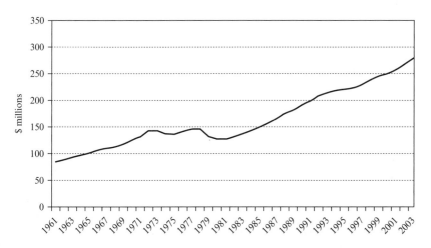

Figure 9.3   Real state and local property tax, 1961–2004 (2000 dollars)

state personal income) imposed by local property taxes across individual states in 2006 was equal to 3 percent of state personal income. This is down 27 percent from 1972 levels (3.8 percent) and essentially unchanged (up 0.1 percent) from 1999 (see Table 9.4). The variation between states in this burden is also lower in 2006 than for 1972 and only very slightly greater than 1999. The highest burdens are in the Northeast, specifically New Jersey (5.1 percent), Maine (5.1 percent), Rhode Island (4.7 percent), New Hampshire (4.6 percent), New York (4.5 percent) and Connecticut (4.3 percent). These six states also had the highest relative property tax

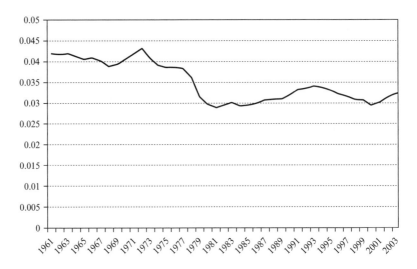

Figure 9.4   Property tax as share of personal income, US totals,
*   1961–2004*

burdens in 1999, though only New Jersey and Connecticut were in the top
eight for 1972. In all cases (except Rhode Island) these burdens were lower
than or equal (Maine) to burdens in 1972. For two, 1999 burdens were
higher than in 2006 (New Jersey and Rhode Island). Lowest burdens are
generally in the South, at less than 2 percent of personal income. Vermont
also enters the ranks of states with the lowest local property tax burden
for 2006 after its 1997 Act 60 education finance reforms. However, in
Vermont, local control of property taxes for education was replaced by
state control. The result is that Vermont has, by far, the highest state property tax burden. For the nation as a whole, the state government property
tax burden is 0.1 percent. Among the other ten states with the lowest local
property tax burdens, the state burden is negligible to non-existent. In
Vermont, state property taxes are 3.7 percent of personal income, resulting in a combined state–local property tax burden of 5.4 percent, making
it tied with New Hampshire for the highest combined (state and local)
property tax burden in the nation. For Vermont, this burden exists under
significantly impaired local choice.

   Property taxes have declined from an average of 40 percent of local
general revenue across states in 1972 to 29 percent in 1999 and 2006.
Irrespective of the growth in housing values and property taxes larger
share of personal income, property taxes as a portion of local revenue did
not grow between 1999 and 2006, as local revenue from other sources kept
pace. Local revenue bases have certainly become more diversified since

Table 9.4   Relative reliance on local property taxes by states, 1972, 1999 and 2006

Rank	Local property taxes as a portion of state personal income			Local property taxes as a portion of local general revenue		
	1972	1999	2006	1972	1999	2006
1	Massachusetts 0.063	New Hampshire 0.054	New Jersey 0.051	New Hampshire 0.68	New Hampshire 0.70	Connecticut 0.557
2	South Dakota 0.063	New Jersey 0.050	Maine 0.051	Massachusetts 0.66	Rhode Island 0.66	New Hampshire 0.543
3	Montana 0.058	Maine 0.049	Rhode Island 0.049	Connecticut 0.66	Connecticut 0.55	Rhode Island 0.533
4	California 0.058	Rhode Island 0.044	New Hampshire 0.044	Vermont 0.65	New Jersey 0.52	New Jersey 0.528
5	New Jersey 0.055	New York 0.040	New York 0.040	Maine 0.65	Maine 0.50	Maine 0.512
6	Connecticut 0.055	Connecticut 0.040	Connecticut 0.040	South Dakota 0.60	Massachusetts 0.42	Hawaii 0.457
7	New Hampshire 0.054	Alaska 0.039	Wisconsin 0.039	Rhode Island 0.59	Hawaii 0.42	Massachusetts 0.423
8	Wisconsin 0.054	Wisconsin 0.038	Indiana 0.038	Montana 0.59	South Dakota 0.38	Texas 0.392
9	Iowa 0.053	Illinois 0.037	Texas 0.037	New Jersey 0.55	Illinois 0.38	Illinois 0.363
10	New York 0.052	Texas 0.035	Illinois 0.035	Indiana 0.52	Texas 0.35	Wisconsin 0.355
11	Vermont 0.052	Iowa 0.035	Nebraska 0.035	Nebraska 0.51	Nebraska 0.34	South Dakota 0.349
12	Minnesota 0.051	Nebraska 0.034	Massachusetts 0.034	Oregon 0.50	Montana 0.33	Indiana 0.342
13	Nebraska 0.051	Montana 0.034	Alaska 0.034	Iowa 0.50	Indiana 0.33	Nebraska 0.335
14	Maine 0.051	South Dakota 0.034	Wyoming 0.034	Kansas 0.49	Virginia 0.32	Virginia 0.322
15	Indiana 0.049	Massachusetts 0.034	Florida 0.034	Illinois 0.49	Wisconsin 0.32	North Dakota 0.322
36	Virginia 0.026	Missouri 0.023	North Carolina 0.023	Virginia 0.31	Utah 0.23	Tennessee 0.231
37	Oklahoma 0.025	California 0.022	Minnesota 0.022	Maryland 0.31	Delaware 0.22	North Carolina 0.228
38	Tennessee 0.025	North Carolina 0.022	Washington 0.022	West Virginia 0.30	Wyoming 0.22	Delaware 0.216
39	Mississippi 0.024	West Virginia 0.022	Maryland 0.022	Nevada 0.30	Mississippi 0.22	Minnesota 0.215
40	North Carolina 0.023	Nevada 0.021	Tennessee 0.021	South Carolina 0.29	Tennessee 0.21	Mississippi 0.207
41	West Virginia 0.022	Washington 0.021	Hawaii 0.021	Arkansas 0.28	North Carolina 0.21	Washington 0.206
42	Hawaii 0.022	Tennessee 0.022	West Virginia 0.019	Tennessee 0.28	Washington 0.20	Nevada 0.205
43	South Carolina 0.022	Hawaii 0.022	Louisiana 0.018	North Carolina 0.27	Nevada 0.19	Kentucky 0.185

Table 9.4 (continued)

Rank	Local property tax as a portion of state personal income			Local property taxes as a portion of local general revenue		
	1972	1999	2006	1972	1999	2006
44	Arkansas 0.022	Arkansas 0.017	Delaware 0.016	Kentucky 0.25	Arkansas 0.19	Oklahoma 0.182
45	Louisiana 0.019	Louisiana 0.016	Oklahoma 0.016	Mississippi 0.24	California 0.17	California 0.181
46	New Mexico 0.019	Oklahoma 0.016	Kentucky 0.016	Delaware 0.23	Kentucky 0.17	Vermont 0.165
47	Alaska 0.019	Delaware 0.015	New Mexico 0.015	Louisiana 0.19	Oklahoma 0.17	Louisiana 0.149
48	Delaware 0.018	New Mexico 0.015	Vermont 0.015	New Mexico 0.18	Louisiana 0.15	New Mexico 0.134
49	Kentucky 0.018	Kentucky 0.014	Alabama 0.014	Alaska 0.18	New Mexico 0.12	Alabama 0.112
50	Alabama 0.010	Alabama 0.010	Arkansas 0.010	Alabama 0.12	Alabama 0.10	Arkansas 0.102
Cross-50-state average	0.038	0.029	0.030		0.4	0.29
Coefficient of variation	37.11	33.2	33.7		34.74	37.6
1	Vermont 8.68	Rhode Island 5.55	Connecticut 4.13	New Hampshire 5.71	Hawaii 5.45	Hawaii 4.174
2	Connecticut 8.50	Connecticut 5.10	Rhode Island 3.84	Massachusetts 5.04	Connecticut 3.99	Connecticut 1.848
3	Rhode Island 8.49	New Hampshire 5.00	New Hampshire 3.58	Hawaii 4.48	New Hampshire 2.12	New Hampshire 1.831
4	Maine 7.66	New Jersey 3.27	New Jersey 3.27	South Dakota 3.71	New Jersey 1.84	New Jersey 1.797
5	New Hampshire 6.62	Massachusetts 3.24	Maine 3.24	Connecticut 3.35	Rhode Island 1.76	Rhode Island 1.749
6	Massachusetts 6.54	Maine 3.15	Massachusetts 3.15	Maine 3.05	Maine 1.72	Maine 1.714
7	New Jersey 5.48	Vermont 2.43	Wisconsin 2.16	Montana 2.71	South Dakota 1.42	Texas 1.586
8	South Dakota 4.42	Illinois 1.94	Hawaii 2.14	Vermont 2.58	Texas 1.29	South Dakota 1.349
9	Montana 4.06	South Dakota 1.92	South Dakota 1.77	Nebraska 2.56	Illinois 1.24	Illinois 1.304
10	Illinois 3.97	Wisconsin 1.79	Virginia 1.73	Rhode Island 2.23	Nebraska 1.2	Nebraska 1.286
11	Wisconsin 3.72	Virginia 1.64	New York 1.68	Oregon 2.15	Colorado 1.12	Florida 1.225
12	Hawaii 3.46	Maryland 1.54	Illinois 1.68	New Jersey 2.11	Massachusetts 1.09	Massachusetts 1.140
13	California 3.27	Hawaii 1.50	Texas 1.63	Indiana 1.84	Montana 1.03	Colorado 1.071
14	Indiana 3.19	New York 1.49	Maryland 1.55	Ohio 1.83	Virginia 1.01	Indiana 1.039
15	New York 3.03	Texas 1.46	Pennsylvania 1.53	Illinois 1.76	Maryland 0.96	Virginia 0.970

	Oklahoma	Florida	Kentucky	Virginia	Washington	North Carolina
36	Oklahoma 1.48	Florida 0.84	Kentucky 0.02	Virginia 0.88	Washington 0.55	North Carolina 0.600
37	Washington 1.41	South Carolina 0.79	North Carolina 0.02	Minnesota 0.86	Mississippi 0.54	Nevada 0.564
38	Florida 1.36	Washington 0.73	South Carolina 0.03	Maryland 0.80	North Carolina 0.53	West Virginia 0.557
39	South Carolina 1.31	Arkansas 0.71	Minnesota 0.02	Arkansas 0.79	West Virginia 0.52	Mississippi 0.500
40	Tennessee 1.30	Tennessee 0.70	New Mexico 0.02	New York 0.75	Nevada 0.51	Oklahoma 0.496
41	Delaware 1.25	Nevada 0.70	Tennessee 0.02	West Virginia 0.70	Vermont 0.49	Kentucky 0.472
42	Nevada 1.19	North Carolina 0.69	Washington 0.02	Kentucky 0.67	Michigan 0.49	Minnesota 0.470
43	Kentucky 1.15	California 0.69	Nevada 0.03	South Carolina 0.67	Oklahoma 0.47	Delaware 0.459
44	Georgia 1.14	Mississippi 0.63	Oklahoma 0.02	Mississippi 0.54	Delaware 0.46	Louisiana 0.436
45	Louisiana 1.05	Wyoming 0.63	Wyoming 0.04	North Carolina 0.52	Arkansas 0.46	California 0.419
46	New Mexico 1.03	Kentucky 0.63	California 0.02	Delaware 0.48	Kentucky 0.44	Alabama 0.328
47	Arkansas 1.02	Louisiana 0.58	Louisiana 0.02	Louisiana 0.45	Louisiana 0.43	New Mexico 0.268
48	Mississippi 0.94	New Mexico 0.57	Mississippi 0.03	Alaska 0.37	California 0.37	Vermont 0.247
49	Alaska 0.72	Oklahoma 0.54	Arkansas 0.01	New Mexico 0.36	Alabama 0.36	Arkansas 0.197
50	Alabama 0.43	Alabama 0.33	Alabama 0.01	Alabama 0.34	New Mexico 0.34	Missouri 0.092
Cross-50-state average	2.92	1.46	1.50	1.48	1.48	0.99
Coefficient of variation	71.16	79.24	74.9	64.62	88.22	68.4

1972, and the extremes of property tax reliance have tempered a little more between 1999 and 2006. With the exception of New York, it is not surprising to find that in states with higher property tax burdens the property tax also comprises a higher portion of local general revenue. Local property tax burdens in New York are the fifth-highest among the states; however, property taxes as a portion of local general revenue are 25th among the states, reflective of the revenue diversification of New York local governments and their significant fiscal presence.

As an offset to the long-term secular decline in the relative role of property taxes in financing local government, the relative importance of fee and charge revenue and intergovernmental transfers from the state have increased. On average, fee, charge and miscellaneous revenue increased from approximately one-third of property tax revenue across states in 1972, to 68 percent of it by 1999, and 66 percent in 2006. Variation in the role of fees and charges across states has been and remains substantial, with a coefficient of variation of 75 percent. States with local governments least reliant on fees and charges are concentrated in the Northeast, with those most reliant concentrated in the South and Southwest. Intergovernmental revenue from states has continued to grow, predominantly driven by changes in the relative state–local role in education finance. In 1972, state transfers were equal to two-thirds of property tax revenue across states. By 2006, state transfers were 8 percent greater than local property tax revenue. The relative importance of transfers continued to increase between 1999 and 2006. The variation between states is also quite substantial and local governments in some states are much more reliant on transfers in 2006 than during earlier periods. Again, New England states (and Hawaii, due to the absence of local responsibility for education) are less reliant on transfers and more reliant on property taxes. At the other extreme, in Missouri, with a moderate property tax burden (due partly to local sales and income taxes) local governments receive approximately ten times more revenue from state aid than from property taxes. Arkansas receives five times as much, and Vermont and New Mexico receive approximately four times. This dependency has significantly increased even since 1999 and has potentially serious implications for local choice.

Distribution of Homestead Property Tax Burdens

Average effective tax burdens
Even with classification, homestead exemptions, circuit-breakers and deferrals, rising property tax burdens and unpopularity of the property tax have aided the imposition of TELs. A major practical concern is the relationship between the property tax payment and the income of the

household. Because homes are purchased on the basis of lifetime economic status, the property tax can become burdensome relative to annual household income. This is a frequent source of discontent and criticism of the tax. The Minnesota Taxpayers Association 50-state property tax study (see Table 9.3) suggests that the average effective tax rate on higher-valued residential homestead property in each state's largest urban areas increased by 25 percent between 2000 and 2004 (from 1.14 to 1.42 percent), with the highest burdens occurring in Michigan, Wisconsin, Connecticut, Maryland, Texas and Oregon (with rates above 2.2 percent). There is great variation within states evident in comparing the 2000 and 2004 studies. Alternatively, data from the American Community Survey (ACS) find that the median household's self-reporting of property tax payments for 2007 across 775 counties results in a cross-county average residential effective tax rate of less than 1.9 percent in each state, with the highs being in Texas, Nebraska, Wisconsin, New Hampshire and New Jersey. The ACS also shows that across surveyed counties in the US, average effective tax rates (taxes as a portion of housing value for the median-valued home) actually declined between 1999 and 2006, suggesting that public choice processes have not been entirely ineffective at mitigating increases.

Still, the ACS also shows that between 2000 and 2006, average household property tax burdens (measured as taxes as a portion of household income) increased in 46 of the 50 states (Mikesell and Mullins, 2008a, Table 4; see Table 9.3) and in 20 states the annual growth rate has been 3 percent or greater. This occurred at a time when median effective tax rates in urban counties actually declined between 1999 and 2006, while median burden increased by 13 percent (Mikesell and Mullins, 2008b). This was due to a 56 percent increase in median property value coupled with a median household income increase of 17 percent. So, unabated, property tax burden increases might have been significantly higher, implying that local rate-setting policy has been responsive to popular and political concerns about this increasing burden in rolling back property tax rates. This suggests that local public choice processes have been more than somewhat successful in holding local officials accountable, calling into question the efficacy of the flurry of statewide intervention.

Vertical equity
However, property tax burdens are not proportional to income. In fact, based on micro-household data for 1999–2006, property tax burdens across the United States are a declining function of income. On average, burdens decline 6 percent for each $10,000 increase in household income (Mikesell and Mullins, 2008a). This suggests that either property tax rates or property valuation methods (or both) and/or the ratio of property value

*Table 9.5   Distribution and determinants of household property tax
           burdens (only quintile coefficients are reported). Dependent
           variable: property tax burden as % of household income, in log
           form*

Quintile distribution	Parameter estimate	t-value
Household income quintile 1	0.85164	1088.37
Household income quintile 2	0.14439	208.03
Household income quintile 3	−0.12260	−183.94
Household income quintile 4	−0.30443	−461.27
Household income quintile 5	−0.56900	−610.56
Coefficient of determination	0.34	
(R-Square)		

Source: Mikesell and Mullins (2008a).

to household income varies across and within states and substate areas in
a manner that levies higher relative taxes on the incomes of lower-income
households. Again, this occurs irrespective of the nearly universal application of homestead exemptions. Table 9.5 displays the relative distribution
of property tax burdens (tax/household income) across income quintiles,
after controlling for household, demographic, fiscal and structural factors.
These results clearly demonstrate a declining property tax burden with
income. This occurs in the face of findings by the Minnesota Taxpayers
Association suggesting that, on average, the effective tax rate on property
is higher for higher-valued property across the states.

Based on the ACS, the lowest household income quintile averages a
property tax burden 85 percent higher than the average across all households (and 97 percent greater than the average for quintile 3), with the
second quintile averaging a 14 percent higher burden (27 percent greater
than quintile 3). Higher-income quintiles face successively and significantly lower burdens (with 30 percent and 57 percent lower relative effective burdens, respectively). Variations in property tax burdens across
states and within household income decile are also considerable. Without
controlling for other factors, burdens for the second income decile are
2.8 times greater than the ninth income decile, and in each decile annual
burdens have increased consistently between 2000 and 2006 (Table 9.6).
Variations in burdens are also most substantial within lower income
deciles. Within individual states, the average coefficient of variation in
property tax burdens across income deciles in 1999 was 98.9 percent; by
2006 this variation had increased slightly to 102.2 percent (Table 9.3).
States experiencing the greatest variation in burdens across income groups

*Table 9.6   Residential property tax burden (as % of household income)
by income decile and coefficient of variation across states,
2000–2006*

Decile	2000		2006	
	(t/i) %	CV	(t/i) %	CV
1	17.7	73.4	25.5	70.7
2	5.8	58.3	8.1	61.1
3	4.2	59.7	5.8	58.2
4	3.5	57.3	4.7	57.8
5	3.1	52.8	4.1	54.8
6	2.8	55.6	3.7	53.3
7	2.5	50.6	3.3	51.7
8	2.4	49.9	3.1	49.2
9	2.3	45.8	2.9	46.8
10	1.9	42.0	2.4	41.6

Source: Mikesell and Mullins (2008a).

include Alaska (165 percent), DC (157 percent), Massachusetts (120 percent), New Mexico (116 percent), Alabama (115 percent) and South Carolina (115 percent). Those with the least variation are Kentucky (75 percent), Idaho (80 percent), Nebraska (76 percent), Iowa (83 percent) and Illinois (83 percent). Still, the least of these variations remain substantial, suggesting that the lack of uniformity in burdens may be a factor in the popular resentment of the property tax.

These outcomes engender opposition to the tax. Administration and structural provisions of property taxation and local finance are not neutral in affecting these burdens. Burdens are affected by classification systems, full disclosure programs, circuit-breakers, deferral programs, alternative revenue options (and home rule), tax base competition, judicial education mandates and acquisition value assessment systems (Mikesell and Mullins, 2008a, 2008b).

NON-LOCAL PURSUITS

Irrespective of issues with the property tax withstanding, the impetus for local limitations appears neither local nor grass-roots.[6] By definition, they provide little local discretion in application of their provisions to individual jurisdictions, and thus seriously limit local choice and the ability of local populations to pursue local community and public service goals.[7] Despite the broad-brush application, effects of these limitations across jurisdiction are non-uniform. They impose differential welfare losses across classes of communities depending on how binding a particular provision is in an individual setting. Governments in different phases of growth and maturity, and with populations with different preferences and capacities for the outputs from the public sector, are affected differently, producing simultaneously arbitrary and biased outcomes. The imposition of fiscal uniformity across areas with diverse preference and population bases is a prescription for inefficiency and dissatisfaction.[8] Adaptive behavior is likely in an attempt to avoid welfare loss created by an arbitrary policy wedge between public service demands and resource access. Adaptations provide second-best solutions and create their own set of distortions. Likely outcomes include: (1) most successful adaptation by localities possessing the greatest resource slack and resource options; (2) emergence of ever greater layers of complexity between citizens of states and localities and the governance structures intended to service their needs and preferences (see Sheffrin, 1998); and (3) a new set of barriers to the maintenance of adequate public service levels in areas of greatest need.

CHARACTERISTICS OF TELS

Detailed inventories of tax and expenditure limitations have been provided elsewhere (Mullins and Cox, 1995; Mullins, 2004; Mullins and Wallin, 2004). Here we provide an updated overview of characteristics and the incidence of their imposition and summary tables.

Local Government TELS

Forty-seven states have some form of constitutional or statutory statewide limitation on the fiscal behavior of their units of local government; only Connecticut, New Hampshire and Vermont have none (Maine adopted limitations on property tax levies and on general expenditures in 2005).[9] Four additional states have adopted only limited full disclosure requirements since 1970.[10] While tax and expenditure limitations on local governments existed as far back as the late nineteenth century, their imposition greatly accelerated in the latter part of the twentieth century. Seventeen states adopted some type of fiscal limitation on their local units of government between 1970 and 1976, and half (50 percent) of those currently in existence were adopted after 1977.

   Local tax and expenditure limitations are generally classified into seven basic forms:

- overall property tax rate limits applying to all local governments;
- specific property tax rate limits applying to specific types of local government (municipalities, counties, school districts and special districts) or specific functions;
- property tax levy (revenue) limits;
- general revenue increase limits;
- general expenditure increase limits;
- limits on assessment increases; and
- full disclosure (truth-in-taxation) (Joyce and Mullins, 1991).

The scope of these limitations vary greatly in terms of the bindingness of the constraint (weak to strong) and the range, types and numbers of local governments affected.

Table 9.7 summarizes local limits across types. The most prevalent is the property tax rate limitation imposed on specific forms of local government (33 states have imposed this,[11] with 31 limiting municipalities, 28 counties, 26 school districts and 23 all three types). Thirty states have limited the size of the tax levy by their local units of government (26 for counties, 25 for municipalities, 17 for school districts and 17 for all three). Twenty-two states have a full disclosure requirement; however, only 18 require a roll-back of property rates to a level not to exceed the previous year's levy. Overall property tax rate limits are in effect in 13 states, while 14 have enacted limits on the growth of property assessments.[12] Most broadly, nine states limit expenditure growth in their local governments, while two limit general revenue increases.[13] A combination of two or more of these limitations exists in 40 states.

While limitations have been enacted throughout the United States (at least 125 overall), there are regional patterns. They are most prevalent in Western states (44), and least employed in the Northeast (13) (Table 9.8). Midwestern states are second in terms of TELS, followed closely by Southern states.[14]

Limitations in the Western states are not only more prevalent, but they are also more restrictive. They often apply to all local government units, and have constraints limits and stronger provisions for override. Western states are also more apt to have multiple limitations in effect.

Most of these restrictions on local revenue raising and spending have come in rather recent times, as noted above, and usually through ballot initiatives. Indeed, during the 1990s there were more than 150 such measures put on the ballot (Brunori, 1999). Very significant limitations have been enacted in several states since 1995, including California, Washington, Oregon, New Mexico, Oklahoma and Maine.[15] While the pace of adoption has slowed, the character of constraints being enacted has strengthened.

Table 9.7 Summary of state-imposed limitations on local governments – number of states by characteristic

Type of Limitation	Occurrence	Scope/classification	Growth provisions	Exclusions	Override provisions
Overall property tax rate limits (13)	Prior to 1978: 8 1978 or after: 5 (Adopted or mod. 1990+: 2)	Multiple Classifications: 12 Residential Only: 1	Not applicable.	Debt service: 9 Special/excess levies: 7 Home rule: 2 Special dst: 1	Referenda: Simple majority: 5 Supermajority: 1 Legislative: 1 Temporary: 2
Specific property tax rate limits (33)	Prior to 1978: 28 1978 or after: 5 (Adopted or mod. 1990+: 8)	Counties: 28 Municipalities: 31 School dst.: 26 All: 23	Not applicable.	Debt service: 23 Special levies: 19 Home rule: 3	Referenda: Simple majority: 20 Supermajority: 3 Legislative: 1
Property tax levy limits (30)	Prior to 1978: 11 1978 or after: 19 (Adopted or mod. 1990+: 9)	Counties: 26 Municipalities: 25 School dst.: 17 All: 17	Fixed %: 16 Base growth: 3 Inflation: 4 Income: 1 Fixed $ amount: 2 Limited to assessment rollback: 7	Debt service: 12 Annex., improvements, construction: 9 Capital improvements: 2 Contracts: 2 Emergencies: 2 Mandates:1 Home rule:1	Referenda: Simple majority: 12 Supermajority: 3 State board: 1 Court appeal: 1 Leg. majority: 1 Petition for referenda:1 Leg. 4/5: 1
General revenue limits (4)	Prior to 1978: 1 1978 or after: 3 (Adopted or mod. 1990+: 2)	Counties: 3 Municipalities: 3 School Dst.: 2 All: 1	Fixed %/$: 2 Base growth: 1 Inflation/CPI: 2 No new tax or rate increase: 1	Debt service: 1 Special assessments: 1 Court judgments: 1	Referenda: Simple majority: 2

General expenditure limits (9)	Prior to 1978: 6 1978 or after: 3 (Adopted or mod. 1990+: 4)	Counties: 5 Municipalities: 6 School dst.: 9 All: 5	Fixed %: 3 Inflation/CPI: 4 Base growth: 2 Income: 3 Pupils: 3	Debt service: 2 Mandates: 2 Emergencies: 3 Special dst.: 2 Special education: 2 Contracts: 2	Referenda: Simple majority: 7 Legislative: Simple majority: 1 Supermajority: 1 State board: 1
Property assessment limits (14)	Prior to 1978: 1 1978 or after: 13 (Adopted or mod. 1990+: 9)	Base: Individual parcel: 11 Aggregate: 2 Residential only: 3	Fixed %: 11 (% range: 2–10, ave. 4.9) Fixed % or CPI: 1	Reassessment on sale: 4 Improvements/new construction: 11	Referenda: Simple majority: 1
Full disclosure limits (22) (18 w/rollback)	Prior to 1978: 7 1978 or after: 15 (Adopted or mod. 1990+: 5)	Counties: 21 Municipalities: 19 School dst.: 14 All: 14 Limited to reassessment: 2	Not applicable.	Debt service: 2 New construction/additions: 2 Annexation: 1 Within specified %: 4	Not applicable.

Source: Mullins (2003), Table 5.2, updated through 2008 from various state websites and sources (see chapter text). Original source based on Mullins and Cox (1995).

235

Table 9.8   Regional distribution of local government tax and expenditure limitations – number of states imposing limitations

Type of limitation	North-east (of 9 states)	Midwest (of 12 states)	South (of 16 states)	West (of 13 states)	U.S. 50 State Total #	U.S. 50 State Total %
Overall property tax rate limit	0	3	3	7	13	26
Specific property tax rate limit	3	10	9	11	33	66
Property tax revenue limit	6	8	6	10	30	60
Assessment increase limit	1	2	6	5	14	28
General revenue limit	0	2	0	2	4	8
General expenditure limit	2	4	0	3	9	18
Full disclosure	1	5	10	6	22	44
Total number of limitations	13	34	34	44	125	
Total number w/o full disclosure	12	29	24	38	103	
Ave. limits per state	1.44	2.83	2.12	3.39		
Ave. limits per state w/o full disclosure	1.33	2.42	1.50	2.92		

Source: Author's update and compilation based on Mullins and Cox (1995).

Formula-based limitations on revenue increases are more prominent, as is broad application across government form (counties, municipalities and school districts).

State Government TELS

The focus of most of the more recent tax and expenditure limitations has been state governments. While before 1970 only two states had TELS in place, there are now 56 limitations in 35 states (see Table 9.9). Thirty-one have been adopted since 1990, in 24 states. The most recent have been enacted in Oregon, Kentucky, Indiana, Massachusetts, Ohio and Wisconsin, with Oregon, Massachusetts and Washington adding newer provisions to their existing state limitations. These TELS range from very stringent to relatively mild. Twenty-seven of these states do allow for legislative override of the limits, but usually with a minimum of three-fifths vote.

Eighteen states have 28 revenue limits in place, while 27 states budget under 28 expenditure limitations. Nine states have provisions limiting both. Direct limits on total taxes or income taxes are in effect in 22 states,

Table 9.9 *State-level tax, revenue and expenditure limitations*

State	Adoption method	Statutory/ constitutional	Revenue limit	Expenditure limit	Growth restriction	Override provision	Exemptions
Alaska	R	Con		1982 (A)	POP/CPI	3/4 L	C
Arizona	R	Con		1978 (AT)	INC	2/3 L	
	R	Con	1979 (T)		T	2/3 L	
	I	Con	1992 (T)		T	2/3 L	
Arkansas	L	Con	1934 (T)		T	3/4 L	
California	I	Con	1978 (T)		T	2/3 L	
	I	Con		1979 (AT)	INC	EM	
Colorado	L	Stat		1991 (GF)	INC or 6%	EM – 2/3 L	
	I	Con	1992(T)		T, Refund	EM – 2/3 L V	
	I	Con		1992 (E)	POP/CPI	EM – 2/3 L V	
	R	Con	2005	Revenue and spending limit suspended until 2011			
Connecticut	R	Con		1992 (A)	INC/CPI	EM – 3/5 L	D,G,M,BR
Delaware	R	Con		1978 (GF)	PCT	EM – 3/5 L	
	I	Con	1980/81(T)		T	3/5 L	D
Florida	R	Con	1971 (CIT)		T	3/5 L	
	R	Con	1994 (R)		INC	2/3 L	
	I	Con	1996 (T)		T	2/3 V	
Kentucky[1]	R	Con	2000 (T)		3/5 L	3/5 L	
Hawaii	CC	Con		1978 (GF)	ECN	2/3 L	Odd years
Idaho	L	Stat		1980/94 (GF)	INC	2/3 L	N-R

237

Table 9.9 (continued)

State	Adoption method	Statutory/ constitutional	Revenue limit	Expenditure limit	Growth restriction	Override provision	Exemptions
Indiana	L?	Stat		2002 (E)	Formula		
Iowa	L	Stat		1992 (GF)	PCT		
Louisiana	L	Stat	1979 (T)		INC	L	
	R	Con		1993 (GF)	INC	2/3 L	
	I	Con	1996 (T)		T	2/3 L	
Maine		Stat		2005 (E)	INC/2.75%		
Maryland	L	Stat		1979 (E)	ECN	L	Advisory
Massachusetts	I	Stat	1986 (T)		WAGES	L	
	I	Con	2000 (IT)				Amendable
Michigan	I	Con	1978		INC	2/3 L-EM	
	R	Con	1994 (SPT)		3/4 L	3/4 L	
Mississippi	R	Con	1970 (T)		3/5 L	3/5 L	
	L	Stat		1992 (A)	PCT		
Missouri	I	Con	1980 (GF, T)		INC, Refund	2/3 L-EM, V	
	L	Con	1996 (T)		V	L-EM, 1 year	
Montana	L	Stat		1981 (A)	INC	2/3 L-EM	
	I	Con	1998 (T)		V	3/4 L	Invalidated
Nevada	L	Stat		1979 (PE)	POP/CPI	Discretionary	
	I	Con	1996 (T)		2/3 L	2/3 L	

State							D,C,G
New Jersey	L	Stat		1990 (GF)	INC		
North Carolina	L	Stat		1991 (GF)	INC		
Ohio	R	Stat		2006 (A)	POP+CPI/3.5%	2/3 L, EM	
Oklahoma	I	Con	1992 (T)	1985 (A)	PCT, CPI	3/4 L	
Oregon	L	Stat		1979/2001 (A)	INC		
	R	Con	1996 (T)		3/5 L	3/5 L	
	I	Con	2000		Refund		
Rhode Island	L	Stat		1935/1994 (A)	FIXED		
	R	Con		1992 (GF)	PCT		
South Carolina	R	Con	1978 (T)	1980/1984 (A)	INC, EMP	2/3 L-EM 1 yr.	
South Dakota	I	Con	1996 (T)		2/3 L, V	2/3 L	
	R	Con			2/3 L, V		
Tennessee	CC	Con		1978 (AT)	INC	L	
Texas	R	Con		1978 (AT)	INC/ECN	L-EM	
Utah	L	Stat		1988/2004 (A)	INC/POP	2/3 L-EM,V	
Virginia	L	Con	1992		EXP		
Washington	I	Stat		1993/2005[2] (E)	POP/CPI	2/3 L-EM	
	I	Stat	1993 (T)		OEL, V		
	I	Stat	1999 (T)		V	V	
Wisconsin		Stat		2001 (A)	INC		

239

Table 9.9 (continued)

Notes:

INC = Per capita income or personal income.
POP = Population.
CPI = Inflation or consumer price index.
C = Capital projects.
L = Legislature.
Con = Constitutional.
Stat = Statutory.
R = Referenda.
I = Initiative.
A = Appropriation increase.
E = Expenditure increase.
T = New or increased taxes and/or fees.
EM = Emergency.
V = Voter approval.
GF = General fund.
PCT = Percentage of revenue, creates a reserve.
D = Debt payment.

CIT = Corporate income tax.
R = Revenue.
ECN = Growth in state economy.
N-R = Non-Recurring general fund appropriations exempt.
WAGES = Growth limited to growth in wages and salaries.
IT = Alters personal income tax rate structure.
FIXED = Fixed percentage allowable growth.
EMP = Limits employment growth.
EXP = Revenue limited to expenditures.
OEL = Limit tax changes to amounts below the expenditure limit w 2/3
L, amounts over expenditure limit requires V.
G = Grants.
M = Court mandates.
BR = Budget reserves.
PE = Proposed expenditures.
CC = Constitutional convention.
At = Appropriation of tax revenue.
SPT = State property tax.

[1] Several sources relying on NCSL tables indicate Kentucky adopted a general tax and fee increase limitation, however, this could not be confirmed via Kentucky statute or constitutional provisions, nor via an examination of tax law votes.
[2] In 2005 Washington's state legislature amended its expenditure limitation to tie expenditure growth for the 'general fund and related funds' to the ten year average growth in state personal income.

Sources: Compiled from Rafool (1996, 1998), James and Rudiuk (2001), Rudiuk (2001) and NCSL (2007).

Table 9.10   Distribution of state revenue and expenditure limitations across regions

Characteristic of state limitations in effect	Northeast (of 9 states)	Midwest (of 12 states)	South (of 16 states)	West (of 13 states)	U.S. 50 State Total #	U.S. 50 State Total %
Either revenue or expenditure limit	6	8	12	9	35	70
Revenue limit	2	3	7	6	18	36
Expenditure limit	5	5	8	9	27	54
States with both	DE	none	LA, MS, OK	AZ,CA, NV, OR, WA*	9	18
Linked to income, population or economic growth	4	6	7	10	27	54
Legislative supermajority override	2	4	7	9	22	44
Initiative adoption	2	3	3	6	15	30

Note: *Montana's expenditure limitation was invalidated and Colorado suspended its revenue limit until 2011.

Source: Compiled based on Table 9.

while 24 of the expenditure limitations restrict growth in general fund expenditures or appropriations. Both types of limits are most frequently (27 cases) tied to growth in population, income, prices, the economy or wages. Twenty of the revenue restrictions allow extra-majority legislative override, as do 16 of the expenditure limitations.

Most (two-thirds) state limitations are constitutional restrictions (24 states). Citizen initiative is increasingly the source of state-level tax and expenditure limitations, accounting for half of all limitations adopted since 1990. State limitations are more prevalent in Southern (12) and Western (9) states than in other regions, the latter likely due in part to the incidence of the initiative (see Table 9.10).

CURRENT INDIVIDUAL STATE DEVELOPMENTS

Colorado TABOR-style restrictions have become more popular as proposals, even as Colorado has suspended its state-level provisions due to the negative consequences TABOR has had on the capacity of the state's governments. These proposals, while numerous, have experienced little success at being adopted. For example, legislative versions of TABOR were considered in 23 states in 2005, but passed in none. TABOR-style proposals were defeated in 16 states during 2006 (Table 9.11). TEL activity over the course of the past 12 years has included the following (also see Table 9.12).

California

Article XIII of the state Constitution was amended via Proposition 218 – Right to Vote on Taxes Act. Effective 1 July 1997, Proposition 218 requires majority voter approval for general taxes and a supermajority (two-thirds) for special taxes, and prohibits the use of fee and charge revenue for general services. All property-related fee and charge increases are subject to majority approval of property owners or two-thirds voter approval (Doerr, 1996).

Oklahoma

New assessment limits took effect on 1 January 1997, limiting residential assessment increases to 5 percent per year, until the property is sold, changed or improved. This was coupled with a freeze on the valuation of homesteads belonging to people over age 65 with household income of $25,000 or less (Hamilton, 1996).

Oregon

A property tax revenue limit (Measure 47) approved by referendum in November 1996 was superseded through referendum (Measure 50) in March 1997. It provides for a revised property tax assessment limit coupled with a levy-based rate freeze. Measure 50 rolled back assessments to 1996 levels less 10 percent and capped annual growth to 3 percent. It also established rates at a level producing a 17 percent reduction over that which would have occurred under Measure 47. New or additional taxes are to be approved at election with a minimum of 50 percent turnout and new fees also require voter approval (Mayer, 1997).

New Mexico

Legislation was enacted (during February 2000) to stiffen the state's limit on assessment increases beginning in 2001. Yearly residential assessment increases are limited to 3 percent, with increases of 5 percent in counties

Table 9.11   State TABOR Proposals – 2006 Legislative Session[1]

1. Arizona	2 bills died in Legislature.
2. Kansas	Bill died in committee.
3. Maine[2]	Initiative was DEFEATED on the November 2006 ballot (54 percent vs 46 percent).
4. Maryland	Bill died in Committee.
5. Michigan	Initiative did not get on November 2006 ballot. Signatures turned in for an initiative but they were rejected by the Board of Canvassers. Court of Appeals upheld decision. 2 bills (carried over from last year) died in committee.
6. Minnesota	Bill died in committee.
7. Missouri	Initiative did not get on November 2006 ballot. Signatures were turned in for an initiative, but they were rejected by the Secretary of State and the courts. Bill died in committee.
8. Montana	Signatures turned in for an initiative (Nov. 2006), but they were rejected by the District and Supreme Court for fraud. Proposal also rejected due to unconstitutionality.
9. Nebraska	Initiative was DEFEATED on the November 2006 ballot (70 percent vs 30 percent).
10. Nevada	Initiative did not get onto November 2006 ballot. Removed from ballot by Supreme Court due non-compliance with rules for ballot questions, i.e. failing to file an accurate copy of the amendment before collecting signatures.
11. Ohio	Initiative taken off Nov. 2006 ballot – Legislature passed a less restrictive statutory version.
12. Oklahoma	Initiative did not get on November 2006 ballot. Removed from ballot by Supreme Court due to insufficient valid signatures. Bill died in committee.
13. Oregon	Initiative DEFEATED on the November 2006 ballot (71 percent vs 29 percent).
14. Pennsylvania	Senate bill passed Senate floor, but died in committee in the House. House bill died in committee.
15. South Carolina	Bill died in committee.
16. Wisconsin	2 bills DEFEATED on the floor of the Senate. 1 bill died in committee.

Notes:
[1]   Unless otherwise noted, proposals listed are constitutional amendments that limit annual growth in state (or state and local) spending or revenue to the rate of growth of population plus inflation and that require voter approval to override the limits.
[2]   The initiative is statutory since citizen initiatives cannot be constitutional amendments.

Source: Center for Budget and Policy Priorities, 18 January 2007.

with existing assessment sales rations of less than 85 percent (Massey, 2000).

Washington

Initiative 695 requiring voter approval of any increase in taxes, or licenses by state or local governments, was adopted in 1999 (Burrows, 2000c). Before it could be implemented, the requirement for voter approval was ruled unconstitutional by the Washington Superior Court, on 14 March 2000 (Alsdorj, 2000), a verdict ultimately concurred with by the State Supreme Court on 26 October (Burrows, 2000b). A substitute provision, Initiative 722, was subsequently approved by voters in November 2000. It voided all taxes enacted without voter approval between certification of I-695 (2 July 1999) and its intended effective date (1 January 2000). It also limited property tax revenue increases to 2 percent per year or the rate of inflation, whichever is less, with similar limits on assessment increases (Brunori, 2000). In December, implementation of 722 was also blocked by the Washington Superior Court (Burrows, 2000a). In early June, the Washington Supreme Court heard arguments to restore implementation (Burrows, 2001a) and, in September, ruled Initiative 722 unconstitutional. A second fall-back petition (Initiative 747) to limit annual property tax revenue increases was approved for signature gathering in February (Burrows, 2001b, 2001c) and adopted at the polls during November 2001. It limits property tax revenue growth to 1 percent per year (beginning 2002) unless approved by voters.

In its fifth year of implementation, June 2006, King County Superior Court ruled I-747 unconstitutional. The lower court's order was stayed by the Washington Supreme Court. However, in November 2007, the State Supreme Court (in a 5 to 4 vote) invalidated I-747. The court found I-747 to be ambiguous and misleading. Its text sought to amend I-722, previously found unconstitutional and, therefore, a non-existent law. The law reverts back to the provisions of Referendum 47. It was approved by voters in 1997 and limits annual property tax revenue (levy) increases to price inflation or a maximum of 6 percent, plus new construction. (Daniels, 2006; Henchman, 2007). Price inflation is defined by the implicit price deflator for personal consumptions as the initial limit for annual levy increases. Increases above this and up to 6 percent are allowable via a supermajority vote of the local legislative body.

Colorado

In November 2005 Colorado voters suspended the spending restrictions imposed by TABOR on state government revenues and expenditures for five years.

South Carolina

In 2006, limited assessment increased to 15 percent over five years.

Wisconsin

The Taxpayer Protection Amendment 2005/2006 was a proposed constitutional amendment limiting growth in revenue collection for every type of government in the state of Wisconsin. Revenue is defined to include taxes, special assessments, licenses, fees, fines, forfeitures and bond proceeds. The state government, counties, special districts and college districts would be limited to an inflation factor plus population growth. School district allowable growth includes enrollment and municipalities includes 60 percent of the value of new construction. Overrides are provided via referenda. After reaching a threshold, state government excess revenue is returned to taxpayers. Unfunded state mandates on localities are also prohibited (Reschovsky, 2006). A version limiting state government general fund revenues narrowly passed the Wisconsin Assembly on 28 April 2006. The joint resolution did not pass the Senate. Constitutional amendments require passage by the legislature in two consecutive sessions and then a referendum of the population.

Texas

During 2003, at least five bills were introduced to limit property assessment increases. Proposed limits ranged from 0 percent on residential homesteads to 5 percent (Moak, Casey & Associates, 2004). The assessment limit, however, remains at 10 percent. On 22 November 2005 the Texas Supreme Court ruled the state's education finance system unconstitutional. The state property tax rate cap combined with mandated education requirements did not provide meaningful local discretion to school districts, creating a de facto state property tax. The court required the state to rectify the situation by June 2006 (Texas Tax Reform Commission, 2006). In response, the legislature reduced the maximum property tax rate for school districts by one-third to $1 per $100 in assessed value by 2007. Taxes on cigarettes were increased by $1 per pack and a business gross receipts tax enacted, intending to shift more of the burden of financing education to the state. Local school district discretion was provided by allowing a rate increase to $1.04 at the discretion of the local school board, with voter approval providing for an increase to $1.17. School districts pursuing override elections have been successful 77 percent of the time (Hamilton, 2007).

The issue of assessment increase and local revenue limits returned by 2006–07, in a proposal sponsored by Governor Rick Perry based on task force recommendations. A constitutional amendment has been proposed that would permit 'taxpayers (including residential, commercial, and industrial properties) in all local taxing entities the option of electing to pay all ad valorem taxes based on the five-year rolling average appraised value'. It also proposes limiting revenue increases for cities and counties to a 5 percent cap without voter approval, and a voter-approved 0.5 percentage point sales tax increase to be exchanged for a more restrictive (5 percent) property tax assessment increase or larger homestead exemptions. It also prohibits unfunded mandates. The homestead exemption would be doubled for municipalities and counties (Shafroth, 2007).

Florida

A proposal was put forward to phase in an increase of the homestead deduction to $50,000, combined with the existing 3 percent assessment increase limitation (Shafroth, 2007), portability of assessment reductions (of up to $500,000) for relocating homesteads, an assessment increase cap of 10 percent on non-homestead property, and a $25,000 exemption for business personal property. A 29 January 2008 referendum was held (and passed) to include these provisions in the state's Constitution (retroactively to 1 January 2008). In February 2008, a subcommittee of the Taxation and Budget Reform Commission approved placing a constitutional amendment enacting state and local spending caps on the November ballot (Follick, 2008). The plan limits spending increases to population growth (or school enrolment for school districts) plus inflation plus 1 percent. The proposal was however rejected by the full commission on 14 April. In June 2007, statutory property tax 'relief' was adopted, requiring local jurisdictions and school districts to roll back 2007–08 property tax levies to 2006–07 levels. School districts were required to reduce levies by 3 percent and local revenue growth is restricted to the rate of growth in population and income (see Box 9.2).

New Jersey

In 2007 the state enacted a homestead credit to replace an existing homestead rebate and established a 4 percent cap on property tax levy increases for municipalities, school districts and counties. The cap goes into effect for budgets adopted after 1 July 2007 and expires on 30 June 2012. Local jurisdictions may override this cap with 60 percent approval in a local election. Credits will provide up to $2000 offset of property tax payments against state income taxes and are completely phased out for income in excess of $250,000 (Shafroth, 2007).

Maine

In January 2005, the state enacted a law (LD1) limiting expenditures of the state, municipalities, counties and schools. Growth in state general fund appropriations are limited (in differing levels of stringency based upon Maine's tax burden relative to other states) in a formula including income growth plus population growth. Emergency legislative override is possible; however, statutory limitations are not binding on the legislature. Levy increase limits were instituted for appropriations of counties and municipalities funded through property taxes based on income growth plus property growth (with offsets for state funding). Similar provisions exist for schools. Limited local legislative overrides are permissible for 'extraordinary events' and via special referenda. These limits are technically levied against appropriations, not revenue increases. Homestead exemptions were increased from $7000 to $13,000 and the circuit-breaker limit from $1000 to $2000.[16]

On 7 November 2006, a stricter Colorado-style (TABOR) amendment to limit revenue and spending of all levels of government was voted on and defeated at the polls. In early January 2007, a resolution calling for a constitutional amendment to freeze resident household valuations for tax purposes was introduced in the Maine House at the urging of Governor John Baldacci. On 29 January 2008 the Maine legislative summary pronounced this legislation 'dead'.

Ohio

A TABOR-style constitutional amendment was removed from the November ballot in 2006. This was replaced by a legislatively enacted state appropriations restriction (SB 321) on 5 June 2006. It requires the Governor to calculate a state appropriations limit (covering most of the General Fund) for the 2008–09 biennium and after. Appropriations

Table 9.12   Selected recent flirtations and enactments

Flirtations (some serious)	Enactments
Wisconsin – Constitutional Amendments to limit revenue growth for every type of government (2005/06).	Colorado – Suspension of TABOR (2005, to 2011).
Texas – Assessment increase limits, local revenue limits (2003, 2006/07). Constitutional amendment proposed.	South Carolina – Assessment increase limit (5 years, 15 percent, 2006). Texas – Rate cap revised under court direction (2007).
Florida – Constitutional amendment setting local spending caps (rejected by Taxation and Budget Reform Commission in April), homestead exemption phase-in with 3 percent assessment increase limit.	New Jersey – Property tax levy increase limits for all local governments (2007–12), homestead credit.
Maine – Colorado-style TABOR defeated 2006, 2007 constitutional freeze on resident homestead valuations legislatively dead.	Maine – Expenditure increase limit on state, municipalities, counties and schools (2005).
Ohio – TABOR-style amendment removed from ballot in 2006.	Ohio – 2006 amendment was replaced by a legislatively enacted state appropriations restriction.
Indiana – Amendment to limit property tax levy (rate) on homesteads to 1 percent of assessed value, 2 percent for other residential, and 3 percent for commercial (expected 30 percent reduction in local revenue), limit levy increase to 2 percent for seniors is still in effect.	Indiana – 2008 statutory enactment of overall property tax rate limit, effective 2008, limiting property tax levy (rate) on homesteads to 1 percent of assessed value, 2 percent for other residential, and 3 percent for commercial (expected 30 percent reduction in local revenue).
Georgia – Proposed constitutional state expenditure limit, resolution adopted by Senate, April 2007 and reported favorably out of House committee, March 2008. Limit spending increase to inflation + population change, two-thirds legislative override.	Rhode Island – property tax levy increase reduction to 4 percent from 5.5 percent by 2013. Florida – 2008 portability of assessment reductions (of up to $500,000) for relocating homesteads due to existing assessment increase limit (see text).
Amendment to freeze 'residential real property tax values'. Introducing acquisition value assessment. Passed Senate, February 2008.	June 2007, statutory property tax 'relief', requiring local jurisdictions and school districts to roll-back 2007–08 property tax levies to 2006–07 levels, school districts required to reduce levies by 3 percent, local revenue growth is restricted to the rate of growth in population and income.
'The GREAT Plan'. Amendment eliminating property taxes for education and establishing a property tax revenue cap and acquisition value assessment.	

increases are limited to 3.5 percent or the sum of inflation and population change. The Governor cannot propose a budget that exceeds these
limits.

Indiana

On 27 March 2008 the state adopted property tax 'relief' for homeowners effective the same year. The package includes a one percentage point
increase in the state sales tax (to 7 percent) to reduce homeowner property tax bills by $870 million (30 percent) in 2008. It imposes a statutory
levy limit of 1 percent of a homestead's assessed value, 2 percent for
non-owner-occupied residential housing and 3 percent for commercial
property. The statute is intended to be followed by a corresponding constitutional amendment. Property tax levy increases would be limited to
2 percent annually for senior citizens. Provisions exist for capital project
referenda. Education aid is being increased for two years to compensate
for levy limits and an expected $524 million reduction in local government
property tax collections by 2010 (Lohrmann, 2008).

Rhode Island

A cap on property tax revenue increases for local governments was
reduced to 4 percent from 5.5 percent by 2013. Allowable school district
property tax revenue growth will move from 5.25 percent in 2008 to 4
percent by 2012. Override is available via a four-fifths vote of the local
governing body (Setze, 2006).

Georgia

A constitutional state expenditure limitation has been proposed. A
Resolution (SR 20) calling for a public referendum on the questions was
adopted by Georgia State Senate on 20 April 2007. Beginning in 2010,
state spending increases would be limited to 'state government inflation
and population change'. Override is possible through a two-thirds vote of
both houses of the General Assembly, will apply for a single year and will
not form a base for successive years. The resolution was reported favora-
bly out of House committee on 28 March 2008.

Proposed was a constitutional amendment to 'require the freezing of
existing residential real property tax values' at 2008 levels and requiring
the implementation of acquisition value assessment and limiting assessment increases to an inflation factor. SR 686 passed the Senate on 12
February 2008.

Also proposed, 'The GREAT Plan' (Georgia's Repeal of Every Ad Valorem Tax), a constitutional amendment eliminating property taxes for education (with exceptions for debt and improvements). It would also provide for a property tax revenue cap, limiting revenue growth to the change in a price index (with overrides through local referenda), in addition to acquisition value assessment, and provides a credit for the personal property tax applied to motor vehicles. Lost local revenue is to be replaced through grants funded partially by expansion of sales taxes to services and local increased sales tax revenue.

WHAT IS THE APPEAL?

Limitations on state and subnational government's autonomy are broadly imposed. Is this simply the result of mistrust of the judgment of representational systems, of the motivations of public officials or of government responsiveness? Why, at a time when mobility and options available to residents are greater than ever before? Why has so much focus been on local government, the level most easily influenced and most responsive to public desires? Why would a uniform statewide approach to issues of local responsiveness be desirable? Explanations are numerous. Some suggest the size of government is inconsistent with voter preferences.[17] However, support for limitations does not coincide with a desire for reduced services.[18]

Voters' Support

Voters desire lower taxes and more efficiency in government, not reduced public services (Ladd and Wilson, 1983, 1982, 1981; Courant et al., 1985; Stein et al., 1983; Alm and Skidmore, 1999; Temple, 1996; Cutler et al., 1999; and Bradbury et al., 1997). Self-interest appears active, with those whose tax burdens would be most clearly affected being most supportive.[19] Support has often been couched in terms of excessive and costly local services. However, expenditure growth at the local level has been significantly below national and state governments.

Many supporters of California's 1978 adoption of Proposition 13 believed that government was inefficient and felt that massive budget reductions would not affect services (Citrin, 1979). Limitation support also emerged from a general dislike of taxes,[20] and objections to particular types of (social) spending (Danziger and Ring, 1982). Voters in many states believed that their own taxes would be reduced without affecting services they desire (Courant et al., 1985; Sears and Citrin, 1982; Ladd and Wilson,

1981). When severe TABOR restrictions were approved in Colorado in 1992, the state was already among the lowest in aggregate state and local tax burden (James, 2001). Polls indicate that dissatisfaction with the 'size and scope' of the state and local public sector has not been a primary motivation; but rather support has been based on 'wish-full' thinking and a self-interested attempt to shift burdens elsewhere (Citrin, 1979). The campaign for limitations in several states has been driven by a combination of external- and narrow self-interested organizations, individuals and entities. The grass-roots nature of support is often highly questionable when campaigns are financed by a limited number of contributors and national advocacy groups and political organizations, rather than through local initiative and contributions (Smith, 2004). The failure of many recent attempts at seriously restricting local jurisdictions suggests that the voting population may have become more sophisticated and nuanced at assessing the potential ramifications and motivations of sweeping statewide action directed to local issues. Still, the current economic climate may be ripe for a resurgence of TEL support.

Political Economy and Principal–Agent Relationships

Initially, passage was not related to the specific features of a limitation. However, evidence suggests that the public is learning and support for the most stringent of limitations appears to be in decline. Alternative service supply- and demand-side factors have been proposed (Alm and Skidmore, 1999; Temple, 1996). Demand explanations include: (1) voter fiscal illusion (or Citrin's 'something for nothing' characterization); and (2) intra-community heterogeneity, asymmetric preference distributions and systematic differences in preference intensities. Explanation (1) reflects a 'free lunch' motivation, explanation (2) suggests risk aversion in local collective decision-making. Supply factors have been suggested to include: (1) public official monopoly power, agenda manipulation and log-rolling; (2) principal–agent difficulties, information asymmetry and difficulties of observing actual service quality; (3) excess interest group influence; and (4) the absence of mechanisms to reveal and incorporate preference intensity. However, few of these factors are found to be of actual consequence in explaining public support.[21]

Local Overrides and Satisfaction with Broad-scale Constraints

Local voter override can be used as an indicator of voter satisfaction with limitations and their constraints. Massachusetts community overrides of Proposition 2½ have been assessed to test voter sentiments, motivations and expectations (Cutler et al., 1999). Some support is found for: (1) agency loss theory, reflecting concern that, without limitations, local governments might undertake spending projects which are not valued by voters;[22] (2) regret theory, indicating that voters ultimately regret the severity of the constraint and seek its relaxation; and (3) personal finance theory which focuses on a voter's own tax burden, with override support tied to a self-interested evaluation of the financing structure.

Illinois home rule votes also suggest that community heterogeneity may affect local support for tax limitations.[23] Heterogeneity suggests differential public service demands and greater variation from the median voter's preference, creating risk that home rule might allow capture of the local agenda by groups preferring higher spending (Temple, 1996). Limitations provide a desired constraint on the range and form of local service, particularly redistributive spending. This outcome is consistent with a fourth voter sentiment theory. Demographic difference theory suggests that voters view waste as spending on groups demographically different from themselves; heterogeneity heightens this perception. These results suggest a variety of motivations rooted in eliminating assumed technical inefficiency, the imposition of reduced tax burdens and preferred spending mixes. However, there is little in the structure of limitations that would assure preferred outcomes. The almost universal public support of local override elections in Colorado (and the five-year suspension of state limitations), suggest both local and statewide dissatisfaction with the severity of TABOR constraints (James and Wallis, 2004).

Allocative Efficiency: Tiebout–Hamilton Distortions and Local Limitations

Massachusetts housing price and school enrollment changes suggest that property tax limitations have had a significant effect on location decisions (and Tiebout–Hamilton efficiency). Public sentiment is demonstrated through market choices. More constrained communities, with presumably lesser abilities to satisfy residents' spending preferences, faced declining (or slower growth in) housing prices (Bradbury et al., 1998; and Bradbury et al., 1997). The effect was greatest for an inability to meet education preferences and has impaired sorting efficiency as: 'families . . . appear to be "voting with their feet" . . . chasing communities that have excess capacity to support schools because they are below their mandated tax limit' (Bradbury et al., 1998, p. 17). The limitation has impaired access to quality education and has likely had the greatest effect on the least mobile (and least affluent). This outcome suggests that despite possible contrary signals in the adoption of limitations, available local revenue capacity is a valued attribute for households seeking residence locations.

Education is also a factor suggested in the appeal of California's Proposition 13. The tax limitation has been argued to have been a result of a previous court restriction. From this view, Proposition 13 was less about the property tax than a revolt against a new education finance system (Fischel, 1989, 2001). Successful passage came in 1978 (after several previously failed attempts) and is linked to the 1971 California Supreme Court ruling in *Serrano* v. *Priest*. This ruling forced statewide redistribution of property taxes, requiring property tax increases in wealthier jurisdictions to maintain net (after transfer) local spending and causing the median voter to lose power over local schools. Prior to *Serrano*, the property tax system had benefited wealthy communities by allowing locally responsive spending. Eliminating local fiscal advantage via property tax financing of local services replaced an efficient benefit-based local revenue structure with one posing a deadweight loss to wealthier communities. After *Serrano*, property values in wealthier communities were suppressed due to the transfer. Post Proposition 13, there was a rapid return in value. The successful adoption of Proposition 13 was, then, a rational fiscal response to a previous court required constraint. Support for Proposition 13 would have been irrational for wealthier communities in the absence of the court's ruling. It was driven by a desire to suppress the effects of redistributive transfers, not dissatisfaction with local public services.

THE EFFECTS OF TELS

Research concerning tax and expenditure limitations has focused on: (1) reasons for voter support; (2) descriptive summaries and projected effects (Peterson, 1981; Ladd, 1978; Shapiro and Morgan, 1978; Bails, 1982); (3) estimates of actual fiscal impacts, including effects on the size of the public sector and its structure; and (4) study of the interlocal ramifications.

As highlighted above, research into public support suggests that limitations have been supported because of a desire for lower taxes and more efficiency in government, not due to a desire for reduced public services. Voters were generally satisfied with the existing service package, but sought a lower tax price. Support is also linked to self-interest, with those whose tax burdens would be most clearly affected supporting the limitations,[24] and to economic growth, with growth in property taxes and local government's share of the state and local public sector more important than demographic or political factors (Alm and Skidmore, 1999). A desire for reduced service does not appear to be a motivation.

Studies of the fiscal effect of tax and expenditure limitations on the state and local sector have focused on tax burdens, the impact of limitations on single jurisdictions, and the effects of limitations on the level and mix of government revenues and expenditures in a cross-section of jurisdictions. Most of these have focused on single states, rather than evaluating effects generally (Kemp, 1982; Danziger, 1980; Shapiro and Sonstelle, 1982; Sherwood-Call, 1987; Reid, 1988; Merriman, 1986; Megdal, 1986; Susskind and Horan, 1983; Fisher and Gade, 1991; Cutler et al., 1997; Bradbury et al., 1997; Dye and McGuire, 1997; Sexton et al., 1999). The earlier cross-sectional studies tested only very general effects, with the most prominent focus being the size and scope of government (Cebula, 1986; Kenyon and Benker, 1984; Howard, 1989). Comprehensive analyses of overall effects of these limitations on the composition and structure of the state and local public sector have also been undertaken (Joyce and Mullins, 1991; Elder, 1992; Preston and Ichniowski, 1991; Mullins and Joyce, 1996; Shadbegian, 1996, 1998, 1999; Skidmore, 1999; Mullins, 2001, 2004; Kousser et al., 2008). The findings of these studies include: (1) little effect on the overall size of the state and local public sector;[25] (2) a decreased use of local broad-based taxes (specifically property taxes) and shifts to state aid, user charges and miscellaneous revenues; and (3) an expanded relative fiscal (revenue and expenditure) role for state governments.[26] Some have also attempted to assess the impact of limitation on long-term public service performance.[27] Others have more specifically focused on public sector employment and wage effects.[28]

TELs have also affected the fiscal structure within the local public sector. Even within the ranks of the individual state studies, there has been limited attention to these types of effects. Tax and expenditure limitations alter the composition of the local public sector, fostering an increased role for special districts, and the constraining interaction between government and local populations (see Mullins, 2004, 2001; Bowler and Donovan, 2004; Carr, 2006). Limitations produce local structural adjustments as governments attempt to evolve mechanisms to continue to satisfy demands for local public services, with implications for the ability of local populations to exercise voice and control over the totality of the public service–tax package made available to them and, thus, the accountability and responsiveness of government. The effect across local jurisdictions is not uniform. Some governments are constrained more than others, resulting in differential abilities to meet the needs of populations. Variations in service availability across jurisdictions increases, driven by differential abilities to respond (Mullins, 2001, 2004).

Likely outcomes of TELs are: (1) reduced efficiencies through lessened ability to meet service preferences (due to resource constraints); (2) increased costs for service delivery due to constraints imposed on governance organizations; (3) lessened ability to coordinate services spatially and across functions (particularly if the role of general-purpose jurisdictions is constrained); and (4) greater compliance costs (for taxpayers) and administrative costs (of government), if service delivery responsibilities are fragmented between providers. Variability in the assignment of public service delivery responsibilities and options, and differences in local fiscal capacities and economic and demographic structures, produce different adaptive responses.

Findings show that TELs affect the organization of government, the package of services they provide and long-term mechanisms of finance. Effects are at times somewhat symbiotic and counterbalancing. Imposing limits on one type of government (general-purpose or school district), reduces competition for non-limited forms and increases their revenue–expenditure flexibility. Research findings suggest an array of effects on the local public sector, including:

- Shifts away from broader-based revenue instruments toward narrow fees and charges.
- Increased reliance on state transfers, increased influence of the state on the delivery of local services and lessened local autonomy.
- Reduced expenditure for critical local services, particularly education, and lowered levels of performance.
- Differential effects on community growth and increased disparities between communities regarding public service provision capacities.
- Increased presence of and reliance on special districts, and shifts in revenue and expenditure authority toward single-purpose districts and away from general-purpose governments, particularly in less prosperous (more constrained) jurisdictions.
- Increased variation in revenue and expenditures across both general-purpose local governments and school districts, with more pronounced effects within older and less prosperous areas serving more dependent populations.
- Increased use of debt finance with growth in outstanding aggregate debt and non-guaranteed debt, particularly in older, less affluent jurisdictions.
- Forms of limitation matter, with more stringent (levy, revenue and expenditure) limitations tending to impose greater overall constraints, with variations between different types of local governments (general-purpose governments versus school districts) and relative to the economic characteristics and conditions of local jurisdictions and populations.

Tax and expenditure limitations do have significant and potentially important substantive effects on the relative levels of local revenue and

expenditures across different jurisdictions and forms of government. Many
are quite unintended and undesirable. TELs produce constraint-induced
differentials in the services available across communities, significantly
affecting the most salient area of local spending: education. Lower-wealth
districts, relying on higher tax rates to produce desired levels of services,
may be prohibited from doing so, while higher-wealth districts experience little such constraint. This effect counters policies advanced in a
number of states to reduce the variability in local education spending (and
outcomes). For example, Michigan's 1994 education finance reform and
Vermont's 1997 Act 60 education reform have both attempted to limit
spending variation. However, in both cases, a rather complicated structure
(with relatively high coordination and transaction costs) has emerged,
predominantly in affluent jurisdictions, to circumvent restriction on the
use of local resources.[29]

Local institutional responses provide mechanisms for the circumvention of limitations. The availability of these mechanisms is related to
relative fiscal capacity. However, local adaptation has become a prominent response to an undiminished demand for local public services. One
of the legacies of the limitations movement is local adaptation to avoid
constraints. While allowing circumvention, these adaptations also entail a
degradation in accountability. Adaptations allow continued local responsiveness to local public service demands, but leave open the question of:
responsive and accountable to whom and to what institutions? While
occurring across states, the elaborate adaptations found in California are
particularly illustrative:

> In order to overcome the obstacles to local finance created by Proposition 13
> and its progeny (most notably Proposition 218) in California, local finance has
> metamorphosed into an overlapping patchwork of disjointed revenue jurisdic-
> tions . . . All of these have differing popular approval requirements ranging from
> a two-thirds vote of the electorate for special taxes to a majority of property
> owners within a district containing fewer than a dozen voters for the assessment
> of flat parcel charges or fees. The result is what Sheffrin refers to as the 'particu-
> larization' of local taxation, as general taxation gives way to levies specifically
> dedicated to particular purposes and narrowly constrained geographic areas
> . . . It is possible for different electoral groupings to be voting on each question
> . . . California voters are left with discretion over everything except what might
> matter most, ad valorem property taxes and education spending . . .
>   The resulting structure is an extremely complicated and almost indecipher-
> able labyrinth to the individual citizen/voter. Local adaptations . . . [to] arti-
> ficial revenue constraints have engendered this complexity and, as a result,
> have created a loss of transparency, responsiveness and accountability at the
> local level . . . [T]he cycle of fiscal innovation leading to a loss in transparency
> is at least partially responsible for demands for more direct citizen control in
> California. As this cycle works its way through a variety of states, the likely

result is that this will foster additional needs for fiscal innovation, additional
losses in transparency and additional initiatives for 'reform'. (Mullins, 2003,
pp. 132–3)

Different types of limitations have different effects. These effects also
vary with the spatial and structural position of the constrained jurisdiction
(urban core or suburban fringe) and with the level of relative community
prosperity. Jurisdictions in the older urban core and those with less prosperous populations are, not surprisingly, most constrained. The outcome
is a reduced capacity to provide services for populations in greatest need,
increasing service disparities. Effects are not confined to directly limited
jurisdictions. Limitations on general-purpose or school district governments
may provide increased revenue or expenditure flexibility for non-limited
forms of government by decreasing competition for shared tax bases.

Revenue and expenditure limitations appear not to have a benign
effect on the structure of the local public sector. They have significant
implications for the functioning of the level of government responsible
for delivering our most basic public services. Too little attention has been
paid to these outcomes. Limitations can significantly alter the relationship
between governments and local populations and significantly affect the
capacity to provide for public needs and wants. Limitations have reshaped
the local public sector in unintended ways. These changes are the results
of local adjustments to the imposition of poorly conceived, haphazard
institutional and structural constraints, and differential abilities to make
such adjustments. While the effects are often asymmetrical, they are not
random. They produce both general and varied effects. Effects vary by
type of government and service subgroup, and by the demographics of
resident populations. These constraints are producing systematic effects,
distorting fiscal and service delivery structures.

Limitations are found to degrade service performance and increase the
variation in per capita revenue collections and expenditures across general-
purpose governments and school districts, through asymmetrically constraining those units under greater fiscal stress, producing increased fiscal
disparity. It is not unwarranted, then, to question the desirability, equity,
efficiency and efficacy of these results and the mechanisms producing
them. The 'tax limitations movement' has resulted in blunt instruments
intended to impose an externally derived definition of fiscal responsibility
on local governments and populations. In so doing, it has often taken its
greatest toll on the jurisdictions and populations which can least afford
a relative decline in resources and in the availability of public services.
Current economic conditions suggest the potential of a resurgence in such
limitations. It is vitally important that the differential effects of what are

too frequently arbitrary one-size-fits-all constraints be considered and understood to avoid crippling public service delivery for communities in heightened need.

NOTES

1. For a more complete review of tax and expenditure limitations, see the 'Characteristics of TELs' section of this chapter.
2. Montana's expenditure limitation was invalidated in 2005, reducing the total from 34.
3. Under this provision, property owners who have benefited from a reduced assessment due to the 3 percent assessment growth cap can transfer the value of the reduced assessment (up $500,000) to newly purchased properties when they change the address of their homestead.
4. As such, the elements surrounding it offer a microcosm of the issues dominant across the broader restructuring of the local public sector. It simultaneously reflects the political agenda and strength of residents, businesses, elderly and 'homeowners' groups. It captures conflicts between the public and government for higher-quality government services at lower cost to particular individuals and groups, and conflict between governments in the use of shared tax bases and the distribution of expenditure responsibilities. The success of the local public sector at adapting and evolving alternative revenue and service delivery structures to compensate for the imposition of constraints has been at least partially responsible for their continued popular support. It has played to a public perception that it is continuously possible to reduce and shift revenue burdens and simultaneously maintain service levels. It has given rise to a popular belief in the proverbial 'free lunch'. This has been furthered by the extraordinary economic prosperity experienced across the nation during the mid-1990s through the turn of the century.
5. Based on calculations of the Minnesota Taxpayers Association for residential housing valued at $150,000 and commercial property valued at $1 million and industrial property valued at $25 million.
6. Advocacy is at the state level (by state-level constituencies and often the result of the initiative of a small group of 'reformers'), resulting in statutory or constitutional provisions of broad scope and wide applicability across virtually all local jurisdictions or classes of jurisdictions within a state.
7. Some point to the existence of local override measures, usually via popular vote (and sometimes requiring supermajorities), as mechanisms for maintaining local control. However, the effectiveness of these measures for such is suspect.
8. The result is opposite of the prescription offered by the leading and most enduring model of local government efficiency articulated by Charles Tiebout (1956) and contrary to median voter prescripts.
9. While not technically in the category of a limitation, in 1997 the state of Vermont adopted an education finance reform (in response to a state Supreme Court decision) which has substantially altered accessibility of the local property tax base for local education. Above a threshold level, a portion of revenues generated by increased local property tax levies are pooled for distribution across school districts in the state. This has significantly altered the role of the property tax in local finance. New Hampshire has also recently instituted a state-wide property tax to fund education in response to an order from its Supreme Court to restructure education finance. The role of the property tax is undergoing redefinition. Connecticut also limits assessment increases related to reassessment.
10. This section draws extensively on, and adapts and updates tables from, Mullins (2003).
11. Table 9.7 identifies the number of states that have imposed any of the seven forms of limitations. It includes all states that have done so, not just those which have limitations currently active. For example two states, Kansas and Minnesota, have repealed specific

rate limitations, resulting in 31 states for which they are active. Likewise, Kansas also repealed its levy limit in 1999, leaving 28 states with limits currently in effect.

12. Washington's assessment increase limit was ruled unconstitutional, leaving 13 active.

13. General revenue limits were repealed in Minnesota and Nevada during 1993 and 1989, respectively. Restrictions remain in Colorado and California, even though Colorado's TABOR state-level restrictions were suspended in 2005.

14. The Midwest and South have the same number of total TELs, however, the Midwest has enacted more per state, and a greater number of the more stringent constraints (that is, those other than full-disclosure).

15. However, Maine's levy and expenditure limits can be overridden by a simple majority vote of local legislative bodies (or through normal school budget approval processes). A public referendum can be triggered by acquiring signatures from citizens equal to 10 percent of the number voting in the last gubernatorial election, to challenge the override.

16. See *Comparison of Tabor (LD 2075) and Current Law*, http://www.maine.gov/ legis/ ofpr/TABOR/TABORsxssum.htm.

17. This point of view is represented by the 'public choice' school, and its most extreme embodiment is probably that offered by the 'Leviathan' champions. See Brazer (1981), Niskanen (1971) and Brennan and Buchanan (1979).

18. In fact, numerous surveys suggest citizens were satisfied with the level of public services and often desired more, but simply wanted to avoid the unpleasantness of paying for them (Brazer, 1981).

19. More recent findings indicate that the passage of limitations is more related to economic growth, property taxes and local government's share of the state and local public sector than to demographic or political factors. See Alm and Skidmore (1999).

20. There was, however, no consensus on displeasure by level of government.

21. Figlio and O'Sullivan's (2001) review of local public officials' response to limitations suggests that supply-side factors may be at play, but that they may be checked by interjurisdictional competition. They find that local officials attempt to reduce direct service staffing levels (for police, fire and education) subsequent to the adoption of a limitation in order to foster support for overrides. The effect is lessened by spatial competition for residency location. This, however, does not imply that officials behave similarly in a limitation's absence, and the correlation of such behavior with the existence of limitations suggests that local officials do not maximize this opportunity under 'unlimited' circumstances.

22. However, use of property taxes up to the limit may only imply that property taxes are the first resort for (or preferred mechanism of) local finance. In and of itself, it indicates nothing about the actual desirability of spending projects to voters. Opinion polls have failed to demonstrate dissatisfaction.

23. Cities with a population less than 25,000 can eliminate property tax restrictions by adopting home rule status.

24. See Ladd and Wilson (1981, 1982, 1983), Courant et al. (1985), Stein et al. (1983) and Alm and Skidmore (1999). Also, see Temple (1996) for an assessment of Illinois's somewhat unique context and the factors affecting a community's electoral choice to opt out of limitations through adoption of a home rule charter. For an evaluation of Massachusetts overrides, see Cutler et al. (1997) and Bradbury et al. (1997).

25. Some studies find this effect to be larger than others; see Shadbegian (1996). Others find little effect associated with state-level TELS; see Kousser et al. (2008).

26. See Joyce and Mullins (1991), Mullins and Joyce (1996), Preston and Ichniowski (1991) and Shadbegian (1999, 1998).

27. Downs and Figlio (1999) provide a summary assessment of limitations effects on school performance based on a review of previous research. The authors conclude that limitations have adversely affected outcomes in schools. They have also negatively affected teacher qualifications (Figlio and Rueben, 2001). Such conclusions are not universal (see Downs et al., 1998). More recent research has considered the differential effect of limitations on education expenditures over time and levels of stringency. Local limitations in Illinois result in increasingly declining property taxes and education

expenditures over time. The restraint on property taxes is more significant than the decline in spending, suggesting a shift toward alternative sources of education budget support (Dye et al., 2005). State-level TELs appear to have little effect on education spending, while stringent local TELs result in reduced spending and higher student–teacher ratios (Shadbegian, 2003).

28. One such study assessed the effect of limitations on employment levels, wages and public sector wage premiums, finding that limitations have a limited effect on employment levels, while reducing relative wages in the local public sector (Poterba and Rueben, 1995).
29. See Mullins (2003) and Rubenstein and Picus (2003).

REFERENCES

Advisory Commission on Intergovernmental Relations (ACIR) (1990, 1992, 1994). *Significant Features of Fiscal Federalism, Volume 1*. Washington, DC: US Government Printing Office.

Alm, J. and Skidmore, M. (1999). Why do tax and expenditure limitations pass in state elections? *Public Finance Review* 27(5): 481–510.

Alsdorj, R.H. (2000). Initiative 695 unconstitutional, says superior court. *State Tax Notes* 20 March: 895.

Anonymous (2008). Hoboken Needs Approval for All Borrowing. *The Bond Buyer*, September 11, p. 24.

Baer, D. (2008). *State Handbook of Economic, Demographic and Fiscal Indicators*, 7th edition. Washington, DC: American Association of Retired Persons.

Bails, D. (1982). A critique of the effectiveness of tax-expenditure limitations. *Public Choice* 38: 129–38.

Bowler, S. and Donovan, T. (2004). Evolution in state governance structures: unintended consequences of state tax and expenditure limitations. *Political Research Quarterly* 57 (2): 189–96.

Bradbury, K., Case, K.E. and Mayer, C.J. (1998). School quality and Massachusetts enrollment shifts in the context of tax limitations. *New England Economic Review* July/August: 3–18.

Bradbury, K., Mayer, C.J. and Case, K.E. (1997). Property tax limits and local fiscal behavior: did Massachusetts' cities and towns spend too little on town services under Proposition 2½? Federal Reserve Bank of Boston Working Paper 97–2. Boston, MA.

Bradley, D. and Lyons, K. (2005). *A Formula for Decline: Lessons from Colorado for States Considering TABOR*. Washington, DC: Center on Budget and Policy Priorities.

Brazer, H.E. (1981). On tax limitations. In N. Walzer and D. Chicoine (eds), *Financing State and Local Government in the 1980s*. Cambridge, MA: Oelgeschlager, Gunn & Hain.

Brennan, G. and Buchanan, J. (1979). The logic of tax limits: alternative constitutional constraints of the power to tax. *National Tax Journal* 32 (2): 11–22.

Brunori, D. (1999). The politics of state taxation. *State Tax Notes* 27 September: 841.

Brunori, D. (2000). Politics of state taxation: the citizens set policy in the 2000 elections. *State Tax Notes* 20 November: 1379.

Burrows, D. (2000a). Judge's injunction blocks property tax limit. *State Tax Notes* 11 December: 1564–7.

Burrows, D. (2000b). State high court rejects measure to require vote on tax, fee increase. *State Tax Notes* 6 November: 1213.

Burrows, D. (2000c). 1999: the year of the citizen tax revolt. *State Tax Notes* 10 January: 96.

Burrows, D. (2001a). High court hears arguments to restore rollback-limit measure. *State Tax Notes* 18 June: 2123.

Burrows, D. (2001b). Activist sees property tax limit petition approved. *State Tax Notes* 12 February: 507.

Burrows, D. (2001c). Activist files new local tax limit initiative. *State Tax Notes* 15 January: 175.

Carr, J.B. (2006). Local government autonomy and state reliance of special district governments: a reassessment. *Political Research Quarterly* 59 (3): 481–92.

Cebula, R.J. (1986). Tax-expenditure limitation in the US: two alternative evaluations. *Economic Notes* 2: 140–51.

Center for Budget and Policy Priorities (2007). State TABOR PROPOSALS – 2006 legislative session. Washington, DC: CBPP, updated 18 January, http://www.cbpp.org/archiveSite/6-1-05tabor.pdf

Chamberlain, A. (2007). What does America think about taxes? The 2007 annual survey of US attitudes on taxes and wealth. Special Report 54. Washington, DC: Tax Foundation.

Chandler, Michael (2008). Supervisors Turn Away Fairfax Schools Proposal. *The Washington Post*, September 23, B1.

Citrin, J. (1979). Do people want something for nothing: public opinion on taxes and government spending. *National Tax Journal* 32 (2):113–29.

Cole, R.L. and Kincaid, J. (2000). Public opinion and American federalism: perspectives on taxes, spending, and trust – an ACIR update. *Publius* 30 (1–2): 189–201.

Courant, P., Gramlich, E. and Rubinfeld, D. (1985). Why voters support tax limitations: the Michigan case. *National Tax Journal* 38 (1): 1–20.

Cutler, D.M., Elmendorf, D.W. and Zeckhauser, R.J. (1997). Restraining the Leviathan: property tax limitation in Massachusetts. NBER Working Paper 6196. Cambridge, MA: National Bureau of Economic Research. September.

Cutler, D.M., Elmendorf, D.W. and Zeckhauser, R.J. (1999). Restraining the Leviathan: property tax limitation in Massachusetts. *Journal of Public Economics* 71: 313–34.

Daniels, J. (2006). Initiative 747 fact sheet. *Freedom Works* 26 September.

Danziger, J.N. (1980). California's Proposition 13 and the fiscal limitations movement in the United States. *Political Studies* 28 (4): 599–612.

Danziger, J.N. and Ring, P.S. (1982). Fiscal limitations: a selective review of recent research. *Public Administration Review* 42 (January/February): 47–55.

Doerr, D. (1996). Voters approve right to vote on taxes. *State Tax Notes* 11 November: 1334.

Downs, T.A. and Figlio, D.N. (1999). Do tax and expenditure limits provide a free lunch? Evidence on the link between limits and public sector service quality. *National Tax Journal* 52 (1): 113–28.

Downs, T.A., Dye, R.F. and McGuire, T.J. (1998). Do limits matter? Evidence of the effects of tax limitations on student performance. *Journal of Urban Economics* 43 (3): 401–17.

Doyle, M. (1994). Property tax limitations and the delivery of fire protection services. Working Paper. Federal Reserve Bank Board of Governors.

Dye, R.F. and McGuire T.J. (1997). The effect of property tax limitation measures on local government fiscal behavior. *Journal of Public Economics* 66 (3): 469–87.

Dye, R.F., McGuire, T.J. and McMillen, D.P. (2005). Are property tax limitations more binding over time? *National Tax Journal* 58 (2): 215–25.

Elder, H.W. (1992). Exploring the tax revolt: an analysis of the effects of state tax and expenditure limitation laws. *Public Finance Quarterly* 20 (1): 47–63.

Figlio, D.N. and O'Sullivan, A. (2001). The local response to tax limitation measures: do local governments manipulate voters to increase revenues? *Journal of Law and Economics* 44 (April): 233–57.

Figlio, D.N. and Rueben, K.S. (2001). Tax limits and the qualifications of new teachers. *Journal of Public Economics* 80: 49–71.

Fischel, W.A. (1989). Did 'Serrano' cause Proposition 13? *National Tax Journal* 42 (4): 465–73.

Fischel, W.A. (2001). Homevoters, municipal corporate governance, and the benefit view of the property tax. *National Tax Journal* 54 (1): 157–73.

Fisher, G.W. (1996). *The Worst Tax? A History of the Property Tax in America.* Lawrence, KS: University Press of Kansas.

Fisher, R.C. and Gade, M.N. (1991). Local property tax and expenditure limits. In T.J. McGuire and D.W. Naimark (eds), *State and Local Finance for the 1990s: A Case Study of Arizona.* Tempe, AZ: Arizona State University.

Follick, J. (2008). Tax panel approves plan to put spending cap on ballot. *State Tax Notes* 47 (12 February): 505.

Gold, S.D. (1979). *Property Tax Relief.* Lexington, MA: Lexington Books.

Hamilton, A. (1996). Voters pass three property tax amendments. *State Tax Notes* 11 November: 1352.

Hamilton, B. (2007). Best laid plans (for property tax relief and school funding). *State Tax Notes* 46 (14 November): 717.

Helderman, Rosalind (2008). Johnson Proposes Two-Week Furloughs. *The Washington Post*, September 16, B5.

Henchman, J. (2007). Washington Supreme Court invalidates property tax limit. *Tax Policy Blog.* 9 November.

Hoene, C. and Pagano, M. (2008). *Cities and State Fiscal Structure.* Washington, DC: National League of Cities.

Howard, M. (1989). State tax and expenditure limitations: there is no story. *Public Budgeting and Finance* 9 (2): 83–90.

James, F. (2001). Tax and spending limits in Colorado. Working paper. Lincoln Land Institute, Conference on Tax and Expenditure Limitations, Graduate School of Public Affairs, University of Colorado, Denver. July.

James, F.J. and Rudiuk, O. (2001). Inventory: tax and spending limits in the United States. Working Paper. Graduate School of Public Affairs, University of Colorado at Denver. July.

James, F.J. and Wallis, A. (2004). Tax and spending limits in Colorado. *Public Budgeting and Finance* 24 (4): 16–33.

Joyce, P.G. and Mullins, D.R. (1991). The changing fiscal structure of the state and local public sector: the impact of tax and expenditure limitations. *Public Administration Review* 51 (3): 240–53.

Katz, Matt (2008). Camden Workers Protest Proposed Layoffs. *The Philadelphia Inquirer*, September 19, B1.

Kemp, R. (1982). California's Proposition 13: a one-year assessment. *State and Local Government Review* 14 (January): 44–7.

Kenyon, D. and Benker, K. (1984). Fiscal discipline: lessons from the state experience. *National Tax Journal* 37: 437–46.

Kousser, T., McCubbins, M.D. and Moule E. (2008). For whom the TEL tolls: can state tax and expenditure limits effectively reduce spending? *State Politics and Policy Quarterly* 8 (4): 331–61.

Ladd, H.F. (1978). An economic evaluation of state limitations on local taxing and spending power. *National Tax Journal* 31 (1): 1–18.

Ladd, H.F. and Wilson J.B. (1981). *Proposition 2½: Explaining the Vote.* Cambridge, MA: John F. Kennedy School of Government.

Ladd, H.F. and Wilson J.B. (1982). Why voters support tax limitations: evidence from Massachusetts Proposition 2½. *National Tax Journal* 35 (2): 121–47.

Ladd, H.F. and Wilson, J.B. (1983). Who supports tax limitations: evidence from Massachusetts' Proposition 2½. *Journal of Policy Analysis and Management* 2 (2): 256–79.

Lay, I.J. and Lyons, K. (2006). The same old TABOR: Maine's 'taxpayer bill of rights' proposal fails to fix flaws of Colorado's TABOR. Center on Budget and Policy Priorities. March. http://www.cbpp.org/3-16-06sfp.htm.

Lohrmann, N. (2008). Indiana enacts major property tax relief for homeowners. *State Tax Notes* 47 (17 March): 900.

Lyons, K., Farkas, S. and Johnson, N. (2007). *The Property Tax Circuit Breaker: An Introduction and Survey of Current Programs.* Washington, DC: Center on Budget and Policy Priorities.

Massey, B. (2000). Governor signs property tax limit. *State Tax Notes* 28 February: 648.

Mayer, J. (1997). Lawmakers put rewrite of property tax limit on May ballot. *State Tax Notes* 7 April: 1059.

McNichol, E. and Lav, I. (2008). State budget troubles worsen. Washington, DC: Center on Budget and Policy Priorities. 10 October.

Megdal, S.B. (1986). Estimating a public school expenditure model under binding spending limitations. *Journal of Urban Economics* 19: 277–95.

Merriman, D. (1986). The distributional effects of New Jersey's tax and expenditure limitations. *Land Economics* 62 (4): 354–61.

Mikesell, J.L. and Mullins D.R. (2008a). The effects of property tax systems on household property tax burdens. *State Tax Notes* 18 February: 533–45.

Mikesell, J.L. and Mullins D.R. (2008b). What shapes property tax rates? An analysis of structural influences on combined rates in large American cities. Paper presented at the Western Social Science Associations Annual Meetings, Denver, CO. April.

Minnesota Taxpayers Association (2001). *50 State Property Tax Comparison Study 2000.* St Paul, MN: Minnesota Taxpayers Association.

Minnesota Taxpayers Association (2006). *50 State Property Tax Comparison Study 2005.* St Paul, MN: Minnesota Taxpayers Association.

Moak, Casey & Associates (2004). *Appraisal Limits: A Wrong Turn on the Road to Property Tax Relief?* Austin, TX: Moak, Casey & Associates.

Mullins, D.R. (2001). *The Effects of Tax and Expenditure Limitations on the Fiscal Structure of Local Government.* Denver, CO: Lincoln Land Institute, Conference of Tax and Expenditure Limitations.

Mullins, D.R. (2003). Popular processes and the transformation of state and local government finances. In D.L. Sjoquist (ed.), *State and Local Finances under Pressure.* Cheltenham, UK and Northampton, MA, USA: Edward Elgar.

Mullins, D.R. (2004). Tax and expenditure limitations and the fiscal response of local government: asymmetric intra-local fiscal effects. *Public Budgeting and Finance* 24 (4):111–47.

Mullins, D.R. and Cox, K.A. (1995). *Tax and Expenditure Limits on Local Governments.* M-194. Washington, DC: Advisory Commission on Intergovernmental Relations.

Mullins, D.R. and Joyce, P.G. (1996). Tax and expenditure limitations and state and local fiscal structure: an empirical assessment. *Public Budgeting and Finance* 16 (1): 75–101.

Mullins, D.R. and Wallin, B. (2004). Tax and expenditure limitations: introduction and overview. *Public Budgeting and Finance* 24 (special issue): 1–43.

National Conference of State Legislatures (NCSL) (2002). *A Guide to Property Taxes: Property Tax Relief.* Washington, DC: NCSL.

National Conference of State Legislatures (NCSL) (2007). *State Tax and Expenditure Limits.* Washington, DC: NCSL.

Niskanen, W.A. (1971). *Bureaucracy and Representative Government.* Chicago, IL: Aldine-Atherton Press.

Pagano, M. and Hoene, C. (2008). City fiscal conditions in 2008. Research Brief on America's Cities, 2008–2. Washington, DC: National League of Cities.

Peterson, J.E. (1981). Tax and expenditure limitations: projecting their impacts on big city finances. In G.C. Kaufman and K.T. Rosen (eds), *The Tax Revolts: The Case of Proposition 13.* New York: Harper.

Poterba, J. and Rueben, K.S. (1995). The effect of property tax limits on wages and employment in the public sector. *American Economic Review* 84 (2): 384–9.

Preston, A.E. and Ichniowski, C. (1991). A national perspective on the nature and effects of the local property tax revolt: 1976–1987. *National Tax Journal* 44 (2): 123–45.

Rafool, M. (1996), State tax and expenditure limitations. *Fiscal Perspective* (NCSL) 18 (5): 14.

Rafool, M. (1998). State tax and expenditure limits: Appendix C. *Fiscal Affairs.* National Conference of State Legislatures (NCSL-electronic publications).

Reid, G.J. (1988). How cities in California have responded to fiscal pressures since Proposition 13. *Public Budgeting and Finance* 8 (1): 20–37.

Reschovsky, A. (2006). The taxpayer protection amendment: a preliminary analysis. Working Paper Series 2006–003. Madison WI: LaFollette School.

Rubenstein, R. and Picus, L.O. (2003). Politics, the courts, and the economy: implications for the future of school financing. In D.L. Sjoquist (ed.), *State and Local Finances under Pressure.* Cheltenham, UK and Northampton, MA, USA: Edward Elgar.

Rudiuk, O. (2001). The new wave of tax revolt: how it is different from the first one? Working Paper. Graduate School of Public Affairs, University of Colorado at Denver.

Saulny, Susan (2008). Financial Crisis Takes a Toll on Already-Squeezed Cities. *The New York Times,* October 7, A16.

Sears, D.O. and Citrin, J. (1982). *Tax Revolt: Something for Nothing in California,* Cambridge, MA: Harvard University Press.

Serrano v. *Priest* (1976). 135 California Reporter 345. 30 December.

Setze, K. (2006). Rhode Island governor approves lowering local property tax cap. *State Tax Notes* 41 (17 July): 206.

Sexton, T.A., Sheffrin, S.M. and O'Sullivan, A. (1999). Proposition 13: unintended effects and feasible reforms. *National Tax Journal* 52 (1): 99–111.

Shadbegian, R.J. (1996). Do tax and expenditure limitations affect the size and growth of state government? *Contemporary Economic Policy* 14 (January): 22–35.

Shadbegian, R.J. (1998). Do tax and expenditure limitations affect local government budgets? Evidence from panel data. *Public Finance Review* 26 (2): 118–36.

Shadbegian, R.J. (1999). The effect of tax and expenditure limitations on the revenue structure of local government, 1962–87. *National Tax Journal* 52 (2): 221–37.

Shadbegian, R.J. (2003). Did the property tax revolt affect local public education? Evidence from panel data. *Public Finance Review* 31 (1): 91–120.

Shafroth, F. (2007). Proper property taxes. *State Tax Notes* 43 (February): 497.

Shapiro, P. and Morgan, W.D. (1978). The general revenue effects of the California property tax limitation amendment. *National Tax Journal* 31 (2): 119–28.

Shapiro, P. and Sonstelle, J. (1982). Did Proposition 13 slay Leviathan? *AEA Papers and Proceedings* 72 (2): 184–90.

Sheffrin, S.M. (1998). The future of the property tax: a political economy perspective. In D. Brunori (ed.), *The Future of State Taxation*. Washington, DC: Urban Institute Press.

Sherwood-Call, C. (1987). Tax revolt or tax reform: the effect of local government limitation measures in California. *Economic Notes*. San Francisco, CA: Federal Reserve Bank, pp. 57–67.

Shields, Jeff and Marcia Gelbart (2008). Five Year Gap in Phila. Spending Could Hit $850 Million. *The Philadelphia Inquirer*, October 9, B1.

Skidmore, M. (1999). Tax and expenditure limitations and the fiscal relationship between state and local governments. *Public Choice* 99 (1): 77–102.

Smith, D.A. (2004). Peeling away the populist rhetoric: toward a taxonomy of anti-tax ballot initiatives. *Public Budgeting and Finance* 24 (4): 88–110.

Stein, R.M., Hamm, K.E. and Freeman, P.K. (1983). An analysis of support for tax limitation referenda. *Public Choice* 40 (2): 187–94.

Susskind, L. and Horan, C. (1983). Proposition 2½: the response to tax restrictions in Massachusetts. In L.E. Susskind (ed.), *Proposition 2½*. Cambridge, MA: Massachusetts Institute of Technology, pp. 159–71.

Temple, J.A. (1996). Community composition and voter support for tax limitations: evidence from home rule elections. *Southern Economic Journal* 62 (4): 1002–16.

Texas Tax Reform Commission (2006). *Tax Fairness: Property Tax Relief for Texans*. March.

Tiebout, C.M. (1956). A pure theory of local expenditures. *Journal of Political Economy* 64 (3): 416–24.

Uchitelle, Louis (2008). Lawmakers Weight Plans for Stimulus. *The New York Times*, October 10, B1.

US Bureau of the Census (2002). 2002 census of governments: government units in 2002, GCO2-1(P). Washington, DC: Department of Commerce.

US Bureau of the Census (2008). Local governments and public school systems by type and state: 2007. Washington, DC: Department of Commerce.

US Department of Commerce (various years). *State and local government finances* series. Washington, DC: Bureau of the Census.

Whittle, Patrick, et al. (2008). Economy Zaps LI Towns. *Newsday*, September 29, A16.

Willon, Phil (2008). L.A. Expects Big Budget Shortfall. *Los Angeles Times*, October 4, part B, p. 3.

Comments on 'Reaching and maintaining structural balance: leaders in the states' and 'Fiscal limitations on local choice: the imposition and effects of local government tax and expenditure limitations'

Kurt Thurmaier

At first glance, there would not seem to be much conjunction of the contributions by Katherine Willoughby and Daniel Mullins in this volume. Willoughby discusses performance management issues at the state level, and Mullins analyzes the cumulative impact of decades of tax and expenditure limitations on local governments. Considered together, however, these contributions are complementary analyses that bring insight into the current and future flexibility of state and local governments to manage the current fiscal crisis and to evolve with emerging fiscal conditions and demands.

Willoughby's analysis of state finances and budgeting focuses attention on how states are reaching and maintaining structural balance. The Government Performance Project (GPP)[1] has provided descriptive reporting of multiple measures of financial performance of states for several years. Willoughby draws our attention to structural balance in the states because there are many fiscal policy issues reflected in whether or not a state has a strong, moderate or weak structural balance performance. Structural balance is defined as: 'the ability of government to support ongoing expenditures with ongoing revenues – this concept is measured by examining tax structures, the existence of countercyclical devices, financial management strategies and various fiscal ratios'. More specifically, the GPP measures structural balance as 'year-end unreserved budget balance (general fund balance plus rainy-day fund balance) as a percentage of general fund expenditures'.

There are two lessons that can be drawn from her analysis. First, the states with the healthiest structural balances have a regular, disciplined approach to fiscal policy and budgeting. They are flexible and rank relatively low on the list for expensive, long-term commitments added to the budget base (see Table 8.8). They are reluctant to add increased employee benefits, or increased retirement benefits, for example. This reluctance to increase benefit commitments may not satisfy employees, of course. Yet the drag of health care costs on organizational budgets in the private, public and non-profit sectors of the American economy are well known. The new Obama administration has made health care reform a central policy goal, but it is unclear what that means now, or what will result from the mix in the 'policy primeval soup' in DC politics. One can be sure, however, that no single state can address this increasing cost alone; the solution must be national. Breaking the link between employment and health care can take many forms, and it could very well free the labor market and truly enhance private and public sector productivity. But the details of this policy are likely to still cost employers, including state governments, substantial sums.

The second lesson reveals some irony. Those states in the top tier of structural balance health are also less constrained by tax and expenditure limitations (TELs) and constitutional balanced budget requirements than the rest of the states. Table 8.7 of Willoughby's analysis is telling. Only 55 percent of the state leaders require a governor to submit a balanced budget, compared to 83 percent of the other states. Only 44 percent of the state leaders prohibit deficit carry-over to the next fiscal year, compared to 61 percent of the other states. None of the leader states have revenue limitations, compared to 15 percent of the other states. Only a third of the leader states are constrained by expenditure limitations, compared to almost half of the other states. What accounts for the counterintuitive data? Willoughby does not explore the issue fully.

One ready hypothesis is that the leader states do not suffer from a structural political leadership deficit. That is, they enjoy a political culture that respects a regular, disciplined approach to fiscal policy. As Wildavsky famously noted, if one wants to change budgetary outcomes, one must change budgetary politics. Process changes are unlikely to yield different results without a political change.

This issue underlies Mullins's analysis of TEL impacts on local governments. Mullins notes that the ability to respond to TELs is a function of underlying fiscal capacity in the face of undiminished demands for local services. This relates directly to an important accountability issue: one of the most important effects of the TELs is an increase in the number of special district local governments (SDLGs). The governance of SDLGs varies widely, but several points are worth noting.

First, many times the governing board is appointed indirectly through 'member' governments (that is, the SDLG is created through some type of interlocal agreement to create a new entity). In this case, voter account-ability is indirect and fees and tax levies can be set without voters having direct recourse to object against (or promote) them.

In a second version, the SDLG is an independent local governing body, and the voters elect the governing board members (for example, park districts in Illinois). While this seems like direct democracy (and it is, technically speaking), the accountability sunlight that shines on these organizations is weak at best, with little media coverage or public interest. Consequently, although citizens' representatives are presented on ballots, the ability for many citizens to discern for whom to cast a ballot (assuming there is any competition – which often there is not) is very low.

In both cases, the impact of TELs that impose 'citizen' control over the taxing powers of general government bodies is to drive taxing decisions to less controllable and less accountable decision-makers. This may not have been the desired outcome of those who initiated the TELs, but Mullins' analysis provides telling evidence that they have squeezed the 'ballooning' taxes on one end, only to find it has ballooned in a different place. In the end, the TANSTAAFL[2] law cannot be avoided: in the face of unrelenting demand for local government services, someone, somewhere, somehow is going to pay.

The other elements of Mullins' analysis do not provide easy answers about how that will work. The forces from state and local TELs combine for an interesting challenge to future state and local fiscal policy. State TELs are increasing pressure to devolve responsibilities (and costs) to local governments and their more limited tax bases; and state TELs are constraining, limiting or leading to diminished state aid to local govern-ments, including schools, in the face of constrained revenue growth. At the same time, TELs at the local level are pressuring states to push service responsibility to the state level, and requiring a statewide response to fiscal stress because local governments have no flexibility to adjust local revenue sources to meet sustained demands for services in the face of declining rev-enues. TELs at the state and local levels also induce increased borrowing by both levels of government, since debt service tax levies are often (but not always) outside the tax caps.

The data in these two contributions prompt important questions but the authors leave them largely unanswered. Willoughby's analysis is largely descriptive. Further analysis should examine why four of the eight states ranked as leaders in 2005 were no longer leaders in 2008. What distin-guishes Delaware, Pennsylvania, South Dakota and Utah from the other nine states that made the leaders list in either 2005 or 2008? What caused the nine to drop from the list or rise to the list? For example, what are the correlations of their structural balance scores with other GPP scores, or basic demographic data?

Another set of questions arises from the strategies presentation. Do state leaders just need to 'do it right' once (whatever that policy change is?) Or must the strategy change be implemented over several years; that is, should we expect to see the 2005 leaders to be making the same decisions in 2008? Are there any constraints (constitutional or otherwise) for the weaker states? Are weaker states chronically trying to 'catch up' or just stay afloat? (One thinks of my home state of Illinois, for example.)

Perhaps more importantly, what are the service impacts of the strategies of the state leaders? What are the service impacts of regular, disciplined fiscal policies of the leaders versus the next tier, for example? Should states be providing the same service and benefits mix as South Dakota and Utah, for example? The GPP appropriately has multiple measures of fiscal performance. States may be enticed by a neighboring state's successful policy outcome, but be unwilling to adopt the entire package of policy changes that produce that outcome.

The Mullins analysis raises important questions about TELs. Does the increased specialization of local government services (that is, the increase in SDLGs) to overcome TELs lead to a paradox? Do SDLGs increase voter power to 'purchase' Tiebout packages of goods and services, but paradoxically decrease the transparency (and, ergo, accountability) that general-purpose local governments have provided with direct representation, because responsibility to create and manage the 'desired' package of goods and services at the desired tax price is transferred from general local governments to unelected officials or SDLGs with low attendance accountability elections?

Finally, some questions link these two research projects to shed light on broader intergovernmental issues that affect future state and local tax policy. Consider the local government expenditure assignments before and after TELs. Do states with increased 'range' of local government spending foster TELs? Does local government spending on services more appropriate at higher levels (counties or the state) have increased probability of TELs being adopted? What are the longer-term impacts of local-level TELs on the long-term fiscal health of states, measured by the long-term structural balance used in the Willoughby study? Do state leaders in structural balance performance have a regular and disciplined fiscal policy regarding local government aid (whether to schools or general local governments)? Are these states quite comfortable fostering a plethora of SDLGs, or do they have a different policy regarding SDLGs than the other states?

While there are many more questions generated by the Willoughby and

Mullins chapters, I am most intrigued by the conflux of fiscal discipline and democratic accountability. If TANSTAAFL indeed governs fiscal policy (and I think it does), scholars would do well to be more explicit about the linkage, the impact of 'fiscal discipline' in its different manifestations, and suggest fiscal policy models that either balance these two objectives, or make the trade-offs between them explicit for policy-makers.

NOTES

1. The GPP is a collaborative effort of Syracuse University, *Governing* magazine, and the Pew Charitable Trusts. More information is available at www.pewcenteronthestates. org.
2. There Ain't No Such Thing As A Free Lunch (TANSTAAFL).

REFERENCES

Wildavsky, A. (1961). Political implications of budgetary reform. *Public Administration Review* 21 (Autumn): 183–90.

10.   Out-of-the-box conference: an epilogue

Bert Waisanen

The conference that led to this volume was held in May 2008 in Atlanta, Georgia. At that time, an atmosphere of uncertainty was beginning to permeate the US economy in numerous regions. A credit crisis was playing out, threatening municipal financing in certain sectors; headline inflation had passed 4 percent and was nearing 5 percent; and energy and food prices in particular were of growing concern. The housing contraction continued to weigh on transaction-based tax revenues. Yet so far, state budgets had held up, due to cautious spending and forecasting in recent quarters. However, signs were emerging that growth was slowing and spending and revenue forecasts would remain uncertain for many states. A straw poll taken at the conference revealed the economic savvy of the group – 90 percent believed the economy would deteriorate in the next six months.

Fisher (Chapter 2) recounts the large and continuing policy challenges affecting tax policy, including education finance, property tax pressures, the fact that one in five Americans depends on Medicaid, and incarceration of young men who are then absent from the workforce and parenting responsibilities. He asked about possible solutions, and questioned whether there is a lack of research, or whether there is a lack of policy change. He posed an out-of-the-box question to ponder: should we engineer and advocate, or just analyze?

Tannenwald et al. (Chapter 3) discuss how state and local governments have turned to creativity in tax policy, because large structural changes face too much push-back to gain a critical mass of support. Meanwhile, rising school costs, obsolete tax systems and income equality still create enough pressure to warrant creative responses, from cost share trigger mechanisms to fees to stopgap solutions.

In Chapter 6 by Rork and Wheeler, the authors examine alternative business tax systems, such as the New Hampshire business enterprise tax structure and performance. The tax includes a low rate on a broad base and is credited against the profits tax. Sjoquist (Chapter 4) reviews revenue systems of states that have no income tax, and their reliance on other revenues, some unique to their economies, as well as greater local government reliance in some cases. In Chapter 5, Wassmer reviews California's Proposition 13 on its 30th anniversary in 2008, a property tax change that shifted reliance to the income tax and changed the state–local fiscal relationship, while Mullins (Chapter 9) considers the history of local fiscal limitations. Wallace (Chapter 7) examines the feasibility of a proposed state–level consumption tax, its structure and impacts.

The complex nature of the effect of the financial markets crisis on the real economy has made pattern recognition difficult. What is clear is that more states face the risk of structural fiscal imbalances, and revenue systems are one-half of that equation. In addition, several authors in this volume have revealed a theme of governments offering short-term approaches to longer-term structural change issues. This raises a question of sustainability for existing state and local tax policy going forward.

In my view, state fiscal trends have remained decidedly inside the box over the past 10 years. Special interest incentives remain plentiful, foregoing existing business activity revenues. Sales tax base erosion continues, and a significant part of the services economy is outside the sales tax system, with few states endeavoring to add services to the base. A few states however, have targeted the corporate income tax for better performance, or broader reform, or both. Tax systems based on gross receipts or a combination of receipts and net income have been approved in Michigan, Ohio and Texas. These actions reflect a willingness to try something new to shore up business tax bases.

Property taxes for homeowners are the subject of one goal: relief. Whether it is state-funded relief, mandated local limits or replacement of revenue with sales taxes, states are responding to calls for residential property tax reductions. These efforts generally trump calls for relief from business and other property owners. Tax swaps were approved by several states during healthier budget times, so revenue stability from reforms has yet to be tested. The prospect of strained economic conditions will increase pressure to cut property taxes, precisely when their reliable revenue may be needed the most to stabilize local economies.

What new developments may be occurring in the state and local tax base? I will offer that green tax issues are rising in the US, and note that Robert Wassmer (Chapter 5) offered an out-of-the-box idea on the prospect of state carbon auctions. Will a fledgling green tax base arise out of the box? Europe, China and Canada are actively debating environmental tax shifts, with carbon-based taxes being the new revenue proposal, and income and payroll taxes being the offset reduction. Is some sort of a green tax shift feasible or appropriate for US taxing entities? More exploration of these topics would be beneficial to inform the debate and would clearly be out-of-the-box approaches to revenue stability in subnational tax systems.

As of May 2008, strong new issues are challenging the federal fiscal structure and long-term commitments. The likelihood of renewed tension in our system of fiscal federalism is growing as federal burdens increase and US revenue adequacy comes into greater focus. The new President will face calls to manage economic policy actively, and the 2010 expiration of federal tax provisions ensures a federal tax reform proposal will emerge early in the new administration and new Congress.

So as our economy changes, how will tax systems and policies adjust? For now, states in some instances continue to fund program commitments with either shorter-term, volatile or narrow revenue sources, such as excise taxes. For example, states are swapping reliable property taxes for more volatile sales taxes, and states are shying away from sales taxes on services, while reluctantly approving rate increases. Since when did a rate increase become more palatable than a base-broadening? These are interesting times.

Going forward, the forces of economic instability may bring to bear enough collective worry to invoke a time-out for well-worn tax policy debates and occasional hyperbole, and usher in a new, more sobering scrutiny of tax system performance in the face of governmental service commitments. The cover has been lifted off of the box. Let us see what ventures outside it.

Index

Overall property tax rate limits 233–4
Owner occupied housing 19, 214, 216, 221

Particularization 256
Political economy 251
Principal–agent 251
Property tax burdens 218–19, 222, 224, 228–30
Property tax levy limits 234
Property tax limitations 6, 252
Property tax reduction fund 197
Property tax 3–6, 10, 19–21, 24, 28, 30, 44–5, 49, 53–4, 58, 69, 71, 81, 85, 87, 90, 92, 94, 96, 98–100, 103, 114–15, 118, 157, 162, 171, 191, 203–9, 212–14, 218–19, 221–6, 228–34, 236, 240, 242, 244–50, 252–3, 258–9, 271–2
Proposition 13 5–6, 20, 98–103, 105, 107, 109–15, 117–19, 121, 125, 127, 222, 250, 253, 256, 272
Public higher education 14–15, 23
Public policy 16, 24
Public safety 4, 10, 16, 18, 58–9, 104, 209, 211
Public sector 8, 126, 232, 251, 253–5, 257, 267
Public services 21, 23–4, 68, 71, 126, 201, 205, 250, 253–4, 256–7

Rainy-day funds 61
Referenda 202, 206–8, 234–5, 240, 245, 247, 249–50
Regions 22, 180, 241, 271
Responsiveness 203, 206, 250, 254, 256
Revenue limitations 202, 267
Revenue sharing 61
Revenue shortfall reserve 196
Revenue shortfall 60, 206, 210–12
Revenue systems 49, 125, 272
Robert W. Wassmer viii, 98
Robert Tannenwald vii, 28
Ronald C. Fisher vii, 9

Sustainability 272
Sales tax – shrinking tax base 59
Sales tax 5, 20, 30–31, 44–5, 49, 51–4, 55, 62, 68–9, 71, 75–6, 83–6, 104, 114–15, 118, 125–6, 132, 134–5,

160, 163, 174, 191, 208, 246, 249–50, 272
Sally Wallace vii, 3, 156
School districts 20, 102–3, 105, 204, 206–9, 233, 236, 245–8, 255, 257
Self-interest 250, 253
Serrano v. *Priest* 99, 101–3, 253
Service package 253
Service preferences 254
Severance tax 85–6
Shirley Franklin 60
Special district 202, 267
Specific property tax rate limits 233–4
Spending and taxes 116
State and local budgets – impact of recessions 59
State government 7, 10–11, 15, 21, 39, 41–4, 89, 116, 157, 183, 185, 190, 224, 236, 245, 249
State income tax 5, 7, 44, 45, 67, 157–8, 162
State lottery 62
State share of 10, 23, 25, 51, 69, 71, 74–81, 86–90, 92, 94, 96, 111
State–local government 4, 10–11, 23–4, 58
State–local spending 11, 16, 23
Statutory rates 28, 30–31, 50, 52–4, 135–6, 156, 166, 168, 206, 208, 232, 246
Streamlined sales tax agreement (SSTA) 28, 53, 55, 62
Streamlined sales tax project (SSTP) 62
Structural balance 7–8, 179, 183, 185–92, 194–5, 197–9, 266–7, 269
Structural deficit 98, 110–11, 118, 128, 183
Sub national 3, 9, 23, 49–50, 157, 201–2, 250, 273
Subprime mortgage 111, 206
Supply factors 251

Tabor 203, 205, 241–3, 245, 247–8, 251–2
Tax incentives 22, 167, 169, 174
Tax limitations 203, 252, 257
Tax pyramiding, cascading 135
Tax relief 21, 44, 196, 205–8, 218
Tax revolt 4, 10, 19–20, 28, 44, 58, 212